Children's Literature Association
Centennial Studies

Kenneth Grahame's
The Wind in the Willows

A Children's Classic at 100

Edited by
Jackie C. Horne
Donna R. White

Children's Literature Association Centennial Studies, No. 5

The Children's Literature Association
and
The Scarecrow Press, Inc.
Lanham • Toronto • Plymouth, UK
2010

Published by Scarecrow Press, Inc.
A wholly owned subsidiary of The Rowman & Littlefield Publishing Group, Inc.
4501 Forbes Boulevard, Suite 200, Lanham, Maryland 20706
http://www.scarecrowpress.com

Estover Road, Plymouth PL6 7PY, United Kingdom

British Library Cataloguing in Publication Information Available

Library of Congress Cataloging-in-Publication Data

Kenneth Grahame's The wind in the willows : a children's classic at 100 / edited by Jackie C. Horne, Donna R. White.
    p. cm. — (Children's Literature Association centennial studies ; 5)
   Includes bibliographical references and index.
  ISBN 978-0-8108-7258-5 (hardcover : alk. paper) — ISBN 978-0-8108-7259-2 (ebook)
  1. Grahame, Kenneth, 1859–1932. Wind in the willows. 2. Children's stories, English—History and criticism. 3. Pastoral fiction, English—History and criticism. 4. Animals in literature. I. Horne, Jackie C., 1965– II. White, Donna R., 1955–
  PR4726.W515K46 2010
  823'.8—dc22
                                          2009027245

For Maddie

Contents

~

Acknowledgments

We would like to thank the Children's Literature Association, and in particular, Teya Rosenberg and the ChLA Publication Committee, for their support of, and hard work on, this project. We would also like to thank Arkansas Tech University for giving Donna a sabbatical to work on it. Special thanks to Roger Michel, who interrupted a London sojourn to visit the Bodleian and review key Kenneth Grahame correspondence. Jackie would like to thank the Traymore Street crowd for their years of support, and Susan Bloom and Cathie Mercier, for allowing her the opportunity to teach *The Wind in the Willows* and other works of children's fantasy at the Center for the Study of Children's Literature at Simmons College.

We have enjoyed working with all our contributors, who responded to our many requests and suggestions with grace and fortitude. Donna especially wants to thank Jackie for doing the lion's share of the work, including all the communication with contributors, ChLA, the publisher, and other interested parties. Jackie especially wants to thank Donna not only for her sound editorial sense and facility with the ins and outs of MLA citation rules, but most importantly, for her unfailing good humor.

~

Introduction

Jackie C. Horne and Donna R. White

"Believe me, my young friend, there is *nothing*—absolutely nothing—half so much worth doing as simply messing about in boats. Simply messing," he went on dreamily: "messing—about—in—boats; messing—" (Grahame, *Wind* 6)

Whenever we happened to mention that we were working on a collection of essays about *The Wind in the Willows*, invariably the person to whom we were speaking would quote back at us, in some form or another, Kenneth Grahame's famous lines about the pleasures of "messing about in boats." Many times, the speaker had never read *Wind*, never even seen a film version of it. But Grahame's words about the necessity of valuing leisure have become a part of not only British, but also American cultural heritage; deeply embedded in the emotional psyche, the idea of messing about in boats can bring a smile at something half-remembered, something vital but half-hidden, bubbling below the surface of conscious everyday life.

Look around with *Wind*-attuned eyes, and references to Grahame's novel are to be found at every turn: a grocery checkout line with an endcap of "Mole Hill candles," adorned with a line drawing of a Mole remarkably similar to Ernest Shepard's, comfortably ensconced in a plush armchair; gourmet foods given cachet due to their distributor's name, "Wind and Willows"; Steiff mohair teddy bears shaped not like bears, but like Toads and Moles; yet another television adaptation of the adventures of the four River Bank friends airing on the BBC, or on PBS; *Wind in the Willows* for the LeapPad Learning System; Michel Plessix's adaptation of *The Wind in the Willows*, the inaugural volume in the newly issued Classics Illustrated graphic novel series. Despite having turned 100 years old, Kenneth Grahame's novel remains one of the few canonical works of children's literature that continues to call to contemporary readers, promising to sate conflicting desires for both lazy riverbank lounging and raucous, uncontrolled carousing—"O bliss! O poop-poop! O my! O my!"—on the open road (Grahame, *Wind* 33).

The Wind in the Willows has long been an object of curiosity for literary critics, including the contributors to this volume. The essays gathered here attempt to draw Grahame's iconic book away from its incarnation as cultural reference used to sell unrelated products and bring it back under a critical gaze. What role did Grahame's novel play in the history of children's literature? What social and historical issues did the novel address? What cultural debates did the novel attempt to intervene in? How did this very English novel influence readers in other parts of the world? And how did a writer who wrote only this one work of literature for children manage to become one of the few authors admitted to the pantheon of the canonical?

The Golden Age and Dream Days

Writing in 1969, Roger Lancelyn Green confidently asserted Grahame's place in the canon of children's literature:

> But back over the whole field of children's literature for the last hundred years, very few books stand out with which *The Wind in the Willows* may worthily be ranked. In their different styles, *Alice*, *The Rose and the Ring*, *The Princess and the Goblin*, *The Carved Lions*, *The Gold of Fairnilee*, *Treasure Island*, *The Enchanted Castle*, *The Jungle Books* and *Peter Pan* (excluding the more adult romances of such writers as Stevenson and Haggard) make, with it, the twelve supreme volumes in this most important branch of literature. And even among these twelve the author of *The Wind in the Willows* holds one of the highest places. (*Tellers of Tales* 245)

Kenneth Grahame might have been surprised to discover his name linked with those of Barrie, Nesbit, Kipling, and Molesworth, for he never set out to become a writer for children. As a schoolboy, he dreamed of attending Oxford University and pursuing either an academic career or a literary one. But his uncle's refusal to pay for any further education killed such dreams. Grahame's biographers[1] consider this refusal one of his greatest disappointments; Peter Green goes so far as to claim that it "was the most crushing blow that Grahame suffered, perhaps, in his whole life" (50). Instead of Oxford, Grahame was sent to London to work for the Bank of England, where he was eventually promoted to the impressive post of secretary of the bank. But his day job did not prevent Grahame from attempting a literary career on the side (sometimes even writing during his office hours). Beginning in 1888, Grahame published occasional essays in the *St. James's Gazette* and the *National Observer*; eventually, he became involved with the notorious *Yellow Book*, an illustrated quarterly published from 1894 to 1897 that featured the work of artists and writers associated with the Decadent movement.[2]

In 1893, John Lane at The Bodley Head published a collection of Grahame's essays in book form. Given the title *Pagan Papers*, this volume's most compelling reads were not its imitative Stevensonian essays, but the six stories, loosely based on Grahame's childhood in rural England, that concluded the book. Although the Grahames were thoroughly Scottish, Kenneth and his siblings had been raised in Berkshire by their maternal grandmother after their mother's death and their father's descent into alcoholism. As a boy, Kenneth had roamed freely in the fields and woods around his grandmother's house, and his love of nature, his fertile imagination, and his keen attention to the ways of late-Victorian childhood infuse his reminiscences with a vitality that is lacking in his other essays. Encouraged by his publisher, Grahame wrote additional stories based on his childhood; the new tales were published along with the original six as *The Golden Age* in 1895.

The Golden Age and its companion volume, *Dream Days* (1898), are largely unfamiliar to readers today. Children's literature scholars know them primarily from reading early reviews of *The Wind in the Willows*, which often compared the latter work unfavorably to the much preferred earlier volumes, for in their day, Grahame's two essay collections for adults were even more popular than *Wind*. *The Golden Age* proved an instant hit: released in February of 1895, the book had to be reprinted six times by 1896. Its initial popularity may have resulted from an encomiastic review of the collection by the poet Algernon Swinburne in the *Daily Chronicle*; Swinburne's rapture over the collection, which he deemed "well-nigh too praiseworthy for praise" (qtd. in Peter Green 160), almost guaranteed the book a strong first-year sale. But the collection proved to be more than a one-year wonder: by 1900, twelve editions had been printed; by 1913, twenty-four editions; by 1930, at least thirty-three. Multiple American editions appeared as well. Between 1932 and 1951, ten editions of a compendium volume, *The Kenneth Grahame Book*, which included *The Golden Age* and its companion volume, *Dream Days*, as well as *The Wind in the Willows*, were printed by Methuen. *The Golden Age* has remained continuously in print; after it fell out of copyright, it was adopted by independent and specialty publishers, particularly those that focused on reissues of the "classics."[3]

What was so appealing about *The Golden Age*? What literary ground did it break? And why did the initial reviewers of *The Wind in the Willows* find it so much less appealing than *The Golden Age* and *Dream Days*? What did these books have that the latter book lacked? Examining *The Golden Age* and its critical reception more closely reveals the innovations of Grahame's earlier writing and how he built upon (or rejected) those innovations when he came to craft *Wind*.

The first innovation that the early reviewers and later literary critics point to is the realism of Grahame's depiction of childhood. As the reviewer in *The Academy* wrote of the protagonists of Grahame's stories (Selina, Harold, Charlotte, Edward, and the unnamed boy narrator), "By a thousand minute touches Mr. Grahame establishes their reality. So typical are their thoughts and actions, misgivings and ambitions, that *The Golden Age* is to some extent every reader's autobiography" ("Mr. Kenneth Grahame" 293). What, though, did such critics mean when they praised Grahame for portraying a character realistically? Historians of children's literature have granted the laurel of "first writer to depict children realistically" to authors as early as Maria Edgeworth and as recent as Paul Zindel, so when the term "realistic" appears, it is best to look more closely at just what critics mean by it. For reviewers of *The Golden Age*, it appears that the realism of Grahame's depiction consists of two quite different aspects. First, reviewers focus on Grahame's ability to portray the imaginative lives of children, which had rarely been depicted with the detail or the sympathy that Grahame brought to bear. As the reviewer in *The Spectator* notes,

> Some of the incidents have an air of truth about them that lead us to suspect Mr. Grahame of having drawn a good deal on his own boyish reminiscences; the love of "pretending" that is inherent in children, and that enables them to become Argonauts or knights of the round table or muffin-men with equal enthusiasm and realism, the thirst for adventure, the charm that overlays the search for a "secret drawer," will all find echoes in the hearts of those who remember their own youthful days. ("The Golden Age" 140)

But depicting the imaginative doings of children was not the only accomplishment that critics cited when discussing Grahame's realism; they also focused on the indifferent, even scoffing attitude Grahame's narrator and his siblings held toward the adults in their lives. The opening story in the collection, "The Olympians," details the children's attitudes toward the aunts and uncles who care for them:

> These elders, our betters by a trick of chance, commanded no respect, but only a certain blend of envy—of their good luck—and pity—for their inability to make use of it. Indeed, it was one of the most hopeless features in their character (when we troubled ourselves to waste a thought on them: which wasn't often) that, having absolute license to indulge in the pleasures of life, they could get no good of it. (Grahame, *The Golden Age* 3)

Regarding the majority of the adults in their lives as both powerful and stupid, openly making fun of their myopic focus on churchgoing and social calls, Grahame's narrator and his siblings do not simply evoke the Victorian cult of the child, always focused on the *adult* as he looks longingly at the elevated, angelic child. Instead, they turn it on its head. Taking the point of view of the child, rather than the adult, Grahame spins out the implication of elevating the child above his elders: the child's inevitable scorn of what this construction of the child devalues, the adult encased like a fly in amber in a world barren of imagination. As Grahame's narrator wonderingly notes,

> They might dabble in the pond all day, hunt the chickens, climb trees in the most uncompromising Sunday clothes; they were free to issue forth and buy gunpowder in the full eye of the sun—free to fire cannons and explode mines on the lawn: yet they never did any one of these things. (4)

Ironically, the unnamed narrator suggests that his pitying attitude toward the "Olympians" stems from his "lack of a proper equipment of parents" (3), but it seemed clear that most readers, orphaned or not, identified with this depiction of the child's scoffing attitude toward unimaginative adulthood. So, too, did subsequent writers for children; despite being written for adults, Grahame's stories influenced many later writers for children, including the groundbreaking E. Nesbit. Even if he had never composed *The Wind in the Willows*, then, Grahame would still be accounted an important figure in the history of writing for the young for his particular brand of realism in depicting children and adults.

Grahame eschewed the child's point of view when he came to write *Wind*, creating animal characters with all the trappings of respectable adulthood—homes, money, social position, (conveniently invisible) servants, and above all, leisure. It was the absence of children from *Wind* that caused many of its readers, expecting more stories about children and their imaginative adventures as they clashed with the prosaic world of adults, such disappointment. Yet while Mole, Rat, Badger, and even at times Toad are depicted as adults, they are adults of a very strange cast. In fact, we might regard them as the embodiment of the adult that the narrator of *The Golden Age* imagined he himself might one day be—one who had "absolute license to indulge in the pleasures of life" and who did so with imaginative flair. No Bank of England to go to every day, no family relationships placing undue restraints upon him, no boring social calls to make or receive—it is as if Grahame, in *Wind*, realized the dream of his earlier narrator to be an Olympian without losing touch with the imaginative pleasures and leisure of the child.

The child's point of view is not the only one present in *The Golden Age*. The second innovation in these early stories is the way that Grahame simultaneously gives the point of view of the child *and* the point of view of the adult looking back with longing at that child. As Barbara Wall perceptively notes, "what was really new in Grahame's work was the rapidity and the skill with which his narrator shifted perspective between child and adult" (135). Readers are simultaneously invited to embody the position of the boy narrator, who cannot understand why an adult would not hunt chickens, play in the pond, and fire cannons on the lawn, *and* the position of the adult, one who knows all too well why the Olympian does not do any of these things with the freedom he has earned. Wall suggests that such a double address is inherently condescending toward the child—Grahame "is always asking his adult reader to join him in laughing at the absurdities of children" (135)—but there is something more complicated going on in these stories. Rather than existing solely to laugh at the absurdities of a child who would climb trees in his Sunday clothes, Grahame's stories allow adult readers to inhabit both positions at the same time. Grahame surely creates an adult/child binary, but because his narrator simultaneously speaks through the eyes of a child and writes in the style of an adult, Grahame seems to urge his reader to reject the hierarchy inherent in that binary.

Many early reviewers found the novelty of Grahame's double address particularly appealing. The *Academy* reviewer singles it out specifically for praise: "The first-person-singular of *The Golden Age* is charming and unique in its mixture of grave juvenility and whimsical humorous manhood" ("Mr. Kenneth Grahame" 493). This reviewer had no difficulty with the double address, asserting that "We never confused the dual character of the historian: we see him as a boy and listen to him as a man, and both boy and man are a delight" (493). Other reviewers, however, had more trouble with Grahame's approach. The reviewer in the *Spectator* asserts that "Mr. Grahame looks through both ends of the telescope, and writes as a small boy with the knowledge and experience of a man, and this causes a sense of artificiality and incongruity about some of the sketches" ("The Golden Age" 140), a view echoed much later by children's literature critic Lois Kuznets, who "finds it hard to sort and categorize the mix of the adult and childlike, especially in those passages where the imaginative faculty is largely solitary and played out not dramatically but in the narrator's mind" (*Kenneth Grahame* 79).

Peter Green suggests that criticism of Grahame's "fluctuating viewpoint" came from the "intellectual periodicals" rather than from the popular press, which seemed unconcerned by (or, perhaps, unaware of) the subtleties of Grahame's narrative stance (161). Grahame seems to have taken the intellectual press's criticism to heart, however, for in the stories that form the sequel to *The Golden Age*, his narrative stance becomes far less nostalgic, far less invested in the adult looking back with longing at the freedoms of imaginative childhood. Although *Dream Days* is still written in the *style* of an adult, the point of view remains far closer to that of the child. In particular, these later stories focus on the child's *desire*—what the child longs for, what the child wants. *The Golden Age* story "Sawdust and Sin" features the narrator imputing sexual desire to a doll, but in *Dream Days'* "The Magic Ring," it is the narrator himself who desires, writing longingly of the ethereal beauty of a bareback rider at the circus:

> It was not only the ravishment of her delirious feats, nor her cream-coloured horse of fairy breed, long-tailed, roe-footed, an enchanted prince surely, if ever there was one! It was her more than mortal beauty—displayed, too, under conditions never vouchsafed to us before—that held us spell-bound. What princess had arms so dazzlingly white, or went delicately clothed in such pink and spangles? Hitherto we had known the outward woman as but a drab thing, hour-glass shaped, nearly legless, bunched here, constricted there, slow of movement, and given to deprecating lusty action of limb. Here was a revelation! From henceforth our imaginations would have to be revised and corrupted up to date. In one of those swift rushes the mind makes in high-strung moments, I saw myself and Coralie, close enfolded, pacing the world together, o'er hill and plain, through storied cities, past rows of applauding relations,—I in my Sunday knickerbockers, she in her pink and spangles. (Grahame 88–89)

Not just sex, but desire in general, characterizes the stories of *Dream Days*: the desire for food, for stories, for acclaim, for adventure, for love. And it is not only the boys who want; even Selina, the eldest girl edging close to dreaded adulthood, longs in the opening story. A naval history buff mourning the fact that Trafalgar Day is no longer celebrated, Selina, taken by a "weird seizure" (8), sets a bonfire and dances around it with the wild abandon of a Mænad (17). Grahame reveals the centrality of desire as his boy narrator invites a girl he likes to share his imaginary dreamland, a place where "if you want anything at all, you've only *got* to want it, and you can have it!" (51). Grahame's accomplishment in this second volume is his unprecedented depiction of childhood desire, desire unfettered by the restrictions of a censoring adult narrative voice. Attempting to reconcile such desire with adult connections and responsibilities (or, perhaps, the impossibility of ever doing so) would become the central theme of his most memorable work: *The Wind in the Willows.*

The Roots of *The Wind in the Willows*

Neither *The Golden Age* nor *Dream Days* had been written for a child audience, but Grahame's child characters were so authentic and his view of childhood so honest and original that he became a de facto expert on English childhood. In the years that followed their publication, he was asked to write reviews of children's books and to contribute prefaces or introductions to the work of children's writers. For the ten years after the publication of *Dream Days*, such small pieces were his only literary output. For by the time Grahame came to write *Wind*, Grahame's later biographers assert, his own desires had been alarmingly constricted by the demands of adulthood. A late marriage to Elspeth Thomson (he was thirty-eight, she thirty-five) proved unhappy, and Grahame often fled their house to be alone in nature or with other male friends. According to Alison Prince, Grahame's most recent biographer, the two took turns trying to out-child the other, particularly after the birth of their only child, Alastair, in May 1900. The boy, nicknamed "Mouse," had been born blind in one eye, and neither parent, argues Prince, could face the fact of their child's disability, or the disappointments of their marriage. Elspeth descended into illness, real or imaginary, and insisted continually that her child was a prodigy. Grahame, in contrast, indulged Alastair as if he were a fellow playmate rather than a child in need of guidance and restraint, attempting, perhaps, to be the idealized late-Victorian father that he himself had never had.

Part of Grahame's fatherly persona included the storyteller who crafted imaginative tales for the toddler Alastair, stories focused on a water-rat, a mole, and later, a dolphin, a mouse, and a skunk.[4] The later introduction of Toad, the character whom Prince reports that Alastair enjoyed the most, allowed Grahame to play more directly with desire, to embody it in a figure simultaneously hideous and admirable for the lack of restraint that characterized his quest for personal pleasure. When Grahame was away from home during 1907, he continued the Toad stories in letters to Alastair; these letters recounting Toad's wild escapades were eventually incorporated almost verbatim into Grahame's masterpiece, *The Wind in the Willows*.

Wind almost never reached an audience beyond the Grahame household, for despite the ongoing popularity and strong sales of *The Golden Age* and *Dream Days*, The Bodley Head, the British publisher of Grahame's earlier bestsellers, refused the book outright. *Everybody's Magazine*, the American periodical that had asked their English agent, Constance Smedley, to persuade Grahame to submit a new book to them, also refused to publish the novel once they had read the manuscript. After these two surprising rejections, Curtis Brown, Grahame's agent, had great difficulties in finding any publisher willing to take *Wind* on, even when he submitted parts of the manuscript as single stories to periodicals—"I tried it with magazine editors all over England and America. They thought it too fantastic and wouldn't have it" (qtd. in Peter Green 291). Only Methuen proved willing to take the risk that the author's reputation would make up for any deficiencies in the book itself. But even its investment was made provisionally; to protect itself in case of the book's failure, the publisher declined to offer Grahame an advance against royalties.

Having finally found a British publisher, Curtis Brown once again sent the manuscript to America. Luckily, Grahame had also sent a copy of the Methuen edition of *Wind* to an influential American fan—President Theodore Roosevelt. Scribner's initially rejected *Wind*, but after receiving a letter from Roosevelt, in which he wrote that *Wind* was "such a beautiful thing that Scribner *must* publish it," the company did an about-face (qtd. in Prince 240).

The initial reviews of *Wind* seemed to confirm the doubts of its publishing detractors. Reviewers expressed puzzlement, displeasure, and above all, incomprehension. Critics expecting a book about human children aimed at an adult audience instead were greeted with a book about animal adults aimed primarily at children. Despite the similarities between *Wind* and Grahame's earlier story collections, readers' disappointment at not being given more of the same was palpable:

as the reviewer for *The Times* put it, "For ourselves we lay *The Wind in the Willows* reverently aside and again, for the hundredth time, take up *The Golden Age*" (qtd. in Peter Green 257).[5]

Despite the book's lackluster critical reception, it proved popular, although it was not reprinted at quite the pace that *The Golden Age* had been. Jackie Wullschläger reports that Methuen reprinted *The Wind in the Willows* four times during the six months after its initial publication, with three additional printings by 1912, although no information about the number of copies printed is included (170).[6] The first mention of a volume with an edition line that WorldCat cites is a twelfth edition in 1919; the Shepard-illustrated edition, first published in 1926, is listed on WorldCat as the nineteenth. After the publication of the Shepard volume, the pace of reprintings increased dramatically, with a thirty-fifth edition appearing by 1930, and a 100th edition by 1951. By the middle decades of the twentieth century, then, what had been a popular novel became the must-own book for every English-speaking child.

Noted illustrators such as Arthur Rackham and Tasha Tudor created new depictions of Mole, Toad, Rat, and Badger during this period, to be followed by an onslaught of scaled-down illustrated editions during the picture-book boom of the 1980s (among them a curious pop-up version by the irreverent Babette Cole). Famous children's book artists such as John Birmingham, Michael Hague, Adrienne Adams, and Michael Foreman all took a hand at providing lush color illustrations for what had become a childhood classic, as did many lesser lights, particularly after the text came out of copyright. Grahame's novel continues to be a staple of publishing lists far and wide, even in the twenty-first century; in its most recent incarnation, published in English in 2007, French illustrator Michel Plessix adapted *Wind* to the graphic novel format.

After the publication of *The Wind in the Willows*, Grahame was to write no more, at least for publication. His later life was marked by disappointment and sadness. Though his early retirement from the Bank of England was presented as his choice, his latest biographer suggests that he was asked to leave, the new governor appointed in 1907 being unhappy with his secretary's frequent absences and short working hours. Grahame's son, Alastair, encountered difficulties at school, and in 1920, while attending the Oxford that was denied his father, was decapitated by a train. While the coroner brought in a verdict of accidental death, both Peter Green and Alison Prince suggest that suicide, not accident, was the true cause of Alastair's death. From this time onward, Grahame, typically reticent in company, withdrew from life even further. He lived, according to Prince, "like a man on the run from his own memories" (313), spending much of the next ten years abroad, in Italy and other parts of Europe. Only in 1930 did he and Elspeth settle permanently back in England; soon after, in July of 1932, Grahame died of a brain hemorrhage. Buried at Oxford, his tombstone inscription reads:

> To the beautiful memory of Kenneth Grahame, husband of Elspeth and father of Alastair, who passed the River on 6th July 1932, leaving childhood and literature through him the more blest for all time. (qtd. in Prince 346)

The Critical Reception of *The Wind in the Willows*

After the initially puzzled reviews when *The Wind and the Willows* appeared, little academic criticism of Grahame's works was published; what did appear tended to focus on Grahame's writing for adults, mentioning *Wind* as an afterthought (Parker; Pryce-Jones). Subsequent critics such as Clayton Hamilton, Roger Lancelyn Green ("Reed"), and Clifton Fadiman continued the praising trend, but shifted their focus away from the early stories and toward *Wind*. That group includes Patrick Chalmers, whose 1933 biography, *Kenneth Grahame: Life, Letters and Unpublished Work*, overseen by Elspeth after her husband's death, presented both a highly edited version of Grahame's life and an overly sympathetic view of his writing; later biographers and critics have taken issue with both.

Only after the appearance of Peter Green's 1959 biocritical study did the academy begin to wrestle with Grahame's complex work. Many literary critics in the 1970s and 1980s built upon Green's approach, which analyzes the novel in terms of Grahame's unhappy life, arguing that the arcadian River Bank Grahame created in *Wind* offered him an escape from his deeply disappointing personal troubles. But other issues joined the biocritical ones during this period: issues of audience, influence, and narrative structure.

Given that Grahame wrote for both children and adults, many critics focused on just who was the intended audience for *Wind*—a child or a grown-up? Or both? Kenneth Sterk begins the discussion by noting the tension that adult writers of children's literature face: they need to create themes and plots that will keep the child reader's interest, while their own interests have developed in other, "alien" directions (20). For Sterk, the child-interest within Grahame's text lies in the Toad stories, while the River Bank sections were written for Grahame and for adult readers. Later critics (Poss; Sale, *Fairy Tales*; Cripps; Robson) would reject this double stance, arguing that the ideal reader of *Wind* is an adult, not a child, one who knows "how it feels to be no longer too young to reach the branches, and has some sense of the 'spirit of divine discontent and longing' from which the work springs" (Poss 90). If a child reader was considered possible, such a reader would not get as much from the novel as the adult reader would (DeForest). Roger Sale would go on to complicate his argument in a later essay, arguing that no great work of children's literature has been written primarily with the restrictions of audience in mind; instead, the best works stem from an author, such as Kenneth Grahame, writing for him or herself ("Audience").

A second trend in this criticism, common to many academic articles on children's texts in a period concerned with justifying the act of analyzing literature for children, works to validate Grahame's novel by linking it to literature for adults. For example, Nicholas Tucker compares Grahame's Toad to Shakespeare's Falstaff; Geraldine Poss traces the epic and pastoral conventions in *Wind*; and Laura Krugman compares his work in *The Golden Age* and *Dream Days* to that of Wordsworth and Dickens. Critics in the 1980s would continue this trend, exploring in more detail the influence of Romantic poets on Grahame's novel (Willis; Gillin). Lesley Willis suggests that Grahame's allusions to Romantic poems highlight the novel's "central tension" between "the paramount value of home and community and the merit of accepting . . . one's own limitations" and the "desire for adventure and change" (108), pointing to a third theme that occupied critics of the 1970s and early 1980s: the dualism of the novel's narrative structure.

This dualism had been noted by critics who discussed issues of audience, as they argued that the Toad strand of the novel appealed to children while the River Bank strand appealed to adults (Robson; Sale, *Fairy Tales*; Carpenter). For those who examined the novel's structure rather than its intended readers, however, the binary shifted away from audience and toward theme, in particular the theme of home versus adventure. Lois Kuznets initiated the discussion of home(s) in the novel, examining the different homes portrayed in Grahame's text in terms of the "topophilic crises" characters experience and the "felicitous spaces" they work to discover ("Toad Hall Revisited"). Michael Mendelson, in contrast to audience-focused critics, argues that instead of setting the two strands of the novel in binary opposition in order to elevate one and devalue the other, critics should recognize how Grahame "not only juxtaposes but interlaces his two different plots and values" and concludes his narrative by "knitting together . . . the novel's contrary states" (128).

In subsequent criticism focusing on the theme of home in the novel, critics began to use their analysis of *Wind* to create larger theories about the nature of literature for children in general. Christopher Clausen suggests that the difference between literature for adults and for children is the way each treats the theme of home. In books for children, home is a privileged place, a place where we should stay or to which we should return. In contrast, adult books portray the need to leave or escape from home. Clausen uses *Wind* as the quintessential example of the first type of book, with *Huckleberry Finn* as the embodiment of the second. Writing only a year later, both Carlee Lippman and Lucy Waddey complicate Clausen's thesis. Lippman takes Clausen's binary of home/away and argues that each requires a different type of "imagining": home requires an imagination focused inward, an imagination that Lippman equates with innocence; away requires an outwardly focused imagination. Waddey shifts from a dual to a triadic conception of home, arguing that children's literature features three different patterns: the Odyssean (freedom to explore then return home); the Oedipal (with home as the center of development); and the Promethean (in which home can be created by the protagonist). While she believes the main pattern in *Wind* is Odyssean, she rejects the Clausen binary by arguing that the other two strands find their articulation in Grahame's novel as well.

Peter Hunt also ties his analysis of *The Wind in the Willows* to an attempt to theorize children's literature as a genre, but in a way that argues against linking works for children to those for adults. Taking *Wind* as his case study, Hunt demonstrates how narrative theory can be useful for analyzing a children's book, but how it also has limitations. Urging critics to "cultivate a double viewpoint," Hunt argues that children read in a way different than adults do, one close to an oral culture's norms and expectations, and thus their literature demands its own theoretical methodology, rather than a methodology based on "an appeal to a common culture" ("Necessary Misreadings" 121, 108).

Many critics in the 1990s, however, did not heed Hunt's call for a genre-specific criticism. In particular, building upon (or sometimes rejecting) Peter Green's Freudian analytical insights, scholars often drew upon various psychoanalytic models developed by literary critics to analyze literature written for adults. Bonnie Gaarden employs Jungian psychoanalysis to explore the characters as different parts of an individual psyche. Toad, rather than the other three main characters, however, proved of particular interest to psychoanalytically inclined critics. Mark West analyzes Toad not as a manic-depressive, as had Peter Green, but rather as a narcissist, while Roger Schlobin discusses Toad as an echo of Robert Louis Stevenson's Mr. Hyde. Andrew McBride narrows Toad's diagnosis even further, discussing Toad as an embodiment of the addict addicted to "joy riding." Perhaps the most interesting use of a psychoanalytic approach is Robert de Board's full-length imagining of Toad in psychotherapy with an invented Doctor Heron. Not intended as a work of literary criticism, de Board's book was created to demonstrate how transactional psychotherapy works in practice. That he would choose Toad for his case study demonstrates that de Board felt that *Wind* still resonates with today's readers. But the changes that de Board imagines Toad and his fellow characters making as a result of his psychotherapy—Badger channels his bossy tendencies into a run for an MP seat; Rat moves to a seaside town in the south to reunite with the Sea Rat; Mole returns to Mole End to turn it into his own restaurant; and Toad sells Toad Hall and goes into business as an estate agent—demonstrate just how the book must be changed to fit late twentieth-century psychosocial ideologies.

While the 1980s saw its share of traditional close readings of *Wind*, focusing on imagery, symbolism, and plot structure (Wolf; Gilead,

"Grahame's"; Kuznets, *Kenneth Grahame*), the advent of cultural criticism witnessed the emergence of essays focusing on ideology in the novel. Peter Hunt combines both approaches in the one book devoted solely to Grahame's novel, *The Wind in the Willows: A Fragmented Arcadia*. Cultural critics were particularly interested in analyzing the novel in terms of gender, of class, and of nationality.

As early as 1975, Geraldine Poss had pointed out the absence of goddesses and women from Grahame's arcadian epic. Peter Green had read the absence of women in *Wind* psychoanalytically, as a reflection of Grahame's early loss of his mother and his wish to escape from his disastrous marriage, but later critics would discuss gender in cultural rather than personal terms. Lois Kuznets, disagreeing with Grahame's assessment that his novel is "free of problems, clear of the clash of sex," asserts that the novel simultaneously "attempts to *repress* the clash of sex" and "*perpetuates* it in the dramatization of certain traditional themes: woman's dangerous power to limit man's freedom, and the male longing to be completely accepted by—and as—the father" ("Kenneth Grahame" 175). While the novel does posit an "attractive androgyny of nurturing males," such androgyny is presented as an option only for men; "women remain forever the Other in *Wind*" (179). Cynthia Marshall echoes many of Kuznets's insights, but urges us to think not in terms of binaries, but rather in terms of gender instability as we analyze *Wind*. Rather than seeing Grahame's text as a misogynist tract, Marshall argues instead that the novel "qualifies its own misogyny with a fairly fluid, even theatrical, notion of gender construction" (65). Marshall urges literary critics to follow Grahame's example and move beyond an "essentialist" feminism, embracing instead a poststructural feminism, with its conception of gender as performative rather than fixed (67). Michael Steig's 1981 article focuses not on gender, but on sexuality, examining *Wind*'s "veiled eroticism," an eroticism that had been quite open in Grahame's earlier *The Golden Age* and *Dream Days*. Grahame's denial of the eroticism in his novel is typical of the Edwardian period, Steig asserts, which features narratives with overt disciplining tendencies that overlie "a strong, though disguised, emotional content of the forbidden" (322). Steig wrote before the advent of gender studies; one wonders how he would approach the subject of sexuality in light of today's queer and homosocial theory, and why so little work to date has been done on the construction of masculinity in Grahame's novel.[7]

Not only gender, but also class proved of interest to critics writing on *Wind* during the closing decades of the twentieth century. Several earlier critics (Robson; Philip) mention the issue of class politics in the novel only to dismiss it—"Considered as a political allegory, *The Wind in the Willows* is reactionary—or, at least, very conservative. But I don't think it is primarily a political book at all" (Robson 106)—but other critics refused to allow Grahame's class ideology to be ignored. Peter Green reads the novel in terms of Grahame's "projection of his own social fears," fears that the "radical *canaille*" would displace the authority and hierarchy of the rural squirearchy (243). Peter Hunt astutely notes that because Grahame is an amazing prose stylist, it is worth analyzing why he rarely used dialect to indicate class affiliation. Such an evasion, Hunt suggests, allows the book as a whole to "evade the confrontations latent in a book which deals obliquely with so many societal issues" ("Dialogue" 160). John David Moore links ideology to genre, arguing that the conservative roots of pastoral find their reflection in Grahame's creation of an idealized Arcadia, one in which the labor of the working class is effaced. For Grahame, Moore argues, the "threat" to pastoral order "is class instability, people not knowing their places" (55). Jan Needle entered the fray not with an essay, but with a work of fiction: *Wild Wood*, which tells the story of *Wind* from the point of view of the working-class ferrets and other denizens of the forest.

Much ink has been spilled trying to situate the four characters in terms of their class. Is Mole part of the middle class? Or is he, as Troy Boone and Hunt assert, closer to a working-class clerk than to a member of the bourgeoisie? Is Badger landed gentry or rustic outsider? Is Toad Hall the sign of a long line of landed Toads or a marker of the nouveau riche, trying to buy its way into the upper classes by purchasing a rural estate? One's reading of the novel can shift dramatically, depending on one's reading of each character's class position.

More recent analyses of *Wind* have shifted the focus from class to nationality. In a novel often identified as quintessentially "English," how is Englishness constructed? Historian Peter Mandler uses *Wind* as one example of a trend which other historians have argued was widespread at the turn of the century, a trend by British elites to construct Englishness as rural idyll in order to counteract the forces of modernism, urbanism, and democracy. Mandler, however, sees the trend as limited to a specific subgroup of artists such as Grahame, middle-class aesthetes rebelling against both democratization and the "stolid barbarians of the aristocracy" (165). Children's literature critic Tony Watkins also writes of *Wind* in the context of nostalgia for a lost Englishness, demonstrating how the use of the characters from the novel were used in an English Tourist Board ad campaign to turn nostalgia into "heritage," Englishness as a commodity to be bought and sold (168). Yet he offers a more hopeful reading, suggesting the possibility that readers might also take up *Wind* as a "utopian" text, reading it as a radical critique of existing social relations rather than simply as conservative nostalgia for a past that never really existed (169).

The Wind in the Willows continues to draw the attention of literary scholars, with critics staking out unique interpretations: Maureen Thum, who links psychological development to landscape; Jane Darcy, who sees in Grahame's depiction of nature in *Wind* the potential for inspiring contemporary readers to recognize their need for connection to the green world; Deborah Stevenson, who attempts to theorize sequels by examining William Horwood's continuations of Grahame's original story. The novel has become such a part of the canon that some critics feel compelled to recount their dislike of it, pushing against the boundaries of the canonical (Meek; Wall). The most recent trend in *Wind* criticism, however, is a historically informed approach. Kathryn Graham demonstrates the parallels between schoolboy novels, public school mores, and the characters and events in *Wind*, while William Greenslade compares Grahame's paganism to that of Stevenson and Forster. The 2007 volume of *Children's Literature* includes two essays that place Grahame in the context of other Edwardian children's writers. Troy Boone emphasizes the way that *Wind*, despite its arcadian cast, incorporates machine culture to "normaliz[e] class relations under industrialism" (88), while Robert Hemmings examines the dual thrust of nostalgia in Grahame, Milne, and Carroll, a nostalgia that simultaneously conceals distasteful aspects of childhood and betrays anxieties of loss and desire. Much critical ground has been covered in studies to date of *Wind in the Willows*, but there are gaps still to be explored, as well as opportunities for extending arguments, as the essays in this collection demonstrate.

Grahame and Style

One gap that Grahame himself would likely find surprising is the lack of attention to the style of the novel. For Grahame, as for many of his initial reviewers, style, more than content, was what made a text a work of art. Noting to Clayton Hamilton that he did not desire fame and had little need of earning money through his writing, Grahame pointed to the joy of crafting prose as his motivation for writing: "a fellow entertains a sort of hope that, somehow, sometime, he may build a noble sentence that might make Sir Thomas Browne sit upward once again in that inhospitable grave of his in Norwich" (73). But he despairs that his efforts will be valued, for living as he does in an age of the eye rather than of the ear, a true appreciation for the "agony, and all the joy" of exquisitely crafted prose has been lost (74).

Grahame's fears seem warranted, for his artistry as a writer has often been overlooked. Early reviewers lauded his style, but said little about just what it was that made it worthy of praise. Later literary scholars have tended to focus on the structure of the novel—either attacking it or defending it—without paying close attention to style and diction. Kuznets, in *Kenneth Grahame*, and Hunt, in *Fragmented Arcadia*, are significant exceptions. Yet the true beauty of *The Wind in the Willows* resides in its language, which captures the cozy familiarity of home, the rhythms of nature, and the simplicity and directness of a bedtime story. We would like to spend a few brief paragraphs pointing out what is praiseworthy about Grahame's style before concluding our introduction with a preview of essays in this collection.

Grahame wrote beautifully poetic prose, but ironically, he wrote terrible poetry. Like many men of his educational background, Grahame fancied himself a poet. We can be thankful that his friend Frederick Furnivall encouraged him to write prose instead, for despite his command of poetic diction, Grahame could not compose memorable verse. *The Wind in the Willows* contains four original poems—songs really—that might be passable if attached to catchy tunes, but most readers would probably share Mole's assessment of Rat's "Duck Ditty": "I don't know that I think so *very* much of that little song, Rat" (Grahame, *Wind* 21). In the context of the novel, most of the verse augments characterization. Rat has a poet's soul, but his talent (like his creator's) is mediocre;

his song exhibits his playful nature and good sense of humor. Toad's two songs reflect his overweening pride and conceit, but they are also full of humor. The fourth song, a Christmas carol, is the only serious offering and the only one that is not used to establish characterization. Without the humor that leavens the other poems, "Carol" shows how clunky Grahame's verse can be:

> Here we stand in the cold and the sleet,
> Blowing fingers and stamping feet,
> Come from far away you to greet—
> You by the fire and we in the street—(*Wind*, 90)

Grahame's prose, on the other hand, can ascend to musical heights, and at its best must be read aloud for a full appreciation of its language. Indeed, like Rudyard Kipling, another writer who infused his children's stories with poetic language (and whom Grahame counted as one of the six men in England besides himself who had "inherited an ear for prose" [Hamilton 74]), Grahame's prose is better poetry than his verse. His description of Mole's escape from spring cleaning provides an excellent example of poetic prose:

> So he scraped and scratched and scrabbled and scrooged, and then he scrooged again and scrabbled and scratched and scraped, working busily with his little paws and muttering to himself, "Up we go! Up we go!" till at last, pop! his snout came out into the sunlight, and he found himself rolling in the warm grass of a great meadow. (*Wind*, 2)

Kipling employs a similar linguistic playfulness in the opening sentences of *Just-So Stories*:

> In the sea, once upon a time, O my Best Beloved, there was a Whale, and he ate fishes. He ate the starfish and the garfish, and the crab and the dab, and the plaice and the dace, and the skate and his mate, and the mackerel and the pickereel, and the really truly twirly-whirly eel. (1)

Both passages use internal rhyme, although it is more noticeable in Kipling. The Grahame passage contains only one example: "his snout came out." Both authors also play with pronunciation to create new words: Kipling's "mackareel" and "pickereel" and Grahame's "scrooged." In both cases, the authors are bouncing the sounds of the new words off words with similar sounds; Kipling is forcing a rhyme while Grahame is extending his alliteration. Grahame's fondness for alliteration is obvious in this passage, although it is even clearer in his description of a bird with its "plumped-out plumage pencilled plainly" on a screen (76).

Imagery also abounds throughout *The Wind in the Willows*, but Grahame's favorite poetic devices are metaphor, simile, and personification. Personification is obviously the basis for his animal characters, but Grahame applies it as a poetic device most often when he depicts nature. For example, describing a winter scene, he writes that "Nature was deep in her annual slumber and seemed to have kicked the clothes off" (41). Nature personified is not always gentle; when Mole is lost in the wood, logs "trip" him (41), and "holes ma[k]e ugly mouths at him" (42). Grahame also applies personification to show the comforts of home, as in this description of Badger's kitchen:

> The ruddy brick floor smiled up at the smoky ceiling; the oaken settles, shiny with long wear, exchanged cheerful glances with each other; plates on the dresser grinned at pots on the shelf, and the merry firelight flickered and played over everything without distinction. (58)

Grahame's metaphors and similes also favor nature. At various times nature is compared to a fairy tale, a pastoral, a parade, a chapter in a book, a stage, a dance, a play, a theater, and even a hotel. Grahame is also prone to comparing manmade things to animals: an approaching motorcar sounds "like the drone of a distant bee" (*Wind*, 30); the Sea Rat compares a line of bobbing casks to "a mile of porpoises" (164); a lonely road seems like "a stray dog" (176). The accumulative effect of these comparisons is to suggest an organic connection between objects in nature and manmade objects. Grahame's choice of metaphors and similes undercuts the critics who argue that he sets nature against technology.

Grahame's poetic language occurs almost entirely in his narrative passages. The third person omniscient narrator, rather than Mole, Toad, or Rat, is the real poet in this novel. Only a few felicitous phrases fall from his character's mouths, and most of those seem appropriate. For example, Badger refers alliteratively to Toad's driving clothes, calling them "hideous habiliments" (98). The phrase is a bit highfalutin for someone who prides himself on plain speaking, but it fits its context. The same cannot be said for Otter's flight of fanciful language after he finds the lost Mole and Rat at Badger's house. Otter generally speaks in incomplete sentences, but the snow inspires him to poetic heights:

> "Here and there great branches had been torn away by the sheer weight of the snow, and robins perched and hopped on them in their perky conceited way, just as if they had done it themselves. A ragged string of wild geese passed overhead, high on the grey sky, and a few rooks whirled over the trees, inspected, and flapped off homewards with a disgusted expression. . . ." (65)

This passage sounds more like Grahame's narrator than Otter, who is prone to short phrases like "Greedy beggars" (11). However, this lapse is unusual for Grahame; in general, his animals' diction is appropriate for their characters. Indeed, most of his diction is appropriate for its subjects. Even the much-criticized Pan chapter, "The Piper at the Gates of Dawn," uses diction that suits its religious topic: an encounter with the divine requires a loftier tone than a riverside picnic.

As Neville Braybrooke observantly notes, Grahame's main goal in writing was to "restore sound to prose" (506). Reading passages out loud not only helps restore the sound but also shows us Grahame's delight in language. At times the author seems deliriously drunk on words, and at other times he is like his River, chattering to us in "a babbling procession of the best stories in the world" (4). Grahame crafted his words carefully to create his desired effects. From the slapstick comedy of Toad's adventures to the high seriousness of "The Piper at the Gates of Dawn," Grahame's word choice and sentence structure reflect his subject matter and prove him to be a master stylist.

The Essays

The writers in this volume take it for granted that Grahame's prose, and his novel, continue to be well worth our time and thought. Their essays revisit some of the issues that have engaged critics of *The Wind in the Willows* from the start—the dual-strand narrative structure; the function of home; the psychological connections between Toad and

Grahame—but extend their arguments by examining them through theoretical lenses heretofore underemployed in Grahame criticism. They also bring to our attention gaps in the scholarship by focusing on issues not addressed in previous analyses of *Wind*, such as the construction of heteronormative masculinity, the appeal of this very English novel to Chinese readers, and the meaning of a text in which animals can be human-like, pets, servants, and even food. With backgrounds in literary criticism, psychology, children's literature, media studies, and even the rhetoric of science and technology, our contributors bring a fascinatingly diverse set of interests and expertise to their readings of Grahame's touchstone work.

In part I, "Competing Discourses," the essayists pick up the thread of earlier critics who analyzed the dualisms of Grahame's text. But they push the discussion of the traditional binaries in exciting new directions. In "*Deus ex Natura* or Nonstick Pan? Competing Discourses in Kenneth Grahame's *The Wind in the Willows*," David Rudd moves beyond the traditional binary discussed by critics (Toad plotline/Mole and Rat plotline) by examining the *numerous* countervailing tendencies in *Wind*, arguing that such competing discourses do not detract from the novel, but instead, grant it a hybrid vigor. Pan, himself a hybrid creature, is an effective symbol for the tensions operating across Grahame's text. Deborah Dysart-Gale applies Max Weber's discussion of *techne* versus technology to examine the existential dislocation Grahame's characters experience in "*Techne*, Technology, and Disenchantment in *The Wind in the Willows*." Weber describes this existential dislocation as "disenchantment," the result of a process in which scientific paradigms supplant other epistemologies and meanings. *Techne*, an older paradigm which seeks harmony with nature, informs the pastoral idyll of Rat and Mole, while technology, which seeks domination over nature, is exemplified by Toad. Toad's exploits with boats, caravans, and motorcars clearly mark the road to technological progress as a dead end and underscore the desirability of *techne* over technology. Yet Grahame's novel does not simply call for reenchantment; rather, the book explores and confronts the process of disenchantment, simultaneously serving as a model for surviving disenchantment and providing an opportunity for readers to reenchant their own existences. Catherine Elick's essay, "'Up [and Down and Back and Forth] We Go!': Dialogic and Carnivalesque Qualities in *The Wind in the Willows*," continues the focus on dualisms by analyzing Grahame's novel in light of Bakhtin's libertarian concepts of polyphony, dialogism, and carnival. Characters who represent dissenting views are consistently unnamed, undifferentiated, and permitted little direct dialogue, suggesting that Grahame's text lacks the true polyphony Bakhtin attributes to the novel as a genre. But *Wind*'s competing narrative strands represent a truly dialogic exchange between the ideas of home and adventure, stasis and motion, Apollonian and Dionysian impulses. Elick concludes by analyzing the text's carnivalesque swings upward out of various forms of oppression and restraint into positions of power or riotous abandon, followed by downward swings or decrowning moments, in which characters experience harsh reality once more.

In "It's a Mole-Eat-Hare World: The River Bank, the School, and the Colony," Meg Worley turns us from competing narrative strands to competing depictions of humaneness within Grahame's novel. Human language conditions the way we deal with other species; the more we recognize in them something like language, the more intelligent they are assumed to be, and the less likely we are to put them in harnesses, cages, or cooking pots. But Grahame's main characters replicate human relationships toward other animals, conversing with them all the while. Worley argues that the result is a novel that is surprisingly honest about the ways in which the choice to withhold compassion is an inherent feature of human societies. In the final essay of this section, "A Contemporary Psychological Understanding of Mr. Toad and His Relationships in *The Wind in the Willows*," Jonathan Mattanah looks at competing discourses *outside* the novel, in particular, competing discourses in psychoanalysis. Mattanah moves beyond the Freudian discourse employed by previous critics, drawing instead on the self psychology of Heinz Kohut, particularly his reconceptualization of the Freudian concept of narcissism. In the process, Mattanah gives us reason to hope that Toad's reformation may not be as short-lived as many previous readers and critics have believed.

The essays in part II, "Representations of the Edwardian Age," productively bring history and literary analysis together to demonstrate that Grahame's text does not only reflect the times in which it was written, but also actively works to construct representations of class, of gender, and of nationality through its fictional discourse. While the British class system has been the subject of a number of critical essays on *The Wind in the Willows*, the rules of courtesy have been decidedly understudied in such scholarly discussions. In "'Animal-Etiquette' and Edwardian Manners in Kenneth Grahame's *The Wind in the Willows*," Karen A. Keely analyzes *Wind* through the lens of Edwardian courtesy manuals, demonstrating the centrality of manners and rules of politeness in the novel. Opening up the discussion beyond issues of class, Keely shows how Grahame uses animal-etiquette as a source of humor, of accuracy in descriptions of animal behavior, of community delineation, and of social criticism. Class is also a key issue in Ymitri Mathison's "Locating Englishness within the Commodity Culture of the Early Twentieth Century in *The Wind in the Willows*." But class is intricately bound up with constructions of nationality, as Mathison demonstrates as she traces the ways in which *Wind* appears to nostalgically return imperial, capitalist Britain to a pastoral England of a preindustrial bygone era. Yet separating Englishness from Britishness during this period proves especially difficult; both of these identities become open to hybridization as class boundaries became more fluid. Grahame's novel testifies to the importance of the rural landscape for defining a particularly *English* national identity, as well as to the difficulties of sustaining a unique Englishness in an urban, capitalistic, consumer-oriented, and imperialized society. In this section's final essay, "Animal Boys, Aspiring Aesthetes, and Differing Masculinities: Aestheticism Revealed in *The Wind in the Willows*," Wynn Yarbrough examines the issue of gender not through the lens of feminism, but through that of masculinity studies, which reveals a more nuanced view of Grahame's gender politics than previous critics have suggested. For Grahame's text, far from espousing a single normative masculinity, explores multiple constructions of the masculine, including one under great suspicion during the period: masculine aestheticism. In his essay, Yarbrough analyzes Grahame's multiple masculinities, linking them to the historical anxieties surrounding masculinity that plagued England during the Edwardian age. Grahame's novel, the essay suggests, aims to recuperate aspects of aestheticism, particularly in terms of masculinity, while it simultaneously contains the potential threats of homosexuality and class ferment with which aestheticism had become linked in the wake of the Oscar Wilde trial.

The final section of the collection, *Beyond the Text*, examines two very different reinterpretations of Grahame's novel. In "The Wind Blows to the East: On Chinese Translations of Kenneth Grahame's *The Wind in the Willows*," Shu-Fang Lai examines Chinese translations of this quintessentially English children's book. Discussing more than a dozen Chinese translations and adaptations from 1959 to the present, including a serialization in the *Mandarin Daily News*, Lai analyzes why *The Wind in the Willows* has been a best-seller in the Far East. Moving to the United States, Jennifer Geer looks at the Disney adaptation of Grahame's story in "The Pursuit of Pleasure in *The Wind in the Willows* and Disney's *The Adventures of Ichabod and Mr. Toad*." Geer analyzes Disney's film in light of Nicolas Sammond's argument that Disney features of late 1940s and 1950s tend to reflect and reinforce Cold War–era patterns of child rearing, modeling the cooperation, hard work, and respect for the law that would support capitalist democracy while discouraging the extremes of anarchy or conformism that might make citizens susceptible to totalitarianism.

The essays in this volume shed new critical light on *The Wind in the Willows*. Yet there are still many avenues waiting to be explored. How do fantasy writers after Grahame draw upon, or reject, his model of using animals as characters? For example, is Richard Adams in *Watership Down* writing to refute Grahame's method of anthropomorphism? Does Brian Jacques, an author from a quite different class position than Grahame, reject or echo Grahame's class politics in the world of Redwall? Does Grahame's novel, with its rejection of a rule-bound, logically created secondary world, challenge contemporary theories of how fantasy for children works? Can the pantheism of *Wind* help explain the less overtly religious sublimity of later children's fantasy? How have the myriad television adaptations of the novel changed Grahame's canonical text to make it appeal to contemporary audiences? Why did Grahame's often reactionary text appeal to many in the 1960s counterculture?[8] Why have so many classical composers been drawn to the River Bank, and how does their music attempt to capture its appeal?[9] What can theories of illustration contribute to an understanding of the many beautiful (and sometimes irreverent) picture book adaptations that have proliferated during the past twenty-five years? We hope that future critics will, like Rat, return to the River Bank, ready to scribble and suck at the top of their pencils as they attempt to answer these and other, yet-to-be-articulated questions, demonstrating once again the wonders and mysteries of Grahame's ever-intriguing world.

Notes

1. Grahame has been the subject of three biographies. The first was written shortly after Grahame's death by Patrick Chalmers, under the supervision of Grahame's widow, Elspeth. It is generally considered less than reliable, marred by Elspeth's deep investment in creating a palatable myth of her husband's life for public consumption. Peter Green's 1959 *Kenneth Grahame* takes a biocritical tack, reading the characters in *Wind* as manifestations of Grahame's own psyche, an approach unsurprising in a time when Freudian psychoanalysis was in great vogue in Western culture. Grahame's most recent biographer, Alison Prince, often echoes Green's psychological approach, but her research, which brings new facts about Grahame's family and work life to light, provides additional validation for her psychological speculations. The editors have drawn on all three sources in crafting these introductory notes.

2. Even though Oscar Wilde was banned from the *Yellow Book* because art editor Aubrey Beardsley disliked him, Wilde was mistakenly linked to the publication when he was arrested with a yellow book under his arm. His trial for homosexuality destroyed the magazine's reputation. See Wynn Yarbrough's essay in this collection for more information on Grahame and the Aesthetic Movement.

3. Information about editions comes from a review of listings of *The Golden Age* on the WorldCat database.

4. *First Whisper of "The Wind in the Willows"* and *My Dearest Mouse: "The Wind in the Willows" Letters* both reprint Grahame's letters to Alastair from 1907 and cite them as the source of his later novel. But Grahame's letters to Elspeth from 1903 to 1905, sent while she was away taking rest cures at places such as Woodhall Spa, include many references to stories of Mr. Mole and the Water Rat that Grahame was sharing with Alastair. See the Kenneth Grahame papers at the Bodleian Library at Oxford, #43839, "Letters from Grahame to his wife, 1903–5." Our thanks to Roger Michel for taking time away from his London holiday to visit the Bodleian and examine its holdings of Grahame's papers on our behalf.

5. For a detailed discussion of the book's initial reviews, see Hunt, *Wind* 14–18.

6. Wullschläger does not cite her sources for these sales figures, unfortunately. Her assertion that the first version illustrated by Ernest Shepard appeared in 1931, rather than in 1926, makes her assertions open to question.

Unfortunately, the editors did not have the opportunity to consult the royalty statements in the Kenneth Grahame papers at the Bodleian Library, which may have given a more detailed picture of the sales figures for *Wind* (although the catalog lists statements only from 1933 to 1946).

7. Sandra Martina Schwab discusses masculinity in "The Reluctant Dragon," but not in *Wind*.

8. See for example the 1968 CD by the band The Wind in the Willows, best known for featuring the debut of Blondie's Deborah Harry, and the rock opera *Wind in the Willows* written by Eddie Hardin in the 1980s and recorded in 1991.

9. See for example John Rutter's "The Reluctant Dragon"; William Bolcom's "Three Songs from *The Wind in the Willows*"; Laurie Johnson's "The Wind in the Willows—Tone Poem for Small Orchestra"; and Charles Bestor's "A Wind in the Willows" for solo flute.

Works Cited

Bestor, Charles. "Wind in the Willows." Perf. Grzegorz Olkiewicz and Gerald Ranck. *Night Thoughts and Fancies: New Music for Flute and Piano*. Capstone, 1998.

Bolcom, William. "Three Songs from *The Wind in the Willows*." Perf. Carole Farley and William Bolcom. *William Bolcom: Songs*. Naxos, 2005.

Boone, Troy. "'Germs of Endearment': The Machinations of Edwardian Children's Fictions." *Children's Literature* 35 (2007): 80–101.

Braybrooke, Neville. "Rereading *The Wind in the Willows*." *Horn Book* 46 (1970): 504–07.

Carpenter, Humphrey. *Secret Gardens: A Study of the Golden Age of Children's Literature*. Boston: Houghton, 1985.

Chalmers, Patrick. *Kenneth Grahame: Life, Letters and Unpublished Work*. London: Methuen, 1933.

Clausen, Christopher. "Home and Away in Children's Fiction." *Children's Literature* 10 (1982): 141–52.

Cripps, Elizabeth A. "Kenneth Grahame: Children's Author?" *Children's Literature in Education* 12 (1981): 15–23.

Darcy, Jane. "The Representation of Nature in *The Wind in the Willows* and *The Secret Garden*." *Lion and the Unicorn* 19 (1995): 211–22.

de Board, Robert. *Counselling for Toads: A Psychological Adventure*. London: Routledge, 1998.

DeForest, Mary. "*The Wind in the Willows*: A Tale for Two Readers." *Classical and Modern Literature* 10 (1989): 81–87.

Fadiman, Clifton. "Professionals and Confessionals: Dr. Seuss and Kenneth Grahame." *Only Connect: Readings on Children's Literature.* Ed. Sheila Egoff, G. T. Stubbs, and L. F. Ashley. Toronto: Oxford UP, 1969. 316–22.

Gaarden, Bonnie. "The Inner Family of *The Wind in the Willows.*" *Children's Literature* 22 (1994): 43–57.

Gilead, Sarah. "Grahame's *The Wind in the Willows.*" *Explicator* 46 (1987): 33–36.

Gillin, Richard. "Romantic Echoes in the Willows." *Children's Literature* 16 (1988): 169–74.

"The Golden Age." Rev. of *The Golden Age,* by Kenneth Grahame. *The Spectator* 25 Jan. 1896: 140–41.

Graham, Kathryn. "School and the River: *The Wind in the Willows* and its Immediate Audience." *Children's Literature Association Quarterly* 23 (1998–1999): 181–86.

Grahame, Kenneth. *Dream Days.* 1898. London: John Lane/The Bodley Head, 1902.

_____. *First Whisper of "The Wind in the Willows."* 1944. Ed. Elspeth Grahame. London: Methuen, 1946.

_____. *The Golden Age.* 1895. London: John Lane/The Bodley Head, 1899.

_____. Letters to Elspeth Grahame, 1903–1905. Kenneth Grahame Papers 43839. Bodleian Lib., Oxford.

_____. *My Dearest Mouse: "The Wind in the Willows" Letters.* London: Pavilion, 1988.

_____. *Pagan Papers.* London: John Lane/The Bodley Head, 1898.

_____. *The Wind in the Willows.* 1908. London: Puffin, 1994.

Green, Peter. *Kenneth Grahame 1859–1932: A Study of His Life, Work and Times.* London: John Murray, 1959.

Green, Roger Lancelyn. *Tellers of Tales: Children's Books and Their Authors from 1800 to 1968.* London: Kaye & Ward, 1969.

_____. "'Reed Talk': The Genius of Kenneth Grahame." *The Scots Magazine* July 1945: 262–67.

Greenslade, William. "'Pan' and the Open Road: Critical Paganism in R. L. Stevenson, K. Grahame, E. Thomas and E. M. Forster." *Outside Modernism: In Pursuit of the English Novel, 1900–1930.* Ed. Lynne Hapgood and Nancy L. Paxton. Basingstoke: Macmillan, 2000. 145–61.

Hamilton, Clayton. "Fater Ave Atque Vale: A Personal Appreciation of the Late Kenneth Grahame." *Bookman* Jan. 1933: 69–74.

Hardin and York's Wind in the Willows: Rock Concert. By Eddie Hardin. 1991. DVD. Angel Air Waves, 2003.

Hemmings, Robert. "A Taste of Nostalgia: Children's Books from the Golden Age—Carroll, Grahame, and Milne." *Children's Literature* 35 (2007): 54–79.

Hunt, Peter. "Dialogue and Dialectic: Language and Class in *The Wind in the Willows*." *Children's Literature* 16 (1988): 159–68.

_____. "Necessary Misreadings: Directions in Narrative Theory for Children's Literature." *Studies in the Literary Imagination* 18 (1985): 107–21.

_____. *The Wind in the Willows: A Fragmented Arcadia*. New York: Twayne, 1994.

Johnson, Laurie. "The Wind in the Willows—Tone Poem." *The Music of Laurie Johnson*. Unicorn-Kanchana, 1992.

Kipling, Rudyard. *Just So Stories*. 1902. New York: Weathervane Books, 1978.

Krugman, Laura Ray. "Kenneth Grahame and the Literature of Childhood." *English Literature in Transition* 20 (1977): 3–12.

Kuznets, Lois. *Kenneth Grahame*. Boston: Twayne, 1987.

_____. "Kenneth Grahame and Father Nature, or Whither Blows *The Wind in the Willows*." *Children's Literature* 16 (1988): 175–81.

_____. "Toad Hall Revisited." *Children's Literature* 7 (1978): 115–28.

Lippman, Carlee. "All the Comforts of Home." *Antioch Review* Autumn 1983: 409–20.

Mandler, Peter. "Against 'Englishness': English Culture and the Limits to Rural Nostalgia, 1850–1940." *Transactions of the Royal Historical Society*, Sixth Series 7 (1997): 155–75.

Marshall, Cynthia. "Bodies and Pleasures in *The Wind in the Willows*." *Children's Literature* 22 (1994): 58–69.

McBride, Andrew. "Toad's Syndrome: Addiction to Joy Riding." *Addiction Research* 8 (2000): 129–39.

Meek, Margaret. "Blind Spot: The Limits of Delight." *Books for Keeps* May 1991: 24–5.

Mendelson, Michael. "*The Wind in the Willows* and the Plotting of Contrast." *Children's Literature* 16 (1988): 127–44.

Milne, A. A. *Toad of Toad Hall: A Play from Kenneth Grahame's Book*. 1929. New York: Scribner's, 1957.

Moore, John David. "Pottering around in the Garden: Kenneth Grahame's Version of Pastoral in *The Wind in the Willows*." *Journal of the Midwest Modern Language Association* 23 (1990): 45–60.

"Mr. Kenneth Grahame." Rev. of *The Golden Age*, by Kenneth Grahame. *The Academy* 4 Dec. 1897: 493.

Needle, Jan. *Wild Wood*. 1981. London: Methuen, 1982.

Parker, W. M. *Modern Scottish Writers*. Edinburgh: William Hodge & Co., 1917.

Philip, Neil. "*The Wind in the Willows*: The Vitality of a Classic." *Children and Their Books: A Celebration of the Work of Iona and Peter Opie*. Ed. Gillian Avery and Julia Briggs. Oxford: Clarendon Press, 1989. 299–316.

Poss, Geraldine. "An Epic in Arcadia: The Pastoral World of *The Wind in the Willows*." *Children's Literature* 4 (1975): 80–90.

Prince, Alison. *Kenneth Grahame: An Innocent in the Wild Wood*. London: Alison & Busby, 1994.

Pryce-Jones, Alan. "Kenneth Grahame." *London Mercury* Sept. 1932: 446–49.

Robson, William W. "On *The Wind in the Willows*." *Hebrew University Studies in Literature and the Arts* 9 (1981): 76–106.

Rutter, John. "The Reluctant Dragon." *Three Musical Fables*. Collegium, 1993.

Sale, Roger. "The Audience in Children's Literature." *Bridges to Fantasy*. Ed. George E. Slusser, Eric S. Rabkin, and Robert Scholes. Carbondale: Southern Illinois UP, 1982. 78–89.

———. *Fairy Tales and After: From Snow White to E. B. White*. Cambridge, MA: Harvard UP, 1978.

Schlobin, Roger. "Danger and Compulsion in *The Wind in the Willows*, or Toad and Hyde Together at Last." *Journal of the Fantastic in the Arts* 8.3 (1997): 34–41.

Schwab, Sandra Martina. "What is a Man?: The Refuting of the Chivalric Ideal at the Turn of the Century." *Beyond Arthurian Romances: The Reach of Victorian Medievalism*. Ed. Lorretta M. Holloway and Jennifer A. Palmgren. New York: Palgrave Macmillan, 2005. 217–31.

Steig, Michael. "At the Back of *The Wind in the Willows*: An Experiment in Biographical and Autobiographical Interpretation." *Victorian Studies* 24 (1981): 303–23.

Sterk, Kenneth. "Rereading *The Wind in the Willows*." *Children's Literature in Education* 4 (1973): 20–28.

Stevenson, Deborah. "The River Bank Redux? Kenneth Grahame's *The Wind in the Willows* and William Horwood's *The Willows in Winter*." *Children's Literature Association Quarterly* 21 (1996): 126–32.

Thum, Maureen. "Exploring 'The Country of the Mind': Mental Dimensions of Landscape in Kenneth Grahame's *The Wind in the Willows*." *Children's Literature Association Quarterly* 17 (1992): 27–32.

Tucker, Nicholas. "The Children's Falstaff." *Times Literary Supplement* 26 June 1969. Rpt. in *Suitable for Children? Controversies in Children's Literature*. Ed. Nicholas Tucker. London: Chatto and Windus for Sussex UP, 1978. 160–64.

Waddey, Lucy. "Home in Children's Fiction: Three Patterns." *Children's Literature Association Quarterly* 8 (1983): 13–14.

Wall, Barbara. *The Narrator's Voice: The Dilemma of Children's Fiction.* Basingstoke, Hampshire: Macmillan, 1991.

Watkins, Tony. "Reconstructing the Homeland: Loss and Hope in the English Landscape." *Aspects and Issues in the History of Children's Literature.* Contributions to the Study of World Lit. Ed. Maria Nikolajeva. Westport, CT: Greenwood Press, 1995. 165–72.

West, Mark I. "Narcissism in *The Wind and the Willows.*" *Psychoanalytic Responses to Children's Literature.* Ed. Lucy Rollin and Mark I. West. Jefferson, NC: McFarland & Co., 1999. 45–51.

Willis, Lesley. "'A Sadder and Wiser Rat / He Rose on the Morrow Morn': Echoes of the Romantics in Kenneth Grahame's *The Wind in the Willows.*" *Children's Literature Association Quarterly* 13 (1988): 108–11.

The Wind in the Willows. *The Wind in the Willows.* 1968. Fallout, 2007.

Wolf, Virginia. "The Linear Image: The Road and the River in the Juvenile Novel." Eds. Susan R. Gannon and Ruth Anne Thompson. *Proceedings of the Thirteenth Annual Conference of the Children's Literature Association.* West Lafayette, IN: Education Department, Purdue U, 1986: 41–47.

Wullschläger, Jackie. *Inventing Wonderland: The Lives and Fantasies of Lewis Carroll, Edward Lear, J. M. Barrie, Kenneth Grahame and A. A. Milne.* New York: Free Press, 1995.

PART I

COMPETING DISCOURSES

~

Deus ex Natura or Nonstick Pan?: Competing Discourses in Kenneth Grahame's *The Wind in the Willows*

David Rudd

Introduction

Since its initial publication, when *The Times* described it as "negligible as a contribution to natural history" (qtd. in Green 257), *The Wind in the Willows* has been regarded as one of the most contradictory texts in children's literature. It has, in fact, often been the subject of debates as to whether it is a children's book at all (e.g., Gilead; Robson 143). As is well-known, the novel arose from stories about Toad told to Grahame's son, Alastair. But this child's story was then wedded (some would say as uneasily as was Grahame himself) to what is seen as more adult material. The pull between the two can clearly be seen in Grahame's vacillation over titles, ranging from "Mr. Mole and his Mates" to "The Wind in the Reeds."

This tension, along with other contestatory elements, helps give the book a hybrid vigor (that is, using "hybrid" in its original, biological sense of being composed of mixed parts or species) that is personified in Pan, a hybrid figure himself, who manages to hold the book together. This said, the specter of the god having a pipe at the Gates of Dawn does, perhaps, need contextualizing. My notion of "hybrid vigor" is pursued in slightly different terms by Sarah Gilead, who envisages the book as an excellent case study of what is at the heart of "canonical works of children's literature": a "dynamic tension" between an idyllic, childhood realm and the adult world that subverts it. For Gilead, the river symbolizes the "child-kingdom" (151), while the undoing of the childhood idyll occurs in chapter 9 ("Wayfarers All"), where the impossibility of realizing one's "self-indulgent wishfulness" (155) becomes clear. According to Gilead, "Pan . . . seems redundant" as the river "has already demonstrated Grahame's mythopoeia" (155). But it is problematic to see how Pan can epitomize this childish, pleasurable realm while also standing for its opposite, "denigrating adventure in favor of prudence" (153). It is perhaps for this reason that Pan hardly features in Gilead's analysis,[1] whereas I am arguing that his "hybrid vigor," expressing the tensions of the book, is central.

Grahame was quite aware of many of these tensions, seeming to delight in his book's intertextual allusiveness almost in a modernist fashion, as this comment on his own style of composition suggests:

[A] theme . . . is in most cases little more than a sort of clothes-line on which one pegs a string of ideas, quotations, allusions, and so on, one's mental under-garments of all shapes and sizes, some possibly fairly new, but most rather old and patched; they dance and sway in the breeze, they flap and flutter, or hang limp and lifeless. And some are ordinary enough, and some are of a rather private and intimate shape and give the owner away, even show up his or her peculiarities. And, owing to the invisible clothes-line, they seem to have connexion and continuity. (qtd. in Chalmers 216)

At heart Grahame seems to remain the essayist who launched his career with *Pagan Papers*, intermingling narrative with nature writing, mystical musings, parodies, and pastiches. While some critics (e.g., Carpenter) might find these distracting in a novel, such shifts in style and register are undoubtedly deliberate; Grahame moves willfully from the classical to the mystical, from the slapstick to the philosophical and, in style, from the mock-medieval language of popular Victorian historical novelists like Harrison Ainsworth ("Oddsbodkins") to real estate agent pastiche ("Toad Hall . . . is an eligible self-contained gentleman's residence . . . replete with every modern convenience. Up-to-date sanitation. Five minutes from church, post office, and golf-links" [Grahame,

Wind 87, 103]). This discursive mix was all grist to Grahame's mill, for in his own mind, he thought he had a strong enough clothesline on which these disparate elements could not only hang, but dance.

Baldly, these garments—the character types, both animal and human, the descriptions of nature, the intertextual allusions, the stylistic shifts—are linked in his text by his underlying theme, which is about what makes life meaningful. This theme itself comes to life only through the animating wind of the title. Moreover, for Grahame, as for so many Romantics, the wind is itself a metaphor for inspiration, the word *inspirare* meaning to "breathe into" something. It is there, for instance, at the opening of Wordsworth's *The Prelude*, "Oh there is blessing in this gentle breeze" (1), where the wind is invoked in place of the muses, with the added suggestion that it "reaches only the ears of a chosen few," to quote Grahame's own essay, "The Rural Pan" (32).[2] In the course of Grahame's novel, then, the coordinates of a meaningful life are plotted across the three interlinked realms of Wild Wood, Wide World, and River Bank. Indeed, it is of note that Grahame juxtaposes a similar threesome in a lecture he gave in 1921, which touches on the same theme:

> . . . your hill-top may disappoint you, and your sea-coast be too stuffy or too expensive, but the mountain air of dreamland is always recuperating, and there Apollo and all the Muses, or at least Pan and his attendant Fauna, await you. (Grahame, "Ideals" 271–72)

It is of note too that Pan, rather than the Muses, is seen to be the most dependable figure. And for Grahame, as for many others at the *fin de siècle*, Pan is synonymous with the inspirational wind, as he is of all animated nature. Pan is there from the very first page in *The Wind in the Willows*, in the image of the stirrings of the spring air, "penetrating with its spirit of divine discontent and longing" (1).

I shall have more to say about Pan later, arguing that he does indeed make manifest the "invisible" coherence of Grahame's otherwise disparate assortment of garments. But, as suggested in the above quotation, in which Grahame sees Pan as possibly more reliable than the female muses, such coherence seems to come at the expense of the female. For while an inspiring wind might animate the garments on Grahame's fictional clothesline, this would only occur after some invisible female had pegged out the clothes; indeed, just such a lowly washerwoman features in Grahame's novel, where she suffers "[t]he chaff and the humorous sallies" (106) of males. However, before I come to this, let me finish discussing just how disparate these garments are.

A Contradictory Text: Garments of "All Shapes and Sizes"

The shifts in style discussed earlier are linked to the larger debate about whether the book, with its mix of registers, is really for children or adults. The adventures of Toad are frequently seen as being for the former, the parallel story of Mole's exploits slightly less so (especially in "Wayfarers All"), and the intrusions of Pan in "The Piper at the Gates of Dawn" as, for many, "an error of judgement on a grand scale" (Carpenter 169). Undoubtedly the book is a discursive mix (as Grahame seems to have been aware) but, as Bakhtin made most plain, this is very much the nature of the novel *per se*. However, critics still like to pontificate about who, exactly, the intended audience is. Humphrey Carpenter can thus dogmatically claim that "*The Wind in the Willows* has nothing to do with childhood or children, except in that it can be enjoyed by the young, who thereby experience (though they do not rationally understand) what its author has to say, and are able to sense some of its resonances" (168). Not only is his opening generalization unhelpful, but it is itself undermined by the ensuing subordinate clauses. But apart from this criticism, one would want to query the suggestion that it is *adults* who do the understanding. Would we, for instance, include *The Times* reviewer, who finds the book's contribution to natural history minimal? Or what about those whom W. W. Robson accuses of having an "anti-religious bias" in their hostility to "The Piper" chapter: "[a]nyone who could read this chapter and imagine that the author was thinking about politics goes beyond my comprehension" (131–32). Robson, who also avers that the book "ignores sex" (143), would presumably find Peter Hunt equally uncomprehending in his claim that Grahame "seems to have drifted into very questionable sexual waters" in "The Piper" chapter (Hunt 88). Even leaving aside the question of adult rationality, one would still want to question Carpenter's assertion that children lack such a quality, that they are inherently intuitive rather than rational.

While debates about issues of audience are perhaps the most commonly discussed contradiction within Grahame's text, critics have also focused on other contradictions in the novel. For example, several critics have noted the inconsistency of scale in Grahame's depictions of his main animal characters. This inconsistency is of concern to Robson, though he too feels the need to divide and generalize by age: "Children notice these things," he claims (123); thus, "[w]hen Toad is disguised as a washerwoman he seems to be washerwoman size, but when the barge-woman detects him he is toad size (she picks him up by the leg and throws him into the river)" (122). We could, of course, respond by saying that there are many precedents in other shape-changing trickster figures, from Loki, Anansi, and Till Eulenspiegel to Bugs Bunny and Ulysses, Toad being most explicitly linked with the latter. Alternatively, one could respond in the manner of A. A. Milne:

> . . . it is necessary to think of Mole, for instance, sometimes as an actual mole, sometimes as a mole in human clothes, sometimes as a mole grown to human size, sometimes walking on two legs, sometimes on four. He is a mole, he isn't a mole. What is he? I don't know. And, not being a matter-of-fact person, I don't mind. (Milne vii)

A related tension is that between naturalism and anthropomorphism. Ironically, Grahame himself declared that he used animals because he

> felt a duty to them as a friend. Every animal, by instinct, lives according to his nature. Thereby he lives wisely, and betters the tradition of mankind. No animal is ever tempted to deny his nature. No animal knows how to tell a lie. Every animal is honest. Every animal is true—and is, therefore, according to his nature, both beautiful and good. (Hamilton, from a conversation with Grahame, 72)

I say "ironically" because, taking this statement at face value, Grahame's work seems a complete travesty, with Toad most obviously transgressing all such authorial guidelines. Indeed, none of the main characters lives according to its nature—although the supposedly feckless Wild-Wooders might be seen the closest, at least, until their seizure of Toad Hall. It is actually when Grahame tries to write in a more naturalistic way—closer, say, to Beatrix Potter[3]—that he creates more contradictions for his otherwise anthropomorphic characters.

Thus one of the most disturbing images in the book is surely that of the "errant May-fly" swerving across the path of Mole, Rat, and Otter, "in the intoxicated fashion affected by young bloods . . . seeing life" (*Wind* 10). In its anthropomorphism, this episode seems to parallel the equally errant Mole's decision to abandon spring cleaning a few pages earlier. However, the May-fly is promptly devoured by Otter for its errantry, though we are told that animal-etiquette forbids any reference to the activity (Robson's claim that the book "ignores sex and death" [143] is obviously open to challenge on both counts).[4]

The anthropomorphism of the animals, especially the River-Bankers, has led to them being interpreted allegorically, resulting in partial, and sometimes contradictory readings. Thus Peter Green sees them as upper-middle class *rentiers*, with the Wild-Wooders as a "stunted, malevolent proletariat" (Green 246). In this way Grahame can be accused of trying to naturalize a class society in social Darwinian terms. Carpenter, on the other hand, sees the Wild-Wooders as less "working-class mob" than "dissipated gentry" in their treatment of Toad Hall (Carpenter 165), partly basing his reading on the chapter's title, "Return of Ulysses," which links the interlopers formally with Penelope's suitors in *The Odyssey*.[5] In another reading still, Gilead sees the usurpers of Toad Hall as "metaphors for Toad's libidinal aggressive/erotic drives" (156).

To bring this section to a close, let me stress again that my purpose here is not to arbitrate between the different readings of the text. Rather I want to show that the text itself, since its initial reception as *faux* "natural history," has appeared contradictory with its garments "of all shapes and sizes," and has therefore generated contradictory interpretations. But I've also suggested that such critical interpretations arise from partial readings of the text, in which critics ignore certain elements (Gilead with Pan, for instance). In contrast, I maintain that there is unity within Grahame's discursive mix, a unity embodied in the figure of Pan.

Pan as Pandemic

Pan is a demigod from Greek mythology, renowned for his sexual appetite and most often represented as a hybrid being, half-goat, half-human, with horns and legendary panpipes. He obtained these pipes after chasing the nymph Syrinx, who initially escaped Pan by being turned into a reed, only to be then fashioned into one of his reed pipes. His name derives from the Greek word for "pasture," though in folk etymology he has come to be associated with *pan*, Greek for "everything" (as captured in words like "pandemic"); and, in the *fin de siècle* he certainly was everywhere. Peter Green mentions three traditions on which writers drew: one in which Pan "incarnated terror and cruelty, the rejected forces of nature taking their revenge," a second that emphasized "his sexual attributes . . . the fierce unrestrained lechery free of all human conventions" (Green 141), and a third that saw the god in more benign terms, as one who "loveth the more unpretentious humankind" (Grahame, "Rural" 33). Robert Dingley explains Pan's particular appeal at this time as arising from a void that Darwin had created in removing God's hand from creation. Rather than accept existence as a meaningless struggle, many held on to nature as itself spiritually imbued—usefully personified in the figure of the god Pan, as Grahame shows in his essay "The Rural Pan." The key to Pan's appeal for Grahame as a figure in *Wind*, I would suggest, lies in the flexibility of this figure's signification: as a hybrid being that melds the natural (in both the bestial, and unspoilt, senses) and the supernatural (spiritual, disembodied). It is scarcely surprising, then, that he is most readily found between the wilds of the Wild Wood and the byways of the Wide World, at the River Bank.

Pan operates in Grahame's text like a pandemic. He can be detected at levels from the phonological to the thematic, and, between these, he is captured in both imagery and symbol; more indirectly, Pan's presence is also marked by the characters' own levels of awareness of him. But Pan's actual inclusion in the novel was a late decision. As Grahame himself writes, the "invisible clothes-line" seems to emerge only retrospectively, as a result of inspecting the variegated material hung thereon. We certainly know that this was the case in that the "Wayfarers All" and "The Piper at the Gates of Dawn" chapters were added last, making the animating figure of Pan more explicit (Green 206) and thereby giving the text's clothesline an inspiriting lift.

However, as noted earlier, Pan is implicit in the title and from the first page on, being made more overt in the opening chapter when Mole catches, "with his ear to the reed-stems . . . something of what the wind went whispering so constantly among them" (*Wind* 14). Note the repeated /w/ sound here, mixed with the susurrant /s/. Not for nothing is the /w/ known as an "approximant" consonant, such that, in articulating it, the speech organs come close together, yet are then drawn apart in its voicing,[6] simulating what the hybrid Pan does with his reed pipes: forcing the stems apart as his breath blows through them, inspiriting the landscape and inspiring those who witness it.

Grahame's earlier, preferred title, *The Wind in the Reeds*, was not used (owing to its similarity to William Butler Yeats's 1899 work, *The Wind among the Reeds*), but in some ways it does not matter, for the /w/ sound is still neatly linked with the /r/, both phonologically (r is another approximant) and thematically, with the river itself being animatedly forced between its constraining banks. These three elements—reed pipes, river, and Pan himself—are most overtly united in a later sentence from "The Piper," depicting Mole's awe: "Breathless and transfixed the Mole stopped rowing as the liquid run of that glad piping broke on him like a wave, caught him up, and possessed him entirely" (93). But the association is first made when Mole is introduced to the river, which is both fellow animal and a human (another hybrid, of course):

> . . . this sleek, sinuous, full-bodied animal, chasing and chuckling . . . Mole was bewitched, entranced, fascinated . . . he trotted as one trots, when very small, by the side of a man who holds one spellbound by exciting stories; and when tired at last, he sat on the bank, while the river still chattered on to him, a babbling procession of the best stories in the world, sent from the heart of the earth to be told at last to the insatiable sea. (3)

Grahame might have taken this last image from Robert Louis Stevenson's essay, "Pan Pipes" (1878), in which Stevenson writes of "a shaggy world . . . where the salt and tumbling sea receives clear rivers running from among reeds and lilies" (Stevenson 182). This said, Grahame makes Pan's inspirational character more explicit, capable of transforming those who hear his imaginative fictions.[7] It is also worth noting that the river is male, intimated not only in the epithets used ("sinuous, full-bodied") but more explicitly in the simile of Mole being a child to it, to that old "man" river that just keeps rolling along.[8] I shall return to the river's gendering and its association with Pan later.

The eventual title, *The Wind in the Willows*, does have the advantage of yoking together the two other alliterative phrases that Grahame deliberately contrasts in the book, the Wild Wood and the Wide World. The former represents primitive, untamed nature and often seems to be coded female, though its denizens are predominantly male. As noted above, Grahame's animal heroes are precisely *not* true to their nature, being heavily anthropomorphized; the Wild Wood's inhabitants, however, at least earlier in the book, seem less so. The Wide World, in contrast, is the opposite, being associated with civilization and modernity. In fact, if the presiding presence of Pan were to be split in two, it would be tempting to see the Wild Wood as represented by his lower, corporeal half—darker, shaggy, excessive and amoral—as against an upper, relatively depilated, human side (especially as depicted in many sanitized Victorian images). But this would be an oversimplification as each of these realms is seen to lack Pan's more spiritual dimension. The crucial point, then, is where these realms come together: just as the river's energy comes from its containment between two banks, so Pan's animating principle lies in the air he blows through the reeds of his pipe (which is itself fashioned out of the natural and the "human" [i.e., Syrinx]).

In order to move on the argument about the centrality of Pan, let me now explore how his presence, or even his absence in some cases, impacts on each of these three realms, and the characters associated with them. The Wild Wood, as just noted, has connotations of unruliness, of unpredictability, of a place where it is easy to lose oneself.[9] In the "Wild Wood" chapter, nature is not only more red in tooth and claw but is also more sensual, depicted as "bare and entirely leafless . . . deep in her annual slumber," having "kicked the clothes off" and been "stripped of . . . finery" (31–2). In the Wood itself, a predatory, feminine sexuality emerges, with much talk of "[h]oles, hollows, pools, pitfalls, and other black menaces" (37). Mole's fear mounts as the "holes made ugly mouths at him on either side," before he discerns the first "little evil wedge-shaped face, looking out at him from a hole," soon to be followed by "hundreds of them"—that is, holes with faces. Not only is this imagery sexual, it even seems to mount in rhythmic frenzy:

He passed another hole, and another, and another; and then—yes!—no!—yes! certainly a little narrow face, with hard eyes, had flashed up

for an instant from a hole, and was gone. . . . Then suddenly, and as
if it had been so all the time, every hole, far and near, and there were
hundreds of them, seemed to possess its face, coming and going rapidly,
all fixing on him glances of malice and hatred; all hard-eyed and evil
and sharp. (33)

Mole longs to "get away from the holes in the banks," and the sudden appearance of Rat comically stages "the valorous animal," phal-
lically laden with "his pistols, and the great ugly cudgel in his grasp,"
vanquishing the "Terror of the Wild Wood" (34–35).

The Wild Wood thus emerges as a dark and unruly realm, certainly,
but also as one that is effete and tractable, as Rat's "macho" intervention shows. Moreover, it is a realm seemingly bereft of Pan, although
it does seem to contain a figure with the power of a god: Badger, who
not only stands at the Wood's center, but is initially regarded by Mole
as quite god-like: "He seemed, by all accounts, to be such an important
personage and, though rarely visible, to make his unseen influence felt
by everybody about the place" (29). He's someone to whom people
turn when "in any fix," although he often seems "to know of it somehow" (50). His manifestation is also a much-anticipated event: "he'll
be coming along some day, if you'll wait quietly" (30). Certainly, for
Mole, Badger seems the answer to his earlier "divine discontent," and
"he found his thoughts dwelling again with much persistence on the
solitary grey Badger, who lived his own life by himself, in his hole in
the middle of the Wild Wood" (30).

However, when Mole finally reaches Badger, he (and we) soon
sees that Badger is no god at all (not that he ever pretends to be).
Whereas Mole was initially aroused by the whisperings of the wind,
Badger delights in its absence, declaring, "I *hate* a draught myself"
(53). Badger and his kind, "an enduring lot" (54), seem to lack any
spiritual dimension, which is perhaps why this otherwise central character is conspicuously absent from the rescue of Portly in "The Piper"
chapter.[10] He is also shown to be unsuccessful in making converts,
significantly failing to make Toad see "the error of his ways" (78),
although Badger initially thinks otherwise. All that Badger does do
effectively is play a leading role in the clunky *deus ex machina* at the
novel's end. Both here, and in keeping a lid on the feminized realm
of the Wild Wood—"Any friend of *mine* walks where he likes in this

country, or I'll know the reason why!" (55)—he is also a stereotypically male figure.

If the Wild Wood is painted as a benighted realm, then the Wide World is its opposite: a civilized realm of modernity, although such modernity comes at the expense of losing touch with nature. In fact, Grahame seems to see these realms as in many ways similar, especially when we are told that the Wild Wood was once a "city of people" who thought they "would last for ever" (54). Patricia Crain, speaking about Susan Warner's *The Wide Wide World*, notes how common this phrase, "the Wide World," was in nineteenth-century literature, being linked to "friendlessness and loneliness" (Crain 144).[11] In Grahame's novel, the Wide World is generally a philistine realm, overrun by machinery—which, of course, is what appeals to Toad, who, in common with Badger, seems to lack any spiritual dimension. Unlike Rat and Mole, who are most closely associated with the River Bank, these other two are never seen communing mystically with nature. But whereas Badger is content to live ingenuously in the wild, Toad is not: he is the one most attracted by the Wide World, lacking any affinity with nature. The river itself seems alien to him; even in a boat he is observed "splashing badly and rolling a good deal" (10); and when he does actually enter its waters, it is only as a result of being flung there by a barge-woman, in the opposite of a baptismal, spiritual experience. The sound of the wind in the reed stems thus remains closed to him. He might exhibit the trance state of those inspired, being described as alternately "dreamy" and in "violent paroxysms" (*Wind* 25, 80), but it is only in response to the call of false gods, those of Mammon, with his punts, his houseboats, his caravans, and, ultimately, his cars.[12] Toad, then, never hears what is close to home, "always" reaching for "somebody else's horizon" (25). But though different from Badger in this regard (Badger likes to stay in his womb-like burrow), the characters are alike in showing no signs of development, either spiritually or in terms of self-knowledge.[13]

In contrast to these two figures—one down-to-earth (in the Wild Wood), the other always eyeing the horizon (the Wide World)—are Rat and Mole, both linked to the River Bank and its spiritual offerings, where the wind is indeed in the willows and among the reeds. They too, though, are not immune from temptation by false gods. Mole, as I've already discussed, is initially captivated by Badger, as is Rat later by the wayfarer, the Sea Rat: "O, those southern seaports! The smell of them, the riding-lights at night, the glamour!" (123). The alluring alliteration (southern seaports . . . smell), the assonance and rhyme (riding-lights . . . night) make explicit the Sea Rat's resemblance to one of Ulysses's Sirens, as well as to Coleridge's "Ancient Mariner." But the Sea Rat's vision of the Wide World is shown to be as false as Toad's; indeed, the language is often similar, each fastening on the distant horizon (25, 122), whether it is Toad observing the "glittering plate-glass and rich morocco" of a car (24) or the Sea Rat describing the "flash and shimmer" of lights "on the polished steel prows of the swaying gondolas" (124). The Sea Rat is, notably, also a *male* Siren—whose "wonderful talk" imitates the river's in the way that it "flowed on" (127). Moreover, just as Toad, like Ulysses, needs tying down (being locked in his room) in order to avoid being carried away, so too Rat needs holding down and locking in, his energies eventually being rechanneled by Mole from this false muse into the imaginative realm of "dreamland," of poetic composition. Here I'm invoking Grahame's words from earlier, where "dreamland," attended by Pan, is lauded over "your sea-coast."

Thus instead of staying at home in one's womb-like space, or going where the whim takes one (and risking the loss of home altogether, as Toad almost does), a more liminal zone is suggested. Geographically Grahame represents it as situated between wood and world, and mentally, as an idyllic space where the joys of home (conversation, good food, companionship) can be enhanced by a spiritual awareness of life, of "going with the flow," as the Taoists might put it. It is appropriate, then, that the chapter in which the Piper himself becomes manifest is at the book's center, sandwiched between these two other realms, just as the river is itself contained by its banks.

By making Pan appear, though, Grahame has been accused of overstepping the mark (e.g., Carpenter 169; Sale 189). But it is hard to see where this mark might lie, given that a fantasy world is clearly entered at the outset of this anthropomorphic tale, with a mole whitewashing his house. Unlike naturalistic works such as *Tarka the Otter*, Grahame's novel features hybrid animal-human figures throughout: Mole with his plaster casts of Garibaldi and Queen Victoria; Toad finding the gaoler's daughter a "comely lass," regretting "the social gulf between them" (104), and so on.

But the humorous side of these characters is balanced by their attempts to find a meaningful life (though, with Toad, the two go together). We thus witness each of the three main figures, Mole, Rat, and Toad, going through a crisis linked to the pursuit of his desires. Mole, who initially hears something in the wind, thinks he has found the answer in the person of Badger, and thus experiences his long dark night of the soul in the Wild Wood before eventually gaining entry to the Badger's domain. While Badger is undoubtedly a savior of sorts (for both Mole and Rat), it is not in any spiritual way. There is a parallel, though, between Badger sheltering Mole and Rat in his womb-like space "in the middle of the Wild Wood" (30), and Pan, not only at the center of the whole book, but also on an island at the center of the river, creating an equally womb-like space for Portly. Toad's and Rat's infatuations are, as I've suggested above, more clearly paralleled, with both characters being confined in order to protect them from their seducers; Rat successfully so, Toad not. More generally, the Wild Wood and the Wide World are each shown to lack the spiritual dimension that is to be found at the River itself. The book, then, gestures toward "The Piper" as its climactic episode (in terms of structure and theme) rather than the overt, contrived climax of "Mr. Mole and His Mates," in which the friends emerge from their secret passage to regain control, not only of Toad Hall, but of the text itself, effecting its swift and clunky closure. I use this early alternative title deliberately, because it would have been a more obvious choice *only* if we had not had the psychological crises of Mole, Rat, and Toad, which render the *deus ex machina* ending insufficient.

But, given the way the novel is structured, the parallelisms that have been established, it is fitting that the two more spiritually aware characters—"those who were called and chosen"—are rewarded for their attentiveness to "something of what the wind went whispering" (*Wind* 14). Indeed, it would have been stranger to keep Pan entirely in the wings, as a mere wind-machine (another *deus ex machina*). This said, it needs emphasizing that what Mole and Rat experience is a "Vision" only (95), supplemented, after Pan has vanished, with Rat almost speaking in tongues as he interprets the words behind "the wind playing in the reeds."[14]

As announced by its title, this section has been about the centrality of Pan. I have suggested that critics who argue that Pan's manifestation is out of place often neglect the extent of his presence within the text. Moreover, picking up on Grahame's notion of an "invisible clothesline," in much of the novel Pan's existence is marked precisely by his absence—in draught-free realms like the Wild Wood and the Wide World. The former is a post-Darwinian realm where nature is simply red in tooth and claw; the latter a realm where material trappings are preeminent. Pan, then, must remain discreet. He is central to the book (from the title on) and is physically at its center, yet his appearance occurs in a backwater, as a vision only, and only for the select and prepared few.

Pan—God of "Everything"?

This select few, though, are redoubtably male, as of course is Pan, his gigolo history having been rehearsed earlier. So while this figure animates the text, gesturing toward a deeper and more meaningful life, it is one that is decidedly gendered.[15] Other critics have noted the male-centeredness of this text before (e.g., Hunt; Poss), but this is generally seen in terms of character, whereas I want to suggest that its gendering runs deeper. For, as the Marxist critic Pierre Macherey notes, works do not simply reflect ideology but mobilize it, staging magical resolutions that seek to hide their faultlines and contradictions. Macherey is particularly attentive to a text's absences, to the things *not said*, which, in Grahame's case are not only elided within the text itself, but are endorsed epitextually by the author, who was fond of describing his work as, for example, "clean of the clash of sex" and having only "negative" qualities (once again, things not said), "i.e.—no problems, no sex, no second meaning" (qtd. in Prince 238, 240). As others have pointed out, such repeatedly evasive statements have made us more attentive to the mental nether garments on Grahame's clothesline, though the author must be credited with admitting they might "give the owner away, and show up his or her peculiarities" (qtd. in Chalmers 216).

Thus although we have Mother Nature referred to in the text, it is a male god that stands over and above her. Indeed, it is a male wind that moves nature—whether her reed stems or willows—just as, in the original myth, it was Pan who fashioned the reed-transformed nymph, Syrinx, into "[a] musical instrument," (349) before playing her (as

Elizabeth Barrett Browning's 1862 poem makes explicit). It is also a male river that moves between nature's banks (as Alan Bennett wittily remarked, it sounds "too much like Mellors the gamekeeper" [Bennett 220]). And in "The Piper" chapter, while it is the female moon who "did what she could . . . to help them in their quest," her aid proves for naught: "till her hour came and she sank earthwards reluctantly, and left them" (91). It is Pan who does the actual rescuing.[16] And the family group that we are presented with at this moment is all-male too, comprising Rat, Mole, and Portly, with Pan as *paterfamilias* in his womb-like space. So, when Green writes that this chapter "forms a mystical testament to [Grahame's] *fin de siècle* faith in the beneficent, personalized powers of Nature" (Green 252), it needs stressing that this Mother Nature is herself under the thumb of a decidedly male god; for, however sanitized Pan is, he still represents "a shaggy world . . . lewd, and cruel," with an "uncouth, outlandish strain," as Stevenson (181–82) describes him. This appropriation by the male occurs elsewhere, too, as I've alluded: the Siren wayfarer is also male; moreover, in that late essay, "Ideals," Pan is accompanied by "Fauna" rather than the traditional female nymphs; finally, in "The Return of Ulysses," there is no Penelope in sight: once again, it is an all-male family.[17] The only females mentioned in these closing paragraphs are the "mother-weasels" who, with their babies, do obeisance to "the great Mr. Toad," "the gallant Water Rat," and "the famous Mr Mole," and threaten their weasel offspring with the bogeyman of "the terrible grey Badger" (*Wind* 184).

In short, the male-centric nature of the text, noted by others, is not only consolidated by making Pan the animating principle, but simultaneously compromises any notions of his spiritual impartiality over "unpretentious humankind" (Grahame, "Rural" 33).

Conclusion

I have argued against the idea that Grahame presents us with a "non-stick" Pan, a being out of place in a work that is essentially a children's adventure story. It might have started out as an oral tale about Toad's adventures, but *en route* it turned into something else. So, rather than seeing Toad's adventures as establishing the norm, with the spiritual as an unwarranted intrusion, I would argue that it is Toad's materialism that is actually found wanting, leading him and others astray. Toad believes in a more literal *deus ex machina*, incarnated in the motor-car, constructing a shrine to this deity in his bedroom. One might, of course, ask why, if the Piper is so important, his chapter doesn't end the book (it could quite easily have done so), but I think that this is part of Grahame's scheme: the spiritual dimension that he was attempting to capture is not for everyone (it "reaches only the ears of a chosen few," to repeat Grahame's words from earlier); neither is it part of the everyday. It can, therefore, be caught only fleetingly, in byways and backwaters, and by those that have been prepared—which is why the vision is at the book's center (and the River's, come to that), as an emotional climax rather than an action-centered one.[18] To have Pan appear for the latter, routing the Wild-Wooders from Toad Hall, would have turned this mystical god into the very *deus ex machina* that Grahame was trying to avoid.

Rat and (especially) Mole, then, have followed a road less traveled (certainly, than one of Toad's), paying attention to a *deus ex natura* instead; although, in the way that Grahame has depicted him, he might more correctly be labeled a *deus supra natura*: a god who rules *over* nature, and a female-coded one at that. So while Grahame's clothes take wing on this inspirited wind, making the clothesline manifest, it is at the expense of the washerwoman and other females who, with this move, might claim that their invisibility becomes equally manifest.

Notes

1. More strangely, Pan is curiously neglected in Hunt's entire monograph.

2. David Sandner, in a chapter called "The 'Correspondent Breeze,'" quotes M. H. Abrams on the way that the Romantics tended to draw less on the muses than the wind as a source of inspiration. Coleridge, in fact, is quoted as using the unfortunate phrase "bottom-wind," which Sandner recycles without a blink (43). This shifting conception of inspiration aside, Sandner omits to note the way that this use makes inspiration, along with the whole process of creativity, a more male phenomenon. Among contemporary children's authors, similar appropriations are to be found elsewhere, as, for instance, in Barrie's *The Little White Bird* and Milne's Pooh books. This male-centric aspect of the text is dealt with at the end of my essay.

3. Potter resented Grahame's lack of attention to natural detail, complaining of Toad "combing his *hair*" (qtd. in Linder 175).

4. Death is more explicit later, from Pan himself, speaking through Rat: *"Lest limbs be reddened and rent—I spring the trap that is set. . . ."* (Grahame, *Wind* 161).

5. One might add that it is not just upper-middle-class adults who celebrate leisure, or who like "messing about" (in boats and elsewhere); children are, in fact, specialists in this area, as well as in feasting on "coldtonguecoldhamcoldbeefpickledgherkins" (5) or, indeed, in acting out their fantasies by piling up chairs to fashion a Toadish car.

6. It is notable that both Jan Needle and William Horwood keep this alliterative /w/ in their very different reworkings: *Wild Wood* and *The Willows in Winter*, respectively.

7. Humphrey Carpenter links it more explicitly to the creative process of writing. In Grahame's description of the river there are clear echoes of Coleridge's "Kubla Khan," with its inspirational subterranean spring. The reference to "Genesis" in Graham Robertson's original frontispiece, "And a river went out from Eden," is thus ambiguous. In Lacanian terms it connotes our entry into the symbolic, which is a move in a fictional direction, from which we establish a tenuous identity. Grahame's clothesline analogy is itself suggestive of Lacan's notion of the *après-coup*, the meaning of anything (even a sentence) being established only retrospectively; we thus move from topic to topic, from signifier to signifier, without any certainty of where we're going till the end, when sense is made.

8. In his essay "The Rural Pan," Grahame actually speaks of "the sinuous Mole" (33), making this link stronger.

9. Scholars have drawn various links between *Wind* and Oscar Wilde, but there's one that is both obvious yet subliminal: in the name itself, the Wild-Wooders, those with whom Rat is "very good friends," despite the fact that "they break out sometimes, there's no denying it" (*Wind* 7). The link is even clearer if one remembers that it is a water-rat who is "The Devoted Friend" in Wilde's collection of fairy tales, *The Happy Prince* (cf. Green 280).

10. One could argue that he is simply a creature of nature, subject to its rhythms, as emphasized in his hibernating tendencies. He and, indeed, the whole Wild Wood therefore represent a nature that lacks a spiritual dimension. Mole comes to appreciate this lack after visiting Badger's home, just as Mole later helps Rat appreciate the spiritual hollowness of his wish to emigrate in "Wayfarers All."

11. Among others, she instances Jane Eyre, "flung . . . friendless on the wide world" and Oliver Twist's "loneliness in the great wide world" (Crain 144).

12. The architect Le Corbusier reacted in a way very similar to Toad when almost knocked down on the Champs Elysées in 1924: "Cars, cars, fast, fast!

One is seized, filled with enthusiasm, with joy . . . the joy of power," he is quoted as saying. As Marshall Berman comments, he identifies himself "totally with the forces that have been bearing down on him" (166).

13. As a trickster figure, in line with Odysseus/Ulysses, of course, Toad stands between realms (apposite for an amphibious creature), the natural and the civilized, and is unlikely to develop. In this reading, it is he who plays the fool to the god Pan.

14. There is an ambivalent hint about Pan appearing in the flesh, though, with Rat finding some "hoof-marks deep in the sward."

15. Attempts like illustrator Michael Foreman's to give him a physical presence therefore seem a mistake. See Foreman in works cited.

16. This would seem another covert reference to Pan's mythological activities: of seducing Selene, the moon goddess, by enticing her from the sky into the woods.

17. It is worth noting that, in at least one version of the myth, Pan's mother was said to be Penelope, visited by Hermes in the guise of a ram.

18. One might also note that Pan's appearance, though it has been anticipated since the beginning, occurs in the seventh chapter; Pan's pipes also traditionally comprise seven reeds.

Works Cited

Bennett, Alan. *Writing Home*. London: Faber & Faber, 1994.

Berman, Marshall. *All That is Solid Melts Into Air: The Experience of Modernity*. London: Verso, 1983.

Browning, Elizabeth Barrett. "A Musical Instrument." *Selected Poems*. Ed. Colin Graham. London: J.M. Dent, 1996.

Carpenter, Humphrey. *Secret Gardens: A Study of the Golden Age of Children's Literature*. London: Allen & Unwin, 1985.

Chalmers, Patrick R. *Kenneth Grahame: Life and Writings*. 1933. 2nd ed. London: Methuen, 1938.

Crain, Patricia. *The Story of A: The Alphabetization of America from* The New England Primer *to* The Scarlet Letter. Stanford: Stanford UP, 2000.

Dingley, Robert. "Meaning Everything: the Image of Pan at the Turn of the Century." *Twentieth Century Fantasists: Essays on Culture, Society and Belief in Twentieth-Century Mythopoeic Literature*. Ed. Kath Filmer. London: Macmillan, 1992. 47–59.

Foreman, Michael, illus. *The Wind in the Willows*. By Kenneth Grahame. London: Pavilion Books, 2001.

Gilead, Sarah. "The Undoing of Idyll in *The Wind in the Willows*." *Children's Literature* 16 (1987): 145–58.

Grahame, Kenneth. "Ideals." *Kenneth Grahame: Life and Writings*. By Patrick R. Chalmers. 1933. 2nd ed. London: Methuen, 1938. 258–73.

_____. "The Rural Pan." *Paths to the River Bank: The Origins of* The Wind in the Willows *from the Writings of Kenneth Grahame*. Introd. Peter Haining. London: Blandford P, 1988. 29–34.

_____. *The Wind in the Willows*. 1908. London: Methuen, 1925.

Green, Peter. *Kenneth Grahame, 1859–1932: A Study of His Life, Work and Times*. London: J. Murray, 1959.

Hamilton, Clayton. "Frater Ave Atque Vale: A Personal Appreciation of the Late Kenneth Grahame." *The Bookman* Jan. 1933. 69–74.

Horwood, William. *The Willows in Winter*. London: HarperCollins, 1993.

Hunt, Peter. *The Wind in the Willows: A Fragmented Arcadia*. New York: Twayne, 1994.

Linder, Leslie. *A History of the Writings of Beatrix Potter*. London: Warne, 1971.

Macherey, Pierre. *A Theory of Literary Production*. Trans. Geoffery Wall. London: Routledge & Kegan Paul, 1978.

Milne, A. A. *Toad of Toad Hall: A Play from Kenneth Grahame's Book* The Wind in the Willows. 1929. London: Methuen, 1940.

Needle, Jan. *Wild Wood*. London: Methuen, 1981.

Poss, Geraldine D. "An Epic in Arcadia: The Pastoral World of *The Wind in the Willows*." *Children's Literature* 4 (1975): 80–90.

Prince, Alison. *Kenneth Grahame: An Innocent in the Wild Wood*. London: Allison & Busby, 1994.

Robson, W. W. *The Definition of Literature and Other Essays*. Cambridge: Cambridge UP, 1982.

Sale, Roger. *Fairy Tales and After: From Snow White to E. B. White*. Cambridge, MA: Harvard UP, 1978.

Sandner, David. *The Fantastic Sublime: Romanticism and Transcendence in Nineteenth-Century Children's Fantasy Literature*. Contributions to the Study of Science Fiction and Fantasy 69. Westport, CT: Greenwood P, 1996.

Stevenson, Robert Louis. "Pan Pipes." *Virginibus Puerisque, and Other Papers*. London: Chatto & Windus, 1916. 181–85.

Wordsworth, William. *The Prelude, or Growth of a Poet's Mind (Text of 1805)*. Ed. Ernest de Selincourt. Oxford: Oxford UP, 1970.

CHAPTER TWO

~

Techne, Technology, and Disenchantment in *The Wind in the Willows*

Deborah Dysart-Gale

Rhetoric is the art and technique of persuasion. Although children's literature is frequently neglected and understudied as a form of rhetoric, it is nevertheless fundamentally rhetorical as it pursues its didactic goal of persuading children to accept certain premises about the world and teaching them how to live and what to value within it. In so doing, children's books provide their readership with what Kenneth Burke characterized as "equipment for living," or "*strategies* for dealing with *situations*" (*Philosophy* 295, emphasis original). The purpose of this chapter is to examine Kenneth Grahame's *The Wind in the Willows* as equipment for living with and adjusting to one of the greatest challenges in early twentieth-century life, namely, technologies of transportation. The boats, trains, and motorcars that figure so prominently in the book's pages had a great effect on the English countryside. Place was changed by displacement, locations were affected by dislocations. With the careening Toad at one extreme and the sedentary Badger at the other, Grahame's characters modeled and tested a variety of strategies for coming to terms with the effects of transportation technology on their lives.

Of course, it is not the tools of technology by themselves that create deep change in a society, but rather how the members of that society conceive and deploy those tools. The full story of technological impact then is not to be found by looking at tools in isolation, but rather at "tools plus theories about tools." Such an inclusive perspective is provided by a return to the etymological root of the word *technology*, in the Greek concept of *techne* as "art" or "craft." I will examine Aristotle's thoughts about technology, as well as those of Max Weber, Grahame's contemporary, who observed the state of technology as it existed in public discourse at the time *The Wind in the Willows* was written. Using Kenneth Burke's dramatistic pentad (*Grammar*, 1969), I argue that the book's characters—Badger, Toad, Rat, and Mole—represent differing models of what he calls equipment for living with the challenges and benefits of technological change.

Nature and Technology

One of the most charming and trenchant observations about *The Wind in the Willows'* appeal comes from A. A. Milne: "One does not argue about *The Wind in the Willows*. The young man gives it to the girl with whom he is in love, and if she does not like it, asks her to return his letters. The older man tries it on his nephew, and alters his will accordingly" (qtd. in Steig 303). It is impossible to find one answer to the question of what accounted for the book's initial popularity. However, I suggest that one reason for its popularity was its success in addressing its audience's concerns regarding technologically driven social change. *The Wind in the Willows* appeared in 1908, a few years before the outbreak of World War I, and concerns about political stasis, economic change, and growing technological (including military) innovation were central in Edwardian public discourse. Familiar, rural lifestyles appeared to be fading under the new social and political organization of modernity, and misgivings about the future were confirmed with the beginning of the Great War.

As if to work against approaching calamities of modernity, Grahame's expressed desire in writing *The Wind in the Willows* was to preserve a space for the pastoral ideal in a story for children "and those who still keep the spirit of youth alive in them: of life, sunshine, running water, woodlands, dusty roads, winter firesides; free of problems" (qtd. in Haining 19). David Gooderham suggests that this pastoral ideal resonated with *The Wind in the Willows*' original audience; readers found reassurance, "not merely in terms of nostalgia for club and Empire, but of an older an more fundamental longing . . . [as] the imaginal themes of the text, layer upon layer, recall the comfort, security, and satisfaction of the child at the mother's breast" (117).

Notwithstanding, in 1908, it was no longer possible to reclaim the pastoral lifestyle of previous centuries. From his essays, we know that Grahame was dismayed about the challenges that technological advance posed to traditional rural lifestyles. Conversely, however, he shared some of Toad's enthusiasm for technological advance, accepting innovative developments as potentially enriching. This ambivalence is apparent in two essays written in 1891 for the *National Observer*. In "Riverside Life," he bemoaned the deleterious effects of the railroad on rural life: "today the iron horse has searched the country through . . . bringing with it Commercialism, whose god is [avarice], and who . . . garrotes the streams with the girder. Bringing, too, into every nook and corner fashion and chatter . . . until the growing tyranny has invaded the last common, spinney, and sheep down" (qtd. in Haining 33–34). Conversely, in his article entitled "The Romance of the Rail," written in the same year for the same journal, Grahame reflected rather positively upon these same changes, hailing the train as a "strange visitant" which "crept by headland and bay" across the rural landscape, bringing with it "a piece of the busy, mysterious outer world" (qtd. in Haining 114). The railroad, Grahame suggested, forged connections between city dwellers and the countryside: "I still hail with a certain affection the call of the engine in the night . . . and pass from one to the other name reminiscent or suggestive of the joy and freedom, Devonian maybe, or savouring of Wessex, or bearing me away to some sequestered reach of the Thames" (qtd. in Haining 115).

The world in which Grahame and his audience lived was a world in transition, one in which technology and modernity disrupted lives and displaced characters. By the time of the publication of *The Wind in the Willows*, the Industrial Revolution was a fait accompli, but the denizens of the River Bank, like Grahame and his readers, were still coming to terms with the influence of modernity, technology, and industrialization upon traditional lifestyles. Grahame's contemporary, sociologist Max Weber, reflected on the society-wide effect of this technological innovation. Weber observed that traditionally, humans had created meaning in their lives through "enchantment"—religion, myth, and mysticism. With the advent of modernity, however, science and scientific thinking emerged as the dominant paradigm for viewing the world and explaining the events within it. In so doing, science replaced the older, enchanted modes of thought. While disallowing traditional, mystic, and spiritual meanings, disenchanted scientific thought remained utterly unable to answer, or even articulate "the only question important for us: 'what shall we do and how shall we live?'" (Weber 19). Weber called this effect the process of *disenchantment*, through which rational and scientific paradigms supplant all other epistemologies and meanings. Through the triumph of science as the dominant public discourse, "there are no mysterious incalculable forces that come into play. . . . [O]ne can, in principle, master all things by calculation. This means that the world is disenchanted. . . . Technical means and calculations perform this service" (14).

Science and rationality acknowledge progress as their only value, Weber argued, giving us only the "answer to the question of what we must do if we wish to master life technically. It leaves quite aside, or assumes for its purposes, whether we should and do wish to master life technically and whether it ultimately makes sense to do so" (20). Weber proposed that because rationality and scientific method calculated how one best leads the technically efficient life, individuals who sought other meanings or asked other questions had no recourse but to seek answers in the personal:

> The fate of our times is characterized by rationalization and intellectualization, and above all, by the "disenchantment of the world." Precisely the ultimate and most sublime values have retreated from public life either into the transcendental realm of mystic life or into the brotherliness of direct and personal human relations. (35)

From this perspective, individuals had two choices: abstain from modernity and cling to the world of enchantment, or renounce the existential questions of enchantment and embrace science.

Inherent in Weber's thought is the notion that in the disenchanted world, science determines the types of questions that can be asked, with technology providing the answers; dissenters must retreat from the discussion. Weber's thought thus envisions a dichotomy between those who choose to embrace science and those who abstain from it. This dichotomy provides a useful perspective from which to view the world of *The Wind in the Willows*. Toad embraces technology; he is saved from himself by his inner circle of friends, who find life's meaning in their brotherhood. However, although Weber's theories are useful in describing the world of the River Bank, there is an alternative formulation of the problem between mysticism and technology, between enchantment and disenchantment that provides an additional perspective on Grahame's rhetorical vision. This formulation entails expanding the notion of technology, viewing it not merely as the tools that provide the solutions to problems posed by science, but rather in terms of the Greek *techne*, defined by R. A. Hodgkin as "the making or mastery of good things" (par. 5).

Hodgkin calls for a reexamination of the Greek concept of *techne* and the etymology of "technology" as a means of obtaining new contemporary insights. Such an examination leads us to Aristotle's reflections on *techne* as a means of both imitating and improving on nature. He noted in *Physics* that nature acts from necessity, not intelligent design; water evaporates, cools, and of necessity falls as rain upon a field of corn, causing the corn to grow. However, lacking design, it might also fall on the harvested grain on the threshing floor, causing it to spoil. Humans then rectify this situation through technical improvements to nature's process (in this case, perhaps by installing a roof). Products produced by the artificial human intervention of *techne* "would move along the same line that the natural process actually takes. . . . Indeed, as a general proposition, *techne* either, on the basis of Nature, carry things further than Nature can, or they imitate Nature" (173; 199a14–20). Joachim Schummer argues that *techne* must imitate or perfect nature's ends, not its form. Contemporary medical technology provides an additional example: vitamins constitute a good technology when imitating the *ends* of nature by improving the body's ability to maintain health. Mechanical ventilators, in contrast, are a bad technology when they imitate the *form* of natural respiration in order to thwart nature's ends by postponing death and prolonging suffering. *Techne* therefore improves human life when complementing or perfecting nature, and increases suffering when rebelling against it. Understood positively as "craft," *techne* was also used pejoratively as "craftiness." In his recuperation of the Greek notion of *techne*, Hodgkin emphasizes that even when innovation is used thoughtfully and purposefully, *techne* can be used not only for the good, but also to the detriment of people.

Hodgkin discerns five categories of technology: (1) *tools* for obtaining desired ends; (2) *scientific instruments*, for enriching our knowledge of nature; (3) *toys* for entertainment, but also for engaging with and exploring our environment; (4) *weapons*; and (5) *artistic technology*, which use various artistic media "in search of meaning and preparing us for 'the unknown'" (par. 26). Although Hodgkin allows that while these five categories may not be exhaustive, they nevertheless describe major areas of human endeavor intended to improve life, or perhaps to make it worse for one's enemies.

Both Weber and Hodgkin offer perspectives on technology that are useful in thinking about Grahame's presentation of transportation technology in *The Wind in the Willows*. Weber observes that science displaces all other systems of meaning, allowing only its own agenda of inquiry and its own answers, which come in the form of technology. From the perspective of science, Toad is correct in his observation that the life of speed is "the real thing" (27), and Pan is right to erase Rat and Mole's memories of their encounter with the divine before they return to the world where disenchantment is the rule. However, bearing Aristotle's observations firmly in mind, we must also understand that technology does not determine human fate; rather, it is for humans to design and deploy technological innovations in ways that are "good," that is, ways that enhance human existence and manifest human values. Thus, we have an alternative to Weber's assertion that we must choose between finding meaning through the embrace of science or through retreat into the private sphere of interpersonal relationships. The alternative is a technology that respects and furthers human values. Hodgkin suggests that this alternative can be achieved, in part, through the technology of art, that is, the use of paint, performance, word, music, and other media to perfect and complement our inner lives, as well as our ability to come to terms with the outer world.

We can thus look upon *The Wind in the Willows* as Grahame's attempt to explore the issue of technology, both its meaning and its use. I do not assert that Grahame was familiar with Weber's writings on disenchantment and technology, but merely that Weber's thesis expressed an opinion on a topic of public deliberation that mirrored Grahame's own concerns addressed in *The Wind in the Willows* and his other writing. Much of *The Wind in the Willows* reflects the loss of fundamental values through the use of technology (the disruptions to self and community wrought by Toad and his motorcars) and the recuperation of values through interpersonal care. *The Wind in the Willows* also offers an example of art designed "to come to terms with the depth and apparent contrariness of phenomena" (Hodgkin par. 24).

The question then becomes how are we, as readers of *The Wind in the Willows*, to come to terms with technologies of transportation—motorcars, boats, trains—that condition the characters' engagement with the natural world and function as metaphors for displacement and (e)motion? What is this world like, and how are we to live in it?

Rhetorical Analysis

The four main characters of the book demonstrate different relationships with nature and technology, providing readers with models for negotiating their own balance between modernity, technology, and tradition. Grahame's persuasive agenda can be observed through the tools of rhetorical analysis. As a scholarly activity, rhetorical analysis is the examination of how texts persuade their audiences of their claims. Such analysis must be purpose-built, as each text will create its own world, make its own claims, and provide its own prescriptions for dealing with the concerns and crises that it invents. In his *A Grammar of Motives*, rhetorical theorist Kenneth Burke identifies five aspects of symbolic action that, when taken together, provide a description of characters' motives. The five parameters, or "basic forms of thought" (xv) of his pentad are *scene* (what is the background of the action; where does the action unfold?), *act* (what happens?), *agent* (who undertakes action?), *agency* (what means is used?), and *purpose* (why does the agent undertake a specific action at a specific time and place?).

These elements typically do not appear in equal balance in a text or oral account, but are manipulated to create a particular explanation or persuasive appeal. Burke identifies these interactions between elements as *ratios*. In children's tales, ratios between pentadic elements serve to demonstrate didactic lessons. For example, Little Red Riding Hood disobeys her mother's admonition not to talk to strangers. However, the actual *act* of speaking to strangers is not central (indeed, the Woodsman with whom she spoke was also a stranger); neither is the *agency* of the path to Grandmother's or her *purpose* of bringing food; the emphasis on the scene-agent ratio reveals that what causes her trouble is her inability to properly size up the Wolf as an evil *agent* within the treacherous *scene* of the forest. The lesson of the tale then is actually not that one must unwaveringly obey one's mother or refrain from talking to strangers. These are default strategies for those who cannot assimilate the real lesson, namely, that one must know how to assess the intentions of unknown agents found in dangerous situations.

When applied to *The Wind in the Willows*, the elements of Burke's pentad offer useful perspectives on the vision of the world that Grahame constructs for his readers. The *scene* suggests that the familiar world is rich and enjoyable. The River Bank is a pastoral idyll, and at its periphery, the characters find an equally romantic agricultural community inhabited by humans, "gathered round the tea-table, absorbed in handiwork, or talking with laughter and gesture" (73). But this familiar world is sometimes constricting. Toad reacts badly to this constriction, and his transgressions take him far into the human world of prison, canals, gypsy camps, and inns. Rat and Mole are more prudent than Toad: the Wild Wood is a treacherous place for the uninitiated, with different social norms (e.g., the Rabbits' unwillingness to help the lost Mole during a blizzard) and natural dangers, a lesson Mole rapidly internalized. But as the characters venture into it, they gain new masteries and find their lives enriched. Nature is perfected through simple technologies such as boats, underground tunnels, and footpaths, and thwarted through motorcars.

Similar to A. A. Milne's depiction of the Hundred Acre Wood in *Winnie the Pooh*, Grahame depicts a world in which one is safe within the familiar domain, especially when surrounded by loved ones. However, in contrast to the Hundred Acre Wood, the familiar River Bank, at length, is found wanting, and one must prudently and courageously move beyond its confines. Like Kingsley's chimney sweep Tom of *The Water Babies*, Rat, Mole, and Toad learn that a full experience of life can only be experienced by leaving one's accustomed domain. The scene of the book, the River Bank, while pastoral, is not static, but rather a site of personal and social tensions in need of resolution.

The *acts* depicted in the book are in one way or another linked to physical and psychological movement and dislocation. As is apparent from the treatment of scene, the denizens of the River Bank enjoy moving about their immediate surroundings, but the plot moves forward through acts of exploration beyond the familiar. The characters' peregrinations may be deliberate (such as the well-provisioned journey in the canary yellow caravan), or unexamined (as when Mole sets out alone to visit Badger in the Wild Wood). They may be a defining part of lifestyle, as when "messing about in boats," or undertaken in search of a new life, as Mole's departure from his hole to the River Bank. Imprudent acts of movement are troubling: Toad's escapades, careening about in motorcars, lead to his near ruin. Emotional experiences are also potent, as both Mole and Rat experience: Mole suffers homesickness when he scents his old home in "Dulce Domum," just as Rat suffers wanderlust in "Wayfarers All."

The four main characters are unique and independent agents, each representing a different way of living within the River Bank (and by synecdoche, the real world of Grahame's audience). Toad is neither satisfied nor sated by his world, while Badger is happy to remain where he is in the status quo. Rat professes satisfaction, and Mole remains the observer. By fully appreciating the centrality of movement and location in the book's scene and action, the intimate connection between *agent* and *agency* becomes evident. Each agent's choice of agency defines the way his life unfolds. Toad's mania for movement lands him in untold tribulations, and fittingly, he chooses agencies that are all beyond his ability to control: he is a poor driver and an incompetent boater, and is even unable to manage his horse cart. In contrast to Toad, Rat professes contentment with the regular, predictably changing rhythms of his river life. His boat is the perfect, nature-perfecting agency through which he can realize this life, conveying him and his lunch hamper to areas of his own choosing, in his own time.

Badger, for his part, is a natural Luddite who resists movement outside his own domain. His agency is not a mode of transportation, but rather his home. Built in the ruins of human habitation that have been reshaped by creatures and natural processes, the warren reminds us of the ultimate fate of all human acts and agencies. Badger's sage acceptance of nature and appreciation for the limits of human endeavor represent a strategy for living in a world shaken by technology. In contrast to Badger, Mole combines characteristics of all three of his friends, and suggests an alternative strategy for dealing with the displacements and opportunities of technology. Mole resembles Toad in seeking meaning in his life through novelty, but (fortunately for himself and his friend Rat) lacks Toad's manic passion in the quest. In the early chapters of the book, he is not an agent with a specific plan of his own and has no specific agency. Thus, he devises no way for getting around except by walking, unless literally and figuratively taken up by others' agency, as riding in Toad's caravan or Rat's boat. By keeping himself open to the events and agents around him, however, he perfects himself, eventually gaining Badger's approval and respect. Although Badger maintains his social dominance, Mole actually transcends Badger in an important way. He develops the Badger-like skills necessary for defeating weasels and maintaining the status quo, but he also demonstrates the ability to adapt to new environments and exigencies, thus becoming a more versatile agent.

This brings us to the final element of Burke's pentad, *purpose*, which encompasses the effects of the previous four elements. This parameter applies both to the purpose of the characters and to Grahame's larger rhetorical purpose for the book. At first glance, "purposeful" is not an adjective that immediately comes to mind in respect to the characters or their actions. Rat and Mole "mess about in boats," organize picnics, and pay visits. They and Badger would be quite undisturbed in their respective pursuits if not for the periodic need to rescue Toad from his irrational actions. Unlike Toad, their purpose is decidedly not the mindless pursuit of modern technology and its exhilarating pleasures. Nor do they, as Weber suggested, retreat into enchantment to seek the deeper existential questions that are disallowed by science, rationality, and technological solution. On the surface, they appear merely to spend time together; in actuality, they use this intimate time to negotiate correct action through "the brotherliness of direct and personal human relations" (Weber 35). Seen from this Weberian perspective, the purpose of their actions, whether quietly enjoying pastoral pleasures or coming heroically to Toad's aid, is to enrich their disenchanted lives through their friendship.

This balance of enchantment and disenchantment gives a clue to Grahame's rhetorical purpose in the text. He creates Toad's "disenchanted" motorcars: they replace questions about the meaning of life with an agenda of speed and power. Grahame also creates the enchanted setting of the River Bank, where the questions of "what shall we do and how shall we live" (Weber 19) are contemplated daily. Grahame then places both enchantment and disenchantment together in a text where both modes must learn to coexist. Motorcars do not satisfy the soul, and perhaps never reappeared at Toad Hall after the rout of the Wild Wood creatures; we are not told. But the characters do not retreat into enchantment, religion, and mysticism—even though the god Pan exists, he must never exert influence upon the characters and must disappear without leaving a trace. The characters are busy, after all, establishing themselves in the disenchanted world, improving their lives, and perfecting nature (e.g., successfully transforming the Wild Wood from a place of danger into a part of their domain). Grahame thus presents a situation—a world poised between tradition and modernity—and proposes a strategy for dealing with it: chart a middle course though the forces of modernity and enchanted mysticism, relying on brotherly love to negotiate the means and meaning of existence.

This Weberian reading of *The Wind in the Willows* remains incomplete, however, as it fails to address the remarkable chapter "The Piper at the Gates of Dawn." From one perspective, Pan appears to have read his Weber; he knows that mystical, spiritual, or religious explanations for phenomena are no longer meaningful in a disenchanted world. Pan directs them to the missing Portly with magic pipes, perhaps, but it is through the technology of the boat (with a healthy admixture of friendship and empathy that sends them out on their search) that the baby is found and returned to his father. From a Weberian perspective, Pan could be erased from the narrative entirely, and in fact, Pan seems to agree by erasing himself from Rat and Mole's memory. Rat and Mole, were they asked, could honestly formulate a rational account that they had found Portly on their own. Yet, despite the characters' amnesia, the audience knows that there is another, enchanted explanation. Through the *techne* of art, Grahame has provided another explanation for coming "to terms with the depth and apparent contrariness of phenomena"

(Hodgkin par. 24). The presence of this remarkable chapter suggests that Weber and the disenchanted world do not have the last word.

Pentadic Ratios

The five elements of Burke's pentad provide us with a comprehensive picture of the world in which Rat, Mole, Badger, and Toad live, a world not unlike the world inhabited by *The Wind in the Willows'* real-life audience. Having established the type of world the River Bank represents, Grahame's rhetorical task is to prescribe how one is to live within it. As stated earlier, the five elements of Burke's pentad can be viewed in relation to each other, as *ratios*, to provide a more thorough understanding of the rhetor's emphasis and concerns (and, conversely, aspects he or she effaces), as well as the dynamic of the elements as they shape the rhetorical impact of the text. Examining the pentadic ratios operative in the depiction of the four main characters can help us to see how each functions in supporting Grahame's claims about the world and how one properly lives in it.

The book's action begins with the Mole's sudden, instinctual act in leaving his home. His purpose in leaving is not to escape the spring cleaning he is engaged in at the time. Rather, he is drawn to something undefined and is arrested by the shining movement of the river. Throughout the book, Mole's emotions repeatedly draw him to seek new things that will enrich his life: he seeks new skills (boating), new vistas (it is he who convinces Rat to join Toad's caravan expedition), and new acquaintances (setting off on his own to seek out the mysterious Badger). In so doing, by the end of the book he develops into a character almost as resourceful and brave as Badger, only more adaptable and open to change.

Mole's development is captured in the tension between act and agent. Burke notes that "[t]he agent does not 'contain' the act, though its results might be said to 'pre-exist virtually' within him . . . and conversely, his acts can make him or remake him in accordance with their nature" (*Grammar* 16). Underscoring the way in which actions shape character (i.e., agent), Peter Hunt argues that the first five chapters of the book constitute Mole's bildungsroman, in which he grows and matures through action: leaving home, taking to the open road, learning of the dangers of the Wild Wood, and arriving at the conclusion that "he must be wise, must keep to the pleasant places in which his lines were laid and which held adventure enough, in their way, to last for a lifetime" (Grahame 71).

Hunt's argument seems plausible, except that Mole reaches this conclusion in chapter four, before the celebrated chapter five, "Dulce Domum," when he experiences the traumatic desire to return to his old home. If we read "Dulce Domum" as a discussion of *scene*, there is little new in this chapter, as it appears to reinforce chapter four's imperative to "keep to the pleasant places in which his lines were laid." However, when viewed as *act*, there is something new—almost a reversal of the lesson of the previous chapter. Chapter five's end "could almost be taken for a textbook on the psychology of children's literature" (Hunt 116) as Mole comes to terms with the call of the upper world: "and he knew he must return to the larger stage" (Grahame 90). While he is to remain in the "places in which his lines were laid," he realizes in chapter five that those lines, like the river, are in flux. He must adapt to, as well as master, change. By the book's final chapters, he is a new agent, a Mole of action.

In depicting Mole's character development through the action-agent ratio, Grahame de-emphasizes the importance of scene, agency, and purpose. This contrasts with Grahame's treatment of Rat, which emphasizes the relationship between scene and act. As Burke notes, the scene functions as a container that must fit the act. Rat's scene is the River Bank, and his actions fit the scene perfectly. It is he who introduces Mole to the glorious life on the river and who has the local knowledge and skills necessary to live there comfortably. He messes about in boats and rescues Toad and Mole from the water as necessary, and his home is always open to them in their hours of need.

Although Rat's actions are perfectly attuned to the scene of his River Bank life, and he is generous and patient in conveying all his knowledge and wisdom to Mole, Rat is ultimately restricted by the scene. Upon meeting Mole, he announces that the river "is my world, and I don't want any other. What it hasn't got is not worth having, and what it doesn't know is not worth knowing" (13). Mole immediately senses the limitations of this scene and worldview ("'But isn't it a bit dull at times?' Mole ventured to ask" [13]). Rat himself comes to realize these limitations in "Wayfarers All." Unlike Mole, however, Rat does not develop new skills and abilities. This is evident on the eve of the liberation of Toad Hall, as Mole spontaneously devises a cagey plan to throw the stoats' defenses into disarray while Rat nervously and ineffectually inventories armaments that will obviously be of no use in the coming action. Nevertheless, Rat is immortalized as "the gallant Water Rat, a terrible fighter" (219) for his participation in the battle because he shares in the brotherly intimacy that Weber suggests replaces the certainty of the enchanted world.

If Rat cannot decide how to break out of his scene and master the technical possibilities of the disenchanted world, Toad has no such misgivings. He continually reinvents himself: "the popular and handsome Toad, the rich and hospitable Toad, the Toad so free and careless and debonair!" (122). Grahame emphasizes Toad's personality as a colorful buffoon; Toad is so colorful a character that he has eclipsed the other main characters as the main focus of *The Wind in the Willows'* many sequels and adaptations, beginning with A. A. Milne's *Toad of Toad Hall.* Personality is explored in the pentadic element *agent,* "the initial origin of a change or rest" (Burke, *Grammar* 228); in Toad's case, *agent* is inextricably linked to *agency,* Toad's motorcars, and other enthusiasms. As agent, Toad is in control, applying *techne* not to improve, but to erase nature: "Here today—in next week tomorrow! Villages skipped, towns and cities jumped—always somebody else's horizon! O bliss!" (35). His well-appointed, comfortable home is too narrow and constraining, and he continually pursues "the real thing, the only genuine occupation for a lifetime" (27). "Toad the terror, the traffic-queller, the Lord of the lone trail, before whom all must give way" (104) is a thrill-seeker, and the purpose of his erratic motion is to satisfy his personal vanity and addiction to speed and novelty. Ultimately, just as Rat is restricted by the confines of the scene he so appears to master, Toad is trapped by his agencies and cannot function as an agent. He cannot judge the boundary where nature, social order, and *techne* coincide.

While Toad is defined in the tension between agent and agency, Badger's personality is firmly rooted in the relationship between agent and scene. Burke describes this ratio as "the synecdochic relation between person and place . . . between the quality of the country and the quality of its inhabitants" (*Grammar* 7–8). Even more than Rat, the autochthonic Badger is firmly anchored in place and lifestyle; his home is a "safe anchorage" in "the cold and trackless Wild Wood" (57). Yet Badger is quite capable of defending himself as well as his friends: "when people were in any fix they mostly went to Badger, or else Badger got to know of it somehow" (63). While Rat is defined by his actions within the scene of the River, Badger is an agent, controlling the actions of others within it. While Rat becomes limited by scene, Badger uses his expert local knowledge and strength of character to preserve order. He determines when it is time to intervene in Toad's badly managed affairs. Together with the other agent, Mole, he devotes himself to the defense of Toad's property against the stoats and weasels, and continues to safeguard it as best he can after he is evicted (an operation from which Rat is strangely absent). It is he who plans and leads the attack to retake Toad Hall, and he is more familiar with that scene (e.g., the secret tunnel and trap door to the pantry) than Toad himself.

Among the characters, Badger has the most Aristotelian approach toward *techne* and the perfection of nature. He needs no boat and certainly no motorcar. He lives as a creature of nature, abiding by its rhythms, and as a result, his timing is perfect. He knows precisely when to mount the battle for Toad Hall; he does not needlessly interrupt his hibernation for what is sure to be an ineffectual intervention as his friend Toad runs amok. He draws his strength from nature and knows that a simple cudgel is the perfect way to improve upon that strength, dismissing Rat's artful pistols and swords. Perhaps his freedom from hubris comes from making his home within the ruins of a once-great city, giving him the chance to observe firsthand that, ultimately, one survives through the grace and goodwill of Nature, who always has the last word.

This might suggest that Grahame is proposing that Badger is the character readers should emulate. However, Badger is a crusty old creature, hardly the creature with whom those intended readers "who still keep the spirit of youth alive in them" (qtd. in Haining 19) would most easily identify. Toad, a buffoon, is likewise an unlikely candidate for identification. Rat is adventurous and capable, but limited to the confines of his familiar River Bank and Wild Wood. Mole, in contrast, is flexible and adaptable. He grows and matures, moving beyond his familiar domains, assimilating new technologies in ways that allow him to develop in meaningful ways. Of the four characters, he is most suited to life under the ambivalent conditions of modern life.

Equipment for Living in Modernity

Taken as "equipment for living," we discern that through his main characters, Grahame presents four distinct strategies for dealing with the questions raised by encroaching modernity, endangered traditional lifestyles, and the loss of the "final and total ontological embrace" (Gooderham 117) of the idealized rural past. Together, the characters of the River Bank live between modernity and tradition. They seek meaning in their lives, and as theorized by Max Weber, must choose to find it through mystical enchantment ("Piper at the Gates of Dawn"), the disenchanted world of science and technology ("The Open Road"), or in intimate, fraternal relations ("The Return of Ulysses"). They must also resolve questions about their proper relationship to nature. Such is the world that Grahame presents to his readers, along with a variety of strategies for dealing with the situations that arise within it.

Toad represents the embrace of science and technology. As an active agent, Toad attempts to swindle or crush nature. Toad's situation is revealed in the agent-agency ratio, as he is quickly drawn in and totally dominated by technology before he is able to develop any mastery of it. He is unable to survive in human society, nor is he able to maintain himself on the River Bank. He lives by inheritance and the goodwill of his friends. In a word, he is overcome by the very agencies he would use to overcome nature.

Rat is a creature of action, and these actions are perfectly contained within the scene of the River Bank. Within that defined world, he knows all there is to know. When Mole is racked by homesickness for his old burrow, Rat knows exactly how to set his friend's mind at ease. And when Rat awakes from his winter's nap to find Mole missing, he instinctively understands that Mole has ventured into the Wild Wood without knowing "pass-words, and signs, and sayings which have power and effect, and plants you carry in your pocket, and verses you repeat, and dodges and tricks you practise" (47). His local knowledge and compassionate understanding of animal instincts make him a kind and generous friend. However, he is limited in his ability to take positive action when his familiar scene changes and becomes threatening and unfamiliar. How else are we to understand his remaining safely at home while Badger and Mole are "living very rough by day and laying very hard by night, watching over" (190) the besieged Toad Hall, or his ineffectual giddiness before the attack to liberate it from the weasels?

Like Rat, Badger has mastery of his scene, although his knowledge is much more comprehensive, being both synchronic and diachronic. He knows the nature of weasels and stoats, and thus can predict their behavior in ways that leave the Rat baffled. Badger knows the ways of nature and the wisdom of living in conformity with it. Badger's venerable character is rooted in his mastery of his environment, as apparent in the agent-scene ratio.

Badger's knowledge of the River Bank and Wild Wood is complete. However, while there is nothing Badger doesn't know, Mole's quite different habits of mind enable him to turn knowledge into action in ways that even Badger does not anticipate. It is Mole who in the end models the most effective strategy for dealing with the situations that emerge in the world that Grahame depicts. Initially, he blindly follows an instinctual urge to improve his life, to improve on his nature as a Mole. By observing, imitating, and learning new skills, he eventually develops mastery of the River Bank. Early on, when lost in the Wild Wood, he marvels at Rat's ability to locate Badger's front door: "If I only had your head, Ratty" (54). Yet, by the end of the book, he outstrips Rat's cleverness, independently formulating a plan to scatter Toad Hall's defenders prior to the friends' attack. This earns him Badger's admiration and approval. He is proclaimed "the best of fellows" (208) and entrusted with the securing of the perimeter, while Toad is commanded to make dinner. Now truly a Mole for all seasons, he demonstrates his ability to assume leadership on the "larger stage" (90).

Perhaps the key to Mole's adaptability is that, for all his love of the River Bank, he is detached from that world in a very significant way. In the beginning of "The Piper at the Gates of Dawn," Mole appears to share fully in the life of the River Bank, suffering the summer heat and enjoying the company of friends. He also shares in Rat's concern for their neighbor's missing offspring and chooses to spend the night searching rather than sleeping. To all appearances, Mole is a member of the River Bank community like any other. But as they search, it is

Rat who hears the irresistible melody of the god, fully enraptured before Mole is able to hear his first note. Mole is smitten, but while Rat is "cowed, stricken, and trembling violently" by the experience, Mole feels "no panic terror—indeed he felt wonderfully at peace and happy" (115). Following the encounter with the god, Rat is immediately released from the spell, while Mole engages with the experience intellectually, "stand[ing] still a moment, held in thought. As one wakened suddenly from a beautiful dream, who struggles to recall it" (117). As they make their way home, Rat is again able to discern and translate the voice of the wind in the reeds. Rat at last hears the words "full and clear . . . at last, it is the real, the unmistakable thing, simple—passionate—perfect—" (121). Mole waits for this revelation, which never comes: the Rat has fallen asleep.

Grahame ends this account without telling us Mole's reaction. Perhaps Mole is angry because Rat has left him helpless at the threshold of a new system of meaning, falling asleep and thereby foreclosing on a reenchantment of the world. Perhaps Mole also falls asleep, content with the world's meaning as it is, and feels no need for further explanation. In any case, Mole is clearly less susceptible to the spell of the River Bank and its enchanted gods than Rat. He can live within that world, but by remaining apart from it, maintains an intellectual distance that enables him to think differently and see different possibilities for action.

The characters—and by extension, Grahame's readers—tacitly accept the fact that they can be satisfied with neither the familiar, pastoral life nor with new technologies and vistas. Mole in particular models the courage, energy, and resourcefulness necessary to live and thrive in the changing world of the River Bank.

Through the tools of rhetorical analysis, we see that Grahame sought to persuade his readers that they will not step into the same River Bank twice. Paradoxically, in order to remain as content and happy as Rat, one cannot *act* like Rat. In order to be as wise as Badger, one cannot *know* like Badger. Rat's contentment and Badger's wisdom depend on the persistence of their familiar world, and as the book's plot confirms, change is inevitable. Contentment and wisdom require Mole's diligence, adaptability, and optimism. One cannot rely, enchanted and passive, on the old gods (Pan disappears without a trace), but likewise cannot fall, unrestrained, into the arms of science and technology, as does Toad. Like Mole, one must learn to move forward, improving one's life as one can, seeking meaning and guidance in friendship and intimate relations. Thus, *The Wind in the Willows* provided the book's readers with just the sort of equipment for living needed for dealing with the challenges of their own world as it came to terms with modernity and the end of the pastoral ideal.

Works Cited

Aristotle. *The Physics.* Trans. Philip Wicksteed and Francis Cornford. Cambridge, MA: Harvard UP, 1929.

Burke, Kenneth. *A Grammar of Motives.* Berkeley: U of California P, 1969.

_____. *The Philosophy of Literary Form.* Baton Rouge: Louisiana State UP, 1941.

Gooderham, David. "Deep Calling unto Deep: Pre-oedipal Structures in Children's Texts." *Children's Literature in Education* 25 (1994): 113–23.

Grahame, Kenneth. *The Wind in the Willows.* 1908. London: Penguin, 1994.

Haining, Peter. *Paths to the River Bank: The Origins of* The Wind in the Willows *from the Writings of Kenneth Grahame.* London: Souvenir Press, 1983.

Hodgkin, R. A. "*Techne*, Technology and Inventiveness." *Oxford Review of Education* 16 (1990): 207–17. *Academic Search Premier.* EBSCO. Concordia University Libraries, Montreal, Canada. 1 Sept. 2008.

Hunt, Peter. "Necessary Misreadings: Directions in Narrative Theory for Children's Literature." *Studies in the Literary Imagination* 18 (1984): 107–21.

Kingsley, Charles. *The Water Babies: A Fairy Tale for a Land Baby.* Mineola, NY: Dover, 2006.

Milne, A. A. *Toad of Toad Hall.* New York: Charles Schribner's Sons, 1957. *Internet Archive.* 2 Oct. 2008 <http://www.archive.org/stream/toadoftoadhall002025mbp>.

Schummer, Joachim. "Aristotle on Technology and Nature." *Philosophia Naturalis* 38 (2001): 105–20.

Steig, Michael. "At the Back of 'The Wind in the Willows': An Experiment in Biographical and Autobiographical Interpretation." *Victorian Studies* 24 (1981): 303–23.

Weber, Max. *The Vocation Lectures.* Ed. David Owen and Tracy Strong. Indianapolis: Hackett Publishing, 2004.

CHAPTER THREE

~

"Up [and Down and Back and Forth] We Go!": Dialogic and Carnivalesque Qualities in *The Wind in the Willows*

Catherine L. Elick

The vitality of a literary text can be measured in part by the active inquiry it continues to generate. For one hundred years now, while readers have expressed great affection for Kenneth Grahame's *The Wind in the Willows*, they have also been bemused by the eccentricities of its structure.[1] During the last fifty years of the novel's reception, while readers have continued to be warmed by its celebration of friendship in an idyllic animal community, they have also awakened to darker undercurrents in the characters' power relations.[2] My own uneasiness about these two issues—the novel's structure and its power systems—has led me to consider Grahame's text in light of the theories of Russian critic Mikhail Bakhtin. Not surprisingly for someone who suffered under the Stalinist regime, Bakhtin accords high praise to literature in which suppressed voices are liberated, oppressive social systems are challenged, and texts become the sites of active dialogue. Although I have come to realize that *The Wind in the Willows* is certainly not what Bakhtin would call polyphonic, since Grahame does not allow equal authority to every character's viewpoint, noting the obvious absence of polyphony in the novel has nevertheless provided a meaningful window through which to view the conflict between the River Bank and the Wild Wood and to understand Grahame's treatment of social class. Considering Bakhtin's concept of dialogism has offered a vantage point from which to perceive that, far from being flawed, the novel's multistrand structure constitutes an active dialogue that readers are invited to join. Finally, Bakhtin's concept of carnival has revealed that in *The Wind in the Willows*, as in the world, laughter can be a source of power and social patterns and hierarchies are always susceptible to inversion.

In *Problems of Dostoevsky's Poetics*, Bakhtin clearly states that Dostoevsky is "the creator of the polyphonic novel" (7), and although he never offers a simple definition of polyphony, Bakhtin argues that "*A plurality of independent and unmerged voices and consciousnesses, a genuine polyphony of fully valid voices is in fact the chief characteristic of Dostoevsky's novels*" (6).[3] According to this description, *The Wind in the Willows* is decidedly not polyphonic, for Grahame actively suppresses the voices of the Wild Wood characters in favor of the viewpoints of his four protagonists, Mole, Rat, Badger, and Toad. Thus, the Wild Wood characters do not escape authorial control "to become full *subjects*, telling their own tales," but instead "remain as objects *used* by the author to fulfill preordained demands" (Booth xxii).

Although Grahame's novel lacks polyphony because the secondary characters in *The Wind in the Willows* do not attain full subject status or the "astonishing internal independence of Dostoevsky's characters" (Bakhtin, *Problems* 13), it nevertheless exhibits dialogic qualities. The central characters' vacillations between home and adventure and the competing narrative strands generated by those conflicting impulses are given free play by Grahame. A dialogic sense of truth develops, one in which neither the peace of home nor the lure of adventure takes precedence. Consequently, Grahame's novel manifests—both in theme and structure—the kind of productive instability that Bakhtin calls unfinalizability.

Finally, in addition to being dialogic, *The Wind in the Willows* is also notably carnivalesque. With both the traditional marketplace festivals of carnival and the entry of the spirit of carnival into the stream of Western literature (what Bahktin calls the carnivalization of literature), "Everything authoritative, rigid or serious is subverted, loosened or mocked" (Selden et al. 41). One set of rules that is subjected to carnival inversion in Grahame's novel is hospitality and, more generally, the polite code of behavior practiced by his inner circle of animal friends. Also symptomatic of carnival's effects in Grahame's novel is the power inherent in carnival laughter. Bakhtin claims in *Rabelais and His World* that carnival laughter "frees human consciousness, thought, and imagination for new potentialities" (49). By granting all characters—even those from the Wild Wood—free access to carnival laughter, Grahame somewhat loosens the authorial grip that is so evident when he suppresses the Wild-Wooders' voices. The most important impact of carnival in *The Wind in the Willows*, however, is the ritual inversion of social hierarchies that accompanies the dualistic act of crowning and decrowning carnival kings. The reversals of fortune experienced by Mole, the Wild Wood characters, and Toad partake in varying degrees of this ambivalent carnival ritual by suggesting both "the *joyful relativity* of all structure and order" (Bakhtin, *Problems* 124) and the possibilities for renewal that attend such swings upward and downward in fortune.

Suppressed Voices

One of the reasons that Bakhtin's aesthetic has been so well received in the West, posits Simon Dentith, is that it represents a "strong and evident ethical imperative" that "affirm[s] the moral and existential irreducibility of the *other*" (43). In the polyphonic novel, "the character is a carrier of a fully valid word and not the mute, voiceless object of the author's words" (Bakhtin, *Problems* 63). Wayne Booth adds a helpful gloss on how characterization is handled in a polyphonic text:

> [S]econdary characters are no longer encompassed by and diminished to their usefulness to heroes—or to the author. Characters are, in short, respected as full subjects, shown as "consciousnesses" that can never be fully defined or exhausted, rather than as objects fully known, once and for all, in their roles—and then discarded as expendable. (xxiii)

This egalitarian approach stands in contrast to that employed in *The Wind in the Willows*, a novel that Bakhtin would not consider polyphonic. Yet the absence of polyphony is as noteworthy as the presence of certain other qualities in the novel, since this lack of polyphony gives insight into Grahame's treatment of social class and power relations generally.

In his 1959 biography of Kenneth Grahame, Peter Green convinc-ingly demonstrates that *The Wind in the Willows* was written out of the author's "need to combat his everlasting fear (shared by many of his class and period) that the structure of society might be destroyed through social revolution" (247). Grahame's polarization of the River Bank and Wild Wood characters into conflicting camps of "Us and Them" (Green 244), noted by Green and other critics, is consistent with Grahame's fears personally and with the Edwardian upper and middle classes' resistance to their loosening grip on class privilege generally. Peter Hunt, pushing this idea further, notes that "we rarely hear the working classes"—the "Them" group—"speak for themselves" ("Dialogue" 162). Far from "renouncing the right to the last word and granting full and equal authority to the word of the characters" (Dentith 42), which is the polyphonic novelist's approach, Grahame actively suppresses the voices of those characters who represent dissent-ing views from his quartet of protagonists. Consequently, the creatures of the Wild Wood, who are consistently unnamed and undifferentiated, are also permitted little direct dialogue.

Because there are so few direct linguistic exchanges between the two groups of animals, it is surprising, then, that the very first conversation in the novel occurs between Mole and an elderly rabbit, one of "Us" and one of "Them." In miniature, this exchange anticipates both the con-flict of the novel and its outcome. Mole dismisses the rabbit's demand for "Sixpence for the privilege of passing by the private road!" leaving him to indulge in recriminations with the other rabbits standing nearby ("'How *stupid* you are! Why didn't you tell him—''Well, why didn't you say—''" [Grahame 3]). A whole gang of extortionate rabbits is no match for a single one of "Us," it seems, just as we will later see the four friends handily supplant a host of stoats and weasels squatting in Toad Hall. Even before his adoption into the inner circle of River Bank life, Mole is an animal entitled. He feels assured of his right to pass through any territory (here a hedgerow, later the Wild Wood) and expresses disdain for those who think otherwise: he feels "impatient and contemptu-ous, . . . chaffing the other rabbits" as he walks by and employs the equivalent of what Bakhtin might term carnival billingsgate, remarking "jeeringly," "Onion-sauce! Onion-sauce!" (3). Bakhtin explains the concept of billingsgate by writing "It is characteristic for the familiar speech of the marketplace to use abusive language, insulting words or expressions, some of them quite lengthy and complex" (*Rabelais* 16). Historically, carnival billingsgate has been "available to both sides," the empowered and the powerless, argues Simon Dentith (75); here, one of the empowered employs it. An open space by a hedgerow substitutes for a carnival marketplace in this scene, and Mole is freed to speak more frankly than he could in a private space. Mole's final act is to "bowl over" the offending rabbit (Grahame 3). In doing so, he resorts to what Green calls "the most time-honoured reactionary's recipe of them all—physical violence" (247), the same strategy the four friends will use to win back Toad Hall.

Paradigmatic though this scene may be, it is important to acknowledge that rabbits are a relatively inconsequential segment of Wild Wood society, "a mixed lot" (Grahame 11), as Rat explains to Mole at their first meeting. According to John David Moore, they represent "a deprecating image of the rustic laboring class as dense, apathetic, healthy, and of course prolific" (54). It's the ferrets, stoats, and weasels, those who "present the lower classes as dangerously vicious and predatory" (Moore 55), that must be reckoned with. Their lack of speech during Mole's encounter with them on his journey to Badger's home—they are known in this scene only by their "whistling" and "pattering" (Grahame 48)—makes them appear more alien than other animals in the novel and therefore more frightening. Yet denying them speech also limits their agency; they remain the undifferentiated mob, trapped between imagery that is at once aggregate—"there were hundreds of them"—and fragmentary—"little evil wedge-shaped face," "little narrow face, with hard eyes" (Grahame 48). To convey "the stunted, malevolent proletariat of contemporary upper-middle-class caricature" (Green 246), Grahame deliberately narrows the reader's range of vision so that we glimpse only parts of bodies (the word "face" or "faces" appears six times) but never fully see an individual predator or hear one speak.

The Back and Forth of Dialogic Structure

It becomes clear that *The Wind in the Willows* cannot be considered polyphonic for the fairly straightforward reason that the Wild Wood characters fail to become fully realized consciousnesses. The claim that Bakhtin makes for the typical Dostoevsky character—that his "word about himself and his world is just as fully weighted as the author's word" (*Problems* 7)—cannot be made for Grahame's secondary characters (I would add that the very notion of "secondary character" is foreign to Bakhtin's egalitarian scheme, since all voices matter in a polyphonic novel). However, this lack of polyphony in *The Wind in the Willows* should not reflect too badly on Grahame. After all, as Gary Saul Morson and Caryl Emerson note, true polyphony is "still relatively rare" (232), even in literature written for adults. Booth states the case even more bluntly: "It is in Dostoevsky and in Dostoevsky alone that Bakhtin finds the polyphonic ideal realized" (xxii). However, Booth also notes Bakhtin's belief that, of all the literary genres, the novel is the best at representing "the inescapably dialogical quality of human life" (xxii). In like fashion, Morson and Emerson stress that, for Bakhtin, "The novel is sure to be the genre that is most dialogic" because "it treats character, society, and knowledge as unfinalizable" and conveys "a sense of the world's essential messiness" (303). I would like to entertain then the claim that, although *The Wind in the Willows* fails to achieve Bakhtin's more exclusive category of polyphony, it reflects his more global concept of dialogue or dialogism. The unresolved competition between the novel's narrative strands—its movement back and forth between the idyllic River Bank chapters and manic Toad escapades—suggests that, as for Dostoevsky's work, "everything in the novel is structured to make dialogic opposition inescapable" (*Problems* 18) and to avoid "*philosophical* finalization—and not because the author has failed in his attempts to achieve it, but because it did not enter into his design" (*Problems* 31).

Guided in part by Green's information regarding Grahame's different stages of composition and the materials he melded in making this novel, many critics have identified three interwoven narratives in *The Wind in the Willows*. To borrow Jay Williams's succinct outline: "It is, in fact, three books pasted together, the adventures of Toad, the tale of the friendship of Rat and Mole, and two prose-poems about the English countryside ('Wayfarers All' and 'The Piper at the Gates of Dawn')" (104). The interworking of these three disparate strands has provoked some critics to decry the novel's lack of unity. Humphrey Carpenter, for instance, considers the structure to be "often shakily executed" (169). If we allow that dialogic interaction may be at work here, and if we agree with M. H. Abrams's claim that "Bakhtin explicitly sets his theory [of dialogism] against Aristotle's *Poetics*" and its elevation of the unity of action (231), then rather than regret the lack of unity in *The Wind in the Willows*, we can acknowledge that Grahame has attempted something different by structuring "the novel as a whole as a '*great dialogue*'" (Bakhtin, *Problems* 40), an open-ended exchange between the ideas of home and adventure, stasis and motion, Apollonian and Dionysian impulses.

Many readers before me have observed thematic tensions at work in Grahame's novel. The designations they have assigned these forces vary: for example, "conservatism and anarchy" (Hunt, *Fragmented* 45), "centripetal" and "centrifugal" forces (Mendelson 127), arcadian and epic or mock-epic impulses (Poss 80–81), to name a few. The most common way of identifying these binaries, however, is home versus adventure.[4] Although critics occasionally plump for one side or the other,[5] more often they acknowledge that the ongoing interplay between the poles of home and adventure enriches the text. For instance, Hunt observes that Mole's and Toad's stories are "symbiotically related, each reverberating off the other" (*Fragmented* 45). Michael Mendelson's essay is especially relevant to the discussion of the novel's structure. Entitled "*The Wind in the Willows* and the Plotting of Contrast," it argues that Grahame's movement back and forth between the adventures of Toad and the more domestic scenes of River Bank life "articulates a complex debate" in which the author "allows his contrary states to interact and reverberate" (134). Mendelson refers to the novel's structure as dialectical, but then acknowledges that, "in the dialectical progress of Grahame's argument, no synthesis is permanent" (137).

I would dispute Mendelson's application of the term dialectic and argue that, if "no synthesis is permanent," then perhaps rather than viewing *The Wind in the Willows* as dialectic, Bakhtin's more dynamic concept of dialogic better describes a reading experience that, as Lesley Willis notes, leaves one with a "sense of not-quite-resolved tension, of reasonably happy compromise" (110) rather than static resolution. For this reason, Bakhtin's assessment of structure in Dostoevsky's novels seems equally apt when applied to *The Wind in the Willows*: "Dialogic relations exist among all elements of novelistic structure; that is, they are juxtaposed contrapuntally" (*Problems* 40). Bakhtin continues, saying that each of Dostoevsky's novels is "constructed . . . as a great dialogue, but one where the author acts as organizer and participant in the dialogue without retaining for himself the final word" (*Problems* 72). Forgoing "the final word," valuing a text's openness and instability—these are hallmarks of Bakhtin's aesthetic and, arguably, qualities of Grahame's novel; for, although by the final chapter Toad Hall has come to represent home restored, the Toad inside Toad Hall remains unregenerate and, like the Wild Wood animals, likely to "break out sometimes" (Grahame 11) into further adventures. Thus, *The Wind in the Willows* resists resolution and allows both polarities of home and adventure to remain in play.

The Power of Carnival Laughter

More than any other Bakhtinian concept, that of carnival—with its possibility for inversions in power systems—helps illuminate the social dynamic at work among Grahame's characters. Although, as we have seen, Grahame does not allow the voices of the Wild Wood creatures to be raised in equal measure to those of his four protagonists, he does grant them a different sort of power: carnival laughter. Carnival laughter "makes us free," write Morson and Emerson (442). In his essay "Epic and Novel," collected in *The Dialogic Imagination*, Bakhtin contends that

> [l]aughter demolishes fear and piety before an object, before a world, making of it an object of familiar contact and thus clearing the ground for an absolutely free investigation of it. Laughter is a vital factor in laying down that prerequisite for fearlessness without which it would be impossible to approach the world realistically. (23)

As the novel's representatives of an oppressed class, the Wild-Wooders do most of the laughing. As the novel's best representative of flagrant class privilege, Toad is the character most laughed at, the one who, more than any other, must be made "an object of familiar contact."

It is for this reason that Toad's misadventures with Wild Wood characters differ significantly from Mole's earlier terrifying encounter with a faceless enemy. For instance, when Toad is on the lam from prison, he is not hunted like Mole but instead has to contend with the sarcasm of a passing fox about his washerwoman garb as well as the fox's "sniggering" (163). Later, when Toad tries to gain reentry into his usurped home, first ferrets fire a bullet at him, and then stoats hurl a stone into his boat; however, it is their deflating laughter—their "horrid thin little laughs," the fact that they "laughed and laughed, supporting each other, and laughed again, till they nearly had two fits"—that injures Toad the most and leaves him "crestfallen" (222–23).

The most sustained example of carnival laughter leveled at Toad occurs just before the recapture of Toad Hall. The Chief Weasel, the only one of the Wild Wood creatures to receive the distinction of an uppercased name,[6] makes a mocking speech in honor of "'our kind host, Mr. Toad. We all know Toad!'—(great laughter)—'*Good* Toad, *modest* Toad, *honest* Toad!' (shrieks of merriment)" (242). Carpenter's assessment of this scene is correct to a degree. He rightly observes that the speech "is not rabble-rousing by a mob leader but a typical piece of after-dinner oratory" (165). Indeed, it is typical because, as a carnival king temporarily supplanting the authority represented by Toad, the Chief Weasel is directly mimicking Toad's style. However, one should not assume, as Carpenter does, that the playfulness of this speech countermands its "revolutionary fervour" (165), for carnival laughter can arouse in its listeners as great a desire for social change as political demagoguery can, albeit through different means.

Let's consider for a moment the nature of carnival laughter. Interpreters of this Bakhtinian concept differ in their assessments of the potency of laughter and the permanence of the change it can effect. Morson and Emerson argue that "laughter rarely alters actual material conditions"; instead, it keeps "evil at bay only by altering people's attitudes" toward those conditions (453). Alternatively, Sue Vice suggests that, when "[c]arnival laughter is directed at exalted objects, . . . [it] forces them to renew themselves" (152). Both these viewpoints merit consideration when assessing the repercussions of carnival laughter in *The Wind in the Willows*. The first understanding of carnival laughter is substantiated by the fact that Toad is master of Toad Hall both at the beginning and end of the novel; therefore, the change in the "actual material conditions" of his wealth and power in the community is only temporary. What does change is the freedom with which the Wild-

Wooders express their irreverence toward Toad. With this reading, we understand that carnival laughter can do its work even when Toad is only an accidental audience, as when he eavesdrops on the Chief Weasel's dinner speech, since it is the Wild Wood animals who are the intended audience and the true beneficiaries of carnival laughter's transformative effects. The second understanding of carnival laughter claims that a change must occur in the "exalted object." Can a case be made for Toad's having been transformed or renewed in any way when he is made to see himself as others see him? For the most part, criticism seems to roll off Toad like water off an amphibian's back. He is occasionally chastened by the disapproval of insiders like Badger or Ratty, as when he responds with "long-drawn sobs" to Badger's "sermon" against reckless driving and spending (Grahame 109), but for the most part he imperiously dismisses the judgments of outsiders like the weasels. Yet having to win Toad Hall back from the rabble (as Toad and Grahame see the Wild Wood characters) is not the same as remaining its unchallenged master. The effort that it takes for Toad to rectify his mistakes, to humble himself to his friends, to submit to Badger's leadership and accept his own role as merely one of the warriors, and not even the most skillful warrior, in the battle for Toad Hall—taken together, these things constitute a kind of renewal for Toad.

Inverted Etiquette

Carnival's effects are apparent not only in the conflict between the "Us" and "Them" groups but also in the social dynamic that bonds the privileged "Us" characters to each other. Although in *The Wind in the Willows* there are none of the raucous Rabelaisian gatherings in market squares that typify traditional carnival festivals or carnivalesque literature, home as sanctuary is constantly being invaded and opened up to convivial celebrations. Early in the novel, the privileges and obligations of hospitality are dealt with straightforwardly, as when Mole is Rat's guest in "The River Bank"; Mole and Rat are Toad's guests in "The Open Road"; Mole, Rat, and Otter are Badger's guests in "Mr. Badger"; and Rat is Mole's guest in "Dulce Domum." As the novel progresses, however, the theme of hospitality is treated more equivocally and ironically. Rat, Mole, and Badger are uninvited guests and

Toad their unwilling host when they attempt to keep him under house arrest after his motoring accidents, foreshadowing a similarly troubled relationship with the Wild-Wooders at the end of the novel. Because the friends' efforts to rein in Toad are not successful, he lands in prison, where, although ostensibly a prisoner of the Crown, he is treated in some respects more like a guest by the gaoler's daughter. When Toad escapes prison, he becomes Rat's unexpected guest. Then, in the final chapter, entitled "The Return of Ulysses," the errant Toad first rids his home of usurpers from the Wild Wood, who are behaving like Penelope's unwelcome suitors in Homer's epic, and then plays host to the friends who have helped restore his home to him.[7]

With this much focus on the vicissitudes of the guest-host relationship, perhaps it is understandable that the "Us" group of animal friends in *The Wind in the Willows* should be so concerned with nuances of proper behavior. The term "animal-etiquette" (Grahame 11, 17) appears twice in the first chapter. According to the rules of polite animal society, as Carpenter interprets them, "No questions must be asked about people's private activities" (156). Moore argues that, just as "[m]uch of the book . . . is concerned with inviting the right people in and keeping the wrong people (weasels, stoats, rabbits) out" (45), "[i]nstinctual etiquette is a matter of polite exclusion" (53). Therefore, touchy subjects like hibernation or predation—subjects that "dehumanize" Grahame's exceedingly anthropomorphized characters—are "either mentioned with polite periphrasis or not mentioned at all" (Moore 53).

Certainly one important part of etiquette, animal or otherwise, is making a good first impression. Like Mole, Kenneth Grahame was an outsider-turned-insider: a Scot who made his home in England, a banker who had been denied a university education but nevertheless hobnobbed with the literati and the Oxford-educated. As Hunt points out, this problematic status helped Grahame see "the way in which one class acknowledges another as a significant (and, no doubt, often painful) indication of their breeding" ("Dialogue" 167). At Mole's first meeting with one of the inner circle, he and Rat act like boys at a public school sizing each other up on the first day: they "stood and regarded each other cautiously," and their nonchalant greeting, using what might be considered surnames in the animal kingdom—"'Hullo,

Mole!'" and "'Hullo, Rat!'"(Grahame 6)—sounds typical of middle-
and upper-class English male naming patterns, as does the later use of
affectionate nicknames like Ratty.[8]

From the first chapter, it is clear that social success within this privileged group of friends depends on striking the right note at any given
moment. Sometimes a chaffing remark cements the clique, as when
Otter excuses both his interruption of Rat's picnic and Rat's oversight
at not inviting him with a bantering "'Greedy beggars!'" (14), or when
the animals feel free, as they frequently do, to call each other "silly ass,"
terms that might be construed as further examples of carnival billingsgate.[9] Rather than being insulting, this badinage proves the strength of
their friendship. It can withstand playful verbal abuse and sometimes
even more serious criticism. In this respect, Toad's sufferance of his
friends' barbed remarks earns approval, as the phrases "like the good
fellow he was" (230) and "like the gentleman he was" (248) suggest.

For the insider or "Us" group, then, a willingness to accept criticism
or to abase oneself before one's friends is often the carnivalesque key
to rising in their good opinion: mortification (decrowning) leads to
social approval (crowning). When not being playfully castigated by
their friends, the animal companions frequently indulge in exaggerated
self-deprecation, whether they wish to be perceived as a welcome guest
or a gracious host. For example, during the picnic just after their first
meeting, Mole "begged as a favour to be allowed to unpack" the basket
by himself, and "Rat was very pleased to indulge him" (12). Soon after,
Mole is brought low with remorse over his reckless attempt at rowing
Rat's boat, which results in capsizing it:

> When all was ready for a start once more, the Mole, limp and dejected,
> took his seat in the stern of the boat; and as they set off, he said in a
> low voice, broken with emotion, "Ratty, my generous friend! I am very
> sorry indeed for my foolish and ungrateful conduct. My heart quite fails
> me when I think how I might have lost that beautiful luncheon-basket.
> Indeed, I have been a complete ass, and I know it. Will you overlook it
> this once and forgive me, and let things go on as before?" (20)

Mole's humbling himself before his new friend ironically raises him in
Rat's good opinion, and Rat responds not only with cheerful forgiveness but also with a further invitation:

"What's a little wet to a Water Rat? I'm more in the water than out of it most days. Don't you think anymore about it; and, look here! I really think you had better come and stop with me for a little time. It's very plain and rough, you know—not like Toad's house at all—but you haven't seen that yet; still, I can make you comfortable." (20–1)

Rat's invitation is made even more gracious by including a denigration of his home.

Roger Sale has noted that "Grahame's animal etiquette resembles English manners in insisting on the virtue of understatement" (179), and I would agree that a gentlemanly code of behavior is much in evidence among Grahame's privileged group of animal friends. By introducing the term "carnivalesque" into the discussion of their behavior, my intention is to argue that, even within the "Us" group, nuances of class difference—as those between the humbler Mole and more elevated Toad—are addressed and overcome by indirect inversion rather than direct confrontation. A complicated social irony is at work in the characters' self-deprecation: laying oneself open for criticism or obligating oneself to another becomes the means to the greatest social praise and influence. For instance, the effect of Rat's humbling himself in his invitation to Mole is to empower Rat and further indebt Mole; Mole is said to be "so touched by his kind manner of speaking that he could find no voice to answer him" (21). In fact, a carnivalesque reversal operates in the main characters' social relationships so that to appear lowly and invite others' criticism results in ennobling oneself in others' eyes and winning their goodwill. This approach works especially well for Mole, who is genuinely humble, but also occasionally for Toad, who only contrives to appear humble but does so charmingly.

The Up and Down Swings of Carnival Kings

In addition to this carnivalesque inversion in the main characters' social dynamic, it is also possible to regard the plot of *The Wind in the Willows* in terms of carnival swings upward out of various forms of oppression and restraint into positions of power or riotous abandon, followed by swings downward or decrowning moments, in which characters experience harsh reality once more.[10] As Bakhtin explains, carnival as it was celebrated seasonally in medieval and Renaissance market squares represents a time when the "laws, prohibitions, and restrictions that determine the structure and order of ordinary, that is noncarnival, life are suspended" (*Problems* 122). He adds that "[t]he primary carnivalistic act is the *mock crowning and subsequent decrowning of the carnival king*," an act that represents "the very core of the carnival sense of the world—*the pathos of shifts and changes, of death and renewal*" (*Problems* 124).

Bakhtin's concept of carnival works well for understanding the progress of Mole in part, of the Wild-Wooders in general, and of Toad in particular. Each of them plays the role of carnival king in turn and to a degree. By experiencing rises and falls in power—dualistic crowning and decrowning moments—they not only underscore the temporary nature of all social power but the potential for refreshment, personal and communal, that carnival inversions represent. As Morson and Emerson explain, "In the carnival symbolic, . . . a casting-down is always a positive gesture as well, a bringing-down-to-earth and thus a renewal and refertilization" (443). The first character in the novel to undergo a sudden change in his social status, Mole is the first to wear the mantle of carnival king, although for reasons I will explore momentarily, he is a less satisfying candidate for this position than some other characters in the novel. The Wild-Wooders' usurpation of and subsequent eviction from Toad Hall are the novel's most indisputable examples of carnival crowning and decrowning acts. Lastly, Toad, this animal society's real king, is also himself a carnival king in the course of Grahame's rich text, suffering numerous humiliations but rebounding with renewed vigor and inflated ego each time.

For Mole, chapter one begins with a carnival swing upward from a home that is described not simply as underground but also as "lowly" (Grahame 1). Thus begins for Mole a festive period, pointedly described as a "holiday" (3), in which he is said to be "emancipated" (22) from a life of labor to one of leisure—from whitewashing and other forms of household drudgery to "messing about in boats" (7) and attending riverside picnics. However, Mole doesn't entirely fit the profile of a carnival king. Although his station at the start is lowly compared to Rat's or certainly Toad's, it is not the lowest. As demonstrated earlier in this essay, he considers himself superior to the nameless rabbits and Wild Wood creatures. And despite Grahame's use of the word "holiday," the change in Mole's life appears to be permanent; he experiences no final return to low estate at the end of the novel. There are some minor decrownings for Mole. For instance, his plummet "down, down, down!" (19) into the river due to his overconfidence while rowing Ratty's boat is set against his "'Up we go! Up we go!'" (2) at the beginning of chapter one. Also, on his way to visit Badger, Mole is brought low by the Wild-Wooders, who force him back into a role he has abandoned by hunting him like the animal he no longer seems to be; one who has dined on the lawns at Toad Hall now finds himself uncomfortably sheltering in a hollow log. But these setbacks are relatively minor, and the pattern for Mole is not one of crowning followed by decrowning but of gradual initiation into permanent membership within a materially comfortable and leisured society. Yet a carnival sense of renewal nevertheless accompanies Mole's development. His rise from a dormant life spent below ground to an active position aboveground follows a triumphant death-birth trajectory that remains more or less stable throughout the text.

The most explicit example of the spirit of carnival in the novel occurs in the occupation of Toad Hall by animals from the Wild Wood. By temporarily supplanting the local authority, the ferrets, stoats, and weasels engage in a communal act of renewal, one that "express[es] both their sense of being victims of power and their own power to subvert institutions" (Guerin et al. 305). Despite the military trappings surrounding both the taking and retaking of the Hall, it is clear that carnival carousing, not serious political revolution, is at issue. As Rat's description to Toad of the Wild-Wooders' behavior suggests, theirs is a classic case of underdogs acting with the same self-indulgence as the top dogs when given half a chance:

> "Lying in bed half the day, and breakfast at all hours, and the place in such a mess (I'm told) it's not fit to be seen! Eating your grub, and drinking your drink, and making bad jokes about you, and singing vulgar songs, about—well, about prisons, and magistrates, and policemen; horrid personal songs, with no humour in them." (220)

All the elements of carnival celebration are present: feasting, drinking, singing, and laughter directed at an elevated being—Mr. Toad, former lord of the manor. As noted earlier, a mock lord of the manor or carnival king in the figure of the Chief Weasel is installed in Toad's place. After the retaking of Toad Hall, the restored lowly status of the Wild-Wooders is emphasized by their being sent upstairs to sweep floors and make up the beds with fresh linen. When the Wild-Wooders want to humiliate their rivals, they treat them like prey. When the River-Bankers want to shame their enemies, they treat them like servants. Although a case can be made that the inevitability of the novel's outcome—the restoration of Toad Hall to its original owner—derives from Grahame's political conservatism or from the Homeric structure he imposes, one can also argue that underlying the plot is an understanding that periods of carnival misrule like that enjoyed by the Wild Wood animals are typically short-lived, and figures of authority, hopefully chastened and reminded of their fallibility, are often reestablished.

Among those figures of authority, Toad is the novel's best embodiment of the many fruitful contradictions inherent in carnival. Yes, he is the lord of the manor temporarily decrowned by the rowdy populace—the "real" king—yet because he experiences more humiliating rebuffs and joyful rebounds than anyone, including the Wild Wood creatures, he exhibits "the carnival pathos of shifts and renewals, the image of constructive death" that Bakhtin attributes to the carnival king (*Problems* 125) better than any other character. Carnival, says Bakhtin, is "a pageant without footlights and without a division into performers and spectators. In carnival everyone is an active participant, everyone communes in the carnival act" (*Problems* 122). By participating in Toad's many swings upward and downward, readers move with him into the carnival square and experience the renewal that attends the crowning and decrowning moments that Toad undergoes.

Let us consider some of the many shifts of fortune that Toad experiences. When he is brought low into the dust of the road by the motorcar's destruction of his horse-drawn caravan, Toad immediately rises up and joins the enemy, as it were, becoming "Toad the terror, the trafficqueller, the Lord of the lone trail" (121). His first decrowning from this position as lord of the highway comes when his three friends strip him of his driving gear and latest motorcar: "A good deal of his blustering spirit seemed to have evaporated with the removal of his fine panoply. Now that he was merely Toad, and no longer the Terror of the Highway, he giggled feebly and looked from one to the other appealingly, seeming quite to understand the situation" (108). Stripping Toad of his "panoply," a word that calls to mind regal robes, underscores the de-crowning nature of his humiliation. Toad resorts in turn to billingsgate, "calling all sorts of names" (108) and "shouting abuse at them through the keyhole" (112). His imprisonment in Toad Hall is a trial run for his later, more official incarceration in the human prison. In both cases, he breaks free: the figure of play and irresponsibility that he represents can't be held in check for long.

Toad is recrowned "Toad the terror" (121) when he escapes his friends and steals a car outside a pub: "As if in a dream he found him-self, somehow, seated in the driver's seat; as if in a dream, he pulled the lever and swung the car round the yard and out through the archway; and, as if in a dream, all sense of right and wrong, all fear of obvious consequences, seemed temporarily suspended" (121). The triple-repetition of the phrase "as if in a dream" underscores that the fever of carnival is closely related to the liminal state of dreaming, as characters like Dostoevsky's Raskolnikov demonstrate. This passage also reinforces that, during carnival, the normal rules of right and wrong seem "temporarily suspended." Before long, "Toad the terror" is decrowned once more when he is tried and sentenced in the dock, loaded in chains, and left "a helpless prisoner in the remotest dungeon of the best-guarded keep of the stoutest castle in all the length and breadth of Merry England" (125). There is a festive extravagance even to Toad's imprisonment!

Toad's dejected state as a prisoner is short-lived, and he rises trium-phant once more, ironically by accepting the disguise and lowly status of a human washerwoman. His "misery [turns] into rapture" (158) when the subterfuge helps him dupe two humans, an engine-driver and a barge-woman, into aiding him in his escape, but he is humiliated when the barge-woman sees through his disguise and, what is more, thinks that his true identity as a toad is more abhorrent than his assumed role of servitude. When she decrowns him with carnival laughter, "laughing unrestrainedly, till the tears ran down her cheeks" (196), she and Toad resort to exchanges of carnival abuse:

"You common, low, *fat* barge-woman!" he shouted; "don't you dare to talk to your betters like that! Washerwoman indeed! I would have you to know that I am a Toad, a very well-known, respected, distinguished Toad! I may be under a bit of a cloud at present, but I will *not* be laughed at by a barge-woman!"

The woman moved nearer to him and peered under his bonnet keenly and closely. "Why, so you are!" she cried. "Well, I never! A horrid, nasty, crawly Toad! And in my nice clean barge, too! Now that is a thing that I will *not* have." (196)

Toad taunts the barge-woman for her lowly position on the social ladder, but the barge-woman counters by taunting him for his lowly position on the food chain and reinforces the insult with physical violence. Toad's animal vulnerability is most apparent when the barge-woman grips him by a "fore-leg"—not arm—and "hind-leg," and he suddenly finds himself "flying through the air, revolving rapidly as he went" (196).[11]

Soon after this unseating, Toad rises from degradation once again by stealing and selling the barge-woman's horse. He recites his recent successful adventures, and afterward he feels "big, and strong, and careless, and self-confident" (203) again. His hated disguise saves him from being recognized by the people whose car he stole, and again he indulges in self-congratulation, with the result that he blows his cover and is chased by the police once more. Toad suffers another downward crash—into the river this time to avoid his pursuers—and another upward swing, as Ratty pulls him out of the river and his friends help him regain Toad Hall. Interestingly, in Toad's triumph during the feasting that follows, he behaves according to the topsy-turvy social code that his River Bank friends have modeled effortlessly all along: that being self-effacing exalts one in others' eyes. Consequently, Toad is pleasantly pleased by the stir his newfound humility causes at the great banquet following his restoration as master: "The animals were evidently puzzled and taken aback by this unexpected attitude of his; and Toad felt, as he moved from one guest to the other, making his modest responses, that he was an object of absorbing interest to everyone" (257). By cannily appearing to cast himself down before his friends, he rises in their esteem. The irrepressible Toad is on top once more!

If animals were the only members of the community depicted in *The Wind in the Willows*, then Toad would occupy an unambiguous position of privilege and thereby signify this society's true king and the rightful target of the Wild-Wooders' merry deposing. However, Grahame depicts his animal microcosm as engulfed by the Wide World of humanity, a place that is dangerous for the animals even to mention—"Don't ever refer to it again, please," Rat admonishes Mole (12)—much less visit. The fact that so much of the degradation Toad suffers comes at the hands of human beings far more powerful than he allows us to see him both as the real king within the animal society and the animals' carnival king vis-à-vis human society. Power struggles between groups of animals may swing first one way and then another, suggests Grahame, because there is a fundamental equality among them; but between animals and humans, only escape or, at the most, brief suspensions of human authority are possible for the animals. This desire to engineer occasional triumphs for Toad over human characters is in keeping with Grahame's deep love of animals and his preference for them over humankind, attitudes that have been well documented. For instance, Green details both Grahame's "growing aversion to humanity" (274) and his belief that "the beasts of the field are morally equal, if not superior, to Man" (275). For this reason, I would contend that, underlying Toad's carnivalesque encounters with the police, the court system, and individual humans like the barge-woman is Grahame's desire to redress the inequity in human-animal power relations. Even though a lowly toad cannot gain lasting ascendency in a world run by people, Toad's temporary triumphs spark hope in those readers who, like Grahame, wish for a world where animals are freer and more empowered.

Lingering on the Threshold

Bakhtin argues that, in Dostoevsky's case, carnivalization in his novels "proved remarkably productive as a means for capturing in art the developing relationships under capitalism" (*Problems* 166). Having risen to the position of secretary in the Bank of England, Kenneth Grahame understood both the privilege and the constraint upon personal freedom that success in a capitalist system engenders. Consequently, although he feared social upheaval, as his biographer Green has shown, he nevertheless harbored an "anti-authoritarian streak" (37). "Protest, unorthodoxy, disobedience"—at least when mediated through the imagination—appealed to him (Green 53). This obliquity in

Grahame's nature makes plausible the presence of covertly subversive, carnivalesque qualities in The Wind in the Willows. He seems prepared to tweak the nose of the middle class that had so closely regulated his life but prefers not to bite the hand that continued to feed him. In the society he creates in The Wind in the Willows, Grahame cannot therefore sanction an ultimate overturning of authority by the Wild Wood rabble, but he—and his readers—can enjoy Toad's crowning moments as a carnival king, especially when his triumph is over human opponents. Grahame fails to grant the Wild Wood creatures their own voices with which to do "battle with . . . definitions of their personality in the mouths of other people" (Bakhtin, Problems 59), although he allows all his characters the disruptive power of carnival laughter. Despite this slight to the Wild Wood, Grahame's presentation of an animal society endangered by the encroachment of the Wide World attests to his determination to combat the "reifying devaluation" of the natural world created "under the conditions of capitalism" (Bakhtin, Problems 62). Those crowning swings upward that prove possible for Toad renew hope in the carnival crowd of readers who like to see the human hegemony over animals suspended now and then.

We also love Toad in part because, as Otter says of him early in the novel, he has "no stability" (Grahame 16), not in boats or anywhere else. According to Bakhtin's aesthetic, Dostoevsky's characters are admirable precisely because they refuse externally or authorially imposed stability: "They all acutely sense their own inner unfinalizability, their capacity to outgrow, as it were, from within and to render untrue any externalizing and finalizing definition of them" (Problems 59). A century after the publication of The Wind in the Willows, we continue to value not only the dialogic slipperiness of Grahame's amphibian carnival king, but also, as postmodern readers, we prize his novel's productive instability, the fact that it is structured as a "great dialogue . . . an unclosed whole of life itself, life poised on the threshold" (Problems 63). "Everything . . . lives on the very border of its opposite," as Bakhtin explains, and "opposites come together, look at one another, are reflected in one another, know and understand one another" (Problems 176). For The Wind in the Willows, the forward trajectory of adventure forever butts against the backward turn toward home; the downward curve of defeat forever lifts against the upward swing of joy and freedom.

Notes

1. The novel's unusual structure has given publishers license to pry apart its organically intertwined elements to create abridgments or separate volumes. For instance, illustrator Inga Moore, working for Candlewick Press, split apart Grahame's text to create the two-volume *The River Bank and Other Stories from The Wind in the Willows* (1996) and *The Adventures of Mr. Toad from The Wind in the Willows* (1998).

2. This interest in class conflict—both as it affected Grahame's life and his novel—dates from the 1959 publication of Peter Green's critical biography of Grahame.

3. When italics appear in quotations from Bakhtin's work, they are his own.

4. Many critics have discussed the tension between home and adventure in Grahame's novel. See, for example, Hunt (*Fragmented*) 36 ff.; Kuznets (*Kenneth*) 101 ff.; Moore 53, 55; Nelson 166; Darcy 215; Willis 108 ff.; Watkins 34; and McGillis 186.

5. For instance, Christopher Clausen asserts the primacy of home over adventure and argues that the novel's favoring of this polarity is what qualifies it as children's literature: "I believe that a key to what appeals to children in Grahame's book is this: in *The Wind in the Willows*, the major escape (Toad's) is from prison to home. Although several of the characters are tempted by travel, home is clearly where the characters belong and where, after many vicissitudes, they return" (142).

6. In *The Wind in the Willows: A Fragmented Arcadia*, Peter Hunt observes that Wild Wood society is composed of "the stoats and weasels, undifferentiated by the uppercasing that the novel's other animal characters merit, and ineffectual rabbits (so ineffectual, indeed, that their distant relatives are included in the gipsy's stew)" (79).

7. Hospitality as a sacred duty is just one of the common themes that *The Wind in the Willows* shares with *The Odyssey*. A number of critics have expounded upon the Homeric parallels in Grahame's novel; for example, Green 260 ff., Carpenter 166, Kuznets (*Kenneth*) 100–101, Clausen 144 and 149, Hunt (*Fragmented*) 33, and especially Poss 83–88. In her 1988 article concerning gender in *The Wind in the Willows*, Lois Kuznets emphasizes that "Grahame's Odyssey lacks Penelope" and "males rather than females dispense the hospitality" ("Father Nature" 176).

8. See Kathryn V. Graham's valuable article in which she makes the case that, if we focus on Grahame's "specific addressee," his young son Alastair, then *The Wind in the Willows* can be read as an "obliquely cautionary and

educational tale written by an initiate of the system" (Grahame had had some success as a boy at St. Edward's School, Oxford) posed as "schoolboy lore customized to meet the needs of a one-boy audience" (181). Kathryn Graham notes that the main lessons for survival within the public school culture are negative ones: don't draw attention to yourself, and don't let the side down.

9. In *Rabelais and His World*, Bakhtin explores the ambivalent nature of carnival profanation: "Praise and abuse are, so to speak, the two sides of the same coin. If the right side is praise, the wrong side is abuse, and vice versa. The billingsgate idiom is a two-faced Janus. The praise, as we have said, is ironic and ambivalent. It is on the brink of abuse; the one leads to the other, and it is impossible to draw the line between them. Though divided in form they belong to the same body, or to the two bodies in one, which abuses while praising and praises while abusing. This is why in familiar billingsgate talk abusive words, especially indecent ones, are used in the affectionate and complimentary sense" (165).

10. Several critics have elaborated productively upon the imagery of up and down that pervades *The Wind in the Willows* without connecting it to Bakhtin's idea of the seasonal shifts of carnival or the crowning and decrowning of the carnival king. See, for instance, Hunt (*Fragmented*) 37–38, 41, 54; Gilead 150; and Mendelson 133–34.

11. Toad's vituperative encounter with the barge-woman is also reminiscent of flyting, the ritual exchange of insults found in heroic literature, as well as the African American game of the dozens, a vernacular form involving dueling disparagements. Read in this light, the barge-woman wins the physical conflict but loses the game. As Lewis Hyde explains in *Trickster Makes This World: Mischief, Myth, and Art*, "The loser is the player who breaks the form and starts a physical fight. The point of the game is to play with language, not to take it seriously, or better, to stay in *balance* on the line between the playful and the serious while trying to tip one's opponent *off* that balance, dizzied with a whirl of words" (272–73). Flyting or playing the dozens "requires equilibrium in the force field where all these things join one another. It demands poise in the joints, as it were, balance at the threshold" (Hyde 273–74) and thus represents a true dialogic exchange.

My thanks to my colleague Edward Huffstetler for pointing out this scene's similarity to the game of the dozens and for directing me to Hyde's insightful commentary.

Works Cited

Abrams, M. H. *A Glossary of Literary Terms*. 6th ed. Fort Worth: Harcourt, 1993.

Bakhtin, Mikhail. *The Dialogic Imagination: Four Essays*. Ed. Michael Holquist. Trans. Caryl Emerson and Michael Holquist. U of Texas P Slavic Series 1. Austin: U of Texas P, 1981.

———. *Problems of Dostoevsky's Poetics*. Ed. and trans. Caryl Emerson. Theory and History of Lit. 8. Minneapolis: U of Minnesota P, 1984.

———. *Rabelais and His World*. Trans. Helene Iswolsky. Bloomington: Indiana UP, 1984.

Booth, Wayne C. Introduction. *Problems of Dostoevsky's Poetics*. By Mikhail Bakhtin. Ed. and trans. Caryl Emerson. Theory and History of Lit. 8. Minneapolis: U of Minnesota P, 1984. xiii–xxvii.

Carpenter, Humphrey. *Secret Gardens: A Study of the Golden Age of Children's Literature*. Boston: Houghton Mifflin, 1985.

Clausen, Christopher. "Home and Away in Children's Fiction." *Children's Literature* 10 (1982): 141–52.

Darcy, Jane. "The Representation of Nature in *The Wind in the Willows* and *The Secret Garden*." *Lion and the Unicorn* 19 (1995): 211–22.

Dentith, Simon. *Bakhtinian Thought: An Introductory Reader*. London: Routledge, 1995.

Gilead, Sarah. "The Undoing of Idyll in *The Wind in the Willows*." *Children's Literature* 16 (1988): 145–58.

Graham, Kathryn V. "Of School and the River: *The Wind in the Willows* and its Immediate Audience." *Children's Literature Association Quarterly* 23 (1998–99): 181–86.

Grahame, Kenneth. *The Wind in the Willows*. 1908. New York: Scribner's, 1961.

Green, Peter. *Kenneth Grahame: A Biography*. Cleveland: World, 1959.

Guerin, Wilfred L., et al. *A Handbook of Critical Approaches to Literature*. 3rd ed. New York: Oxford UP, 1992.

Hunt, Peter. "Dialogue and Dialectic: Language and Class in *The Wind in the Willows*." *Children's Literature* 16 (1988): 159–68.

———. *The Wind in the Willows: A Fragmented Arcadia*. Twayne's Masterwork Studies 141. New York: Twayne, 1994.

Hyde, Lewis. *Trickster Makes this World: Mischief, Myth, and Art*. New York: Farrar, Strauss and Giroux, 1998.

Kuznets, Lois. *Kenneth Grahame*. Twayne's English Authors Ser. 449. Boston: Twayne, 1987.

———. "Kenneth Grahame and Father Nature, or Whither Blows *The Wind in the Willows?*" *Children's Literature* 16 (1988): 175–81.

McGillis, Roderick. "Utopian Hopes: Criticism Beyond Itself." *Children's Literature Association Quarterly* 9 (1984–85): 184–86.

Mendelson, Michael. "*The Wind in the Willows* and the Plotting of Contrast." *Children's Literature* 16 (1988): 127–44.

Moore, John David. "Pottering about in the Garden: Kenneth Grahame's Version of Pastoral in *The Wind in the Willows*." *Journal of the Midwest MLA* 23 (1990): 45–60.

Morson, Gary Saul, and Caryl Emerson. *Mikhail Bakhtin: Creation of a Prosaics*. Stanford: Stanford UP, 1990.

Nelson, Claudia. *Boys Will Be Girls: The Feminine Ethic and British Children's Fiction, 1857–1917*. New Brunswick: Rutgers UP, 1991.

Poss, Geraldine D. "An Epic in Arcadia: The Pastoral World of *The Wind in the Willows*." *Children's Literature* 4 (1975): 80–90.

Sale, Roger. *Fairy Tales and After: From Snow White to E. B. White*. Cambridge, MA: Harvard UP, 1978.

Selden, Raman, Peter Widdowson, and Peter Brooker. *A Reader's Guide to Contemporary Literary Theory*. 5th ed. Harlow, England: Pearson, 2005.

Vice, Sue. *Introducing Bakhtin*. Manchester: Manchester UP, 1997.

Watkins, Tony. "'Making a Break for the Real England': The River-Bankers Revisited." *Children's Literature Association Quarterly* 9 (1984): 34–35.

Williams, Jay. "Reflections on *The Wind in the Willows*." *Signal* 21 (1976): 103–7.

Willis, Lesley. "'A Sadder and a Wiser Rat/He Rose the Morrow Morn': Echoes of the Romantics in Kenneth Grahame's *The Wind in the Willows*." *Children's Literature Association Quarterly* 13 (1988): 108–11.

CHAPTER FOUR

~

It's a Mole-Eat-Hare World:
The River Bank, the School,
and the Colony

Meg Worley

The Wind in the Willows is a loving portrait of England's green and pleasant land, beloved and admired for its bucolic setting and loyal companionship. Nonetheless, Mole's first conversation upon emerging from his burrow is an example of the worst that society has to offer: after he has shirked the spring cleaning, the rabbits demand money from him, and he responds with a veiled threat to eat them up with onion sauce (3). *Et in Arcadia ego*, indeed.

If the River Bank is Arcadia, as Humphrey Carpenter, Peter Green, and others have persuasively argued, the *ego* I concern myself with here is not death but inhumane treatment. Children's literature has often taken cruelty as a prominent theme, but as a transgression that must be redressed, corrected, and overwritten by the end of the narrative. *The Wind in the Willows*, however, portrays inhumanity—the choice to withhold compassion—as an inherent feature of societies, something that must be coped with and that cannot be eradicated. Delicious and delightful as Grahame's novel is, it nevertheless contains a number of scenes in which animals enact or threaten to exercise force over other members of their society, frequently in ways that human society considers reprehensible. On the River Bank, it is perfectly acceptable to put one's interlocutors in a dish, in a cage, or in a harness, all the while keeping up a spirited dialogue with the victim.

To act humanely toward someone is to be kind, considerate, and compassionate, as every dictionary tells us; it consists in treating another creature as befits a fellow human being. But the word is packed with tensions, for at the same time that it assumes equality, it implies an unequal relationship between agent and patient, actor and acted-upon. Treating someone humanely asserts that she is a fellow human, but one can only show humane treatment to those who are in one's power in one way or another. "Merciful" as a synonym for "humane" acknowledges this; humane or inhumane behavior occurs when someone is at our mercy. In other words, our choice of behavior centers on the possibility of force. The adjective "humane" is deployed in situations in which the agent has a clear choice between bringing force to bear or forbearing to use force. Humaneness is constituted by the display of power through not exercising it.

Calling someone human or not-human necessarily dates back to the earliest moments of human subjectivity, but "inhumane" is a product of the Age of Exploration. The development of the adjective seems to have been driven by the negative: "inhumane" as clearly distinct from "inhuman" appears a century before comparable use of "human" vs. "humane." Its earliest uses were to modify words like "handlyng," "dealing," "crueltie," and "outrages" in descriptions of barbarian contact and religious persecution. As Shipley notes in *The Origins of English Words*, the suffix "-ane" was separated from "-an" in the late seventeenth century to distinguish between literal and figurative meanings of a word: "The first being physical; the second, of the spirit" (398). The timing, moreover, is hardly accidental, for the period between 1688 and 1793 saw the development of what sociolinguist Richard Watts calls "an ideology of politeness" that addressed its efforts crucially and centrally to the standardization of the English language as the final arbiter of both education and civil conduct (155).

Language is the critical term here, for it sets the terms of our dealings with other creatures. Those with language are human, and thus deserving of humane treatment; those without language make lesser ethical demands upon us, according to mainstream Edwardian views. If I can converse with another creature, then taming, enslaving, or eating it are inhumane. But if we cannot exchange language, I am free to put it to work as a draft animal, take it as a pet, or cook and serve it at table, depending on the role assigned by society to the animal in question. Yet despite these dictates, Mole, Rat, Badger, and Toad act in a way that can be characterized as inhumane, treating the horse, canary, and various other animals in ways that are inconsistent with shared language. In *The Wind in the Willows*, Grahame presages Jean-Paul Sartre ("The important thing is not what you do, but what you do with what has been done to you" [63][1]) in writing a novel that, as Kathryn V. Graham has argued, is a handbook for getting along at school, where institutionalized cruelty is a fact of life. In doing so, he exposes the ways that adults imagine childhood both as a halcyon, protected space and as an alien territory to be exploited.

Ourselves in Fur?

In "Why Look at Animals?" John Berger, following Rousseau, notes that animals constituted the first metaphor, insofar as they were our first experience of something that was simultaneously like and not like ourselves. Animals, like us, are sentient and mortal, but they do not share language with us; thus it is that preliterate cultures often consider animals intermediaries between humans and gods. Lévi-Strauss explores this relationship in the "Totemism From Within" chapter of *Totemism*, arguing persuasively that contact with animals occasions the first differentiation between self and other and that, in fact, the animal is our prototype for binary opposition. In other words, the human-animal distinction is the primordial instance of *us:them*. As Barbara Noske writes, "By drawing a sharp dividing line between human and non-human, a vast gap is created between *subject* (the free acting human agent) and *object* (the passive acted-upon *thing*)" (40). Other binary oppositions follow from *human:animal*—*our tribe:their tribe*, *adult:child*, *male:female*, and so forth[2]—and animals dictate the terms for all these other Others. We use animals as pejorative names for other cultures; we metaphorically categorize children as baby animals (kid, whelp, small fry, and so forth); and we employ animal names to describe women in various roles, from "chick" to "bitch."

In each of these cases, the colon between the terms marks the boundary between civilization and wilderness, culture and nature. Arthur Neal points out that to call someone an animal is to "express the view that important social norms have been violated" (16). And the violation of social norms fundamentally unites animals, children, and the ethnological Other. In all three cases, they are simultaneously like us and not at all like us. John Berger and others have made this point about identity and difference, but it is important to note that in addition to looking different, animals, children, and exotic foreigners cannot be expected to behave according to our social norms. Thus, anyone who doesn't behave correctly is a beast, a brat, a barbarian.

The literary connection between animals and children is made by adults from the earliest hour of children's literature, whether because adults have the controlling hand in both the animal and juvenile kingdoms or because children are seen as gradually growing from a dependent, animalistic state to an autonomous responsible adulthood. For children, animals represent power in an opposite way. The child is subject to the authority of others at every turn: parents, teachers, older siblings, and bullies all act as constraints on their autonomy. But these power dynamics are reversed with animals—now children are the ones calling the shots. This power is physical, and it begins before toddlerhood, as parents watch carefully that the baby doesn't unintentionally harm the family pet. Children can (and do) lead animals around on leashes, ride on their backs, dress them up in doll clothes, and act cruelly to them, at least until adult authority steps in. The early animal story for children exists as an acknowledgment of this fact. As Tess Cosslett and others have observed, books like Mrs. Trimmer's *Fabulous Histories* (1786) and Marshall Saunders's *Beautiful Joe* (1894) were written with the express purpose of teaching children to be kind to animals. The hope was that the lesson might move from symbolic to semiotic space and teach children to be kind to each other as well. In other words, the animal story simultaneously recognizes the child's powerlessness in the world at large and her authority over those below her on the linguistic ladder. To that extent, May Hill Arbuthnot's often-repeated description of animal stories as "ourselves in fur" (462) misses the mark; they may be our *children* in fur, but they are most definitely not us.

Animals and children may sometimes be symbolically interchange-able due to their subject position with respect to the adult world, but in one way they are fundamentally different: the capacity for language. Berger observes that people can (at least potentially) bridge the chasm between minds with speech, but humans and animals must stare at each other "across a narrow abyss of non-comprehension" (3). Children are unlike their parents—and more like animals or foreigners—because their capacity for language is at first merely potential. Their linguistic ability gradually develops over time to become identical with adult lan-guage. The triangulation of language, children, and foreigners is con-cretized in the term "barbarian," which originally meant "to stammer or speak unintelligibly"—it was a term used for children's utterances in classical Rome—and which then took on the meaning of "foreign." And it was English that put the "uncivilized and uncouth" spin on the term. Where the comparison of children to animals erodes, children and outlanders are placed into the same territory of representation.

Interestingly, Grahame posits a language that crosses species lines bidirectionally, in contrast to *Black Beauty* and most other contem-porary animal stories, in which the narrative depends on human non-comprehension. Everyone in Grahame's world shares a language, from the stoats to the gipsy, with variations only in dialect, as in the case of the police sergeant's *Ivanhoe* patois and the gipsy's dropped consonants. The one reference to interspecies linguistic difference—when the gaoler's daughter says, "Squared, I think, is the word you animals use" (138)—denies all opacity, as the young woman displays full knowledge of animal diction even as she calls attention to it. Moreover, that shared language is English, as Rat reminds Toad: "Don't say 'learn 'em,' Toad, [. . .] It's not good English" (221).

Grahame connects language to pedagogy, and specifically to the teaching of social conventions. In their first meeting, Mole exposes his lack of socialization by saying "O, it's all very well to *talk*" (5), and a few pages later his long silence demands a sincere apology: "'I beg your pardon,' said the Mole, pulling himself together with an effort. 'You must think me very rude; but all this is so new to me'" (8). Posi-tive references to manners on the River Bank are similarly focused on language rather than gesture: when inquiring about the mores of Wild Wooders, "Mole knew well that it is quite against animal-etiquette to dwell on possible trouble ahead, or even to allude to it; so he dropped the subject" (10). Later that afternoon, he "recollected that animal-etiquette forbade any sort of comment on the sudden disappearance of one's friends" (14), a rule that suggests something more carnivorous than Otter chasing a mayfly. Even bad manners tend to be verbal in nature, particularly when practiced by Badger, who talks with his mouth full and "hates Society" because it would require him to talk when he doesn't feel like it (2).

At the same time, Grahame is very clear in acknowledging the limits of speech. Ratty is heart-wrenching when he insists "I don't *talk* about my river [. . .] But I *think* about it—all the time!" (29). When they have found Badger's house, Rat asks the uncomprehending Mole if he's "going to sit on the snow all night and *talk*" (55). And Toad almost personifies the limits of language: "Talking to Toad will never cure him" (101); "*Talk* can do little in a case like this" (107); "Talking won't mend matters" (109); "Solid revenge was what he wanted, not cheap, windy, verbal triumphs" (185). In all these cases, the italics are not mine but Grahame's; "talk" is the most frequently italicized word in the novel, reminding us of the importance of talk in this talking-animal story.

Together, these two foundational principles of the River Bank—the importance of language as the vehicle of social conventions and its ultimate limitations—sum up the tensions between culture and nature. Grahame maps them onto competing forms of power: persuasion/culture is at all times preferable, but sometimes one must resort to force/nature. This could in fact be read as the main argument of the novel, from the disastrous caravan jaunt (on which Rat is persuaded to go along but the horse is forced) to the friends' attempt to take Toad in hand to the battle with the stoats and weasels. Grahame even has Badger say it in so many words: "Since you won't yield to persuasion, we'll see what force can do" (104). The two main instances when persuasion rather than force prevails are in the two chapters that most fascinate scholars, "Piper at the Gates of Dawn" and "Wayfarers All." In the one case, physical searching for young Portly is unsuccessful while "the sudden clear call from an actual articulate voice" (120) draws Rat and Mole to the sleeping pup (although it should be noted that even here, language fails in the face of the sublime). In "Wayfarers All," it is Mole's gentle persuasion that brings Rat back to himself, after trying force and failing ("Grappling with him strongly he dragged him inside, threw him down, and held him" [172]). Rat, being a poet, is eternally subject to persuasion, while Toad, ever a creature of impulse, responds far better to force.

All of Grahame's noteworthy examples of inhumane behavior take place necessarily where force and persuasion overlap. In most cases, the mistreatment is an acknowledgment of the failure of language: soft words precede or accompany the firm hand. The talking-animal story is an ideal mode for this lesson, for that is how we deal with domesticated animals. But it is also how we deal with children and with other cultures. When encountering the Other, goodness is defined as succumbing to persuasion, while badness demands force. Note that cruelty is not the same as force. Rather, it is disproportionate force: a display of physical power that is incommensurate with the social expectations for the situation. In other words, cruelty occurs precisely at the seams of power, where language has failed but social conventions continue to prevail.

The Dish, the Cage, and the Harness

Most of the inhumane treatment in *The Wind in the Willows* falls into one of three categories: eating other animals, keeping animals as pets, and using animals for labor. Meat-eating takes primacy of place, not only in terms of total attention given to it in the novel but also literally. Mole's "Onion-sauce! Onion-sauce!" are the first words he says to anyone besides himself (3). Even if he is not threatening to dine on rabbit with onion sauce right there and then, the menace is clear enough: he foresees a delicious, well-seasoned end for the greedy rabbits, one in which he wouldn't mind partaking. Furthermore, Mole is fully aware that he is being mean; Grahame describes his tone as jeering (3), and he is certainly flouting the point of animal-etiquette that he knows perfectly well only a few minutes later (namely, don't allude to trouble that is to come) (10). If more time elapsed between the two scenes, we might assume that Mole had learned consideration from Rat, but he clearly knew the rule before he emerged from his burrow. Extortion attempts—verbal demands rooted in force—may be answered with the possibility of physical harm, but a threat to sauce and serve the extortionists is a disproportionate response. We can even read Mole's jeer as an example of his inexperience; because he does not know how else to respond to the rabbits, he resorts to the promise of force. After a time under Rat's benevolent tutelage, Mole would have less menacing ways of refusing their demands.

Rabbit is not the only meat eaten by the noble company. All of the fine meals in The Wind in the Willows—what C. W. Sullivan III calls "food events"—are centered around meat, from the "coldtongue-coldhamcoldbeefpickledgherkinssaladfrenchrollscresssandwichespot-tedmeatgingerbeerlemonadesodawater" of the first picnic (7) to the cold chicken, tongue, and lobster salad that follow the last battle (232). Elsewhere, the companions tuck into bacon, cold tongue, ham, and a gipsy stew with seven kinds of meat, and when that is not enough, Mole trudges off to buy milk and eggs. In the real world, moles, badgers, toads, and voles (the more common name for the water rat) may eat grasses and small invertebrates, but in Grahame's world, they dine on the best of English butchery. No doubt, lavish descriptions of food are even more satisfying to children at the full-time mercy of institutional kitchens than to the rest of us, but the blithe mention of animals eating animals is an open acknowledgment of certain immovable social roles, effected through muscle, not talk.

Inhumane treatment can include caging other animals as well as eating them. Despite Lesley Willis's description of a single "persistent prison motif" in The Wind in the Willows (108), Grahame seems to draw a distinction between different types of bars. The most obvious example is Toad's incarceration at the end of "Mr Toad," but this is in fact the only case of imprisonment in the novel that takes humane form (that is, as a punishment for a crime). All of the other cases of forcible detention are of the variety reserved for animals and children, namely, those intended to deny independence, forestall autonomy, and satisfy the detainer's desires at the expense of the detainee's. The first case of forcible detention involves the caravan cart, which features "a bird-cage with a bird in it" (25). Willis, noting that the wagon is repeatedly described as "canary-colored," sees it as "a bird within a bird" (110), and I would also point out that songbirds are kept specifically for their pseudoverbal ability. When the caravan crashes, the bird "sob[s] pitifully and call[s] to be let out," but the companions pay no mind to her; instead, Rat "carr[ies] the bird-cage and its hysterical occupant in the other hand" (32). The songbird is obviously the animal most upset and bruised by the caravan crash, but she is the only one who remains in her cage, despite sobbing pleas to the contrary. Sometimes the most gilded tongue cannot talk its way out of a situation.

Toad himself comes in for a great deal of harsh treatment at the hands of friends once Badger decides that the hour has come to knock some sense into him, and while they do not treat him like a pet, they certainly treat him like a small child. After all, Toad above all others exemplifies the failure of persuasion. The friends begin by dragging him inside and stripping him: "They had to lay Toad out on the floor, kicking and calling all sorts of names, before they could get to work properly. Then the Rat sat on him, and the Mole got his motor-clothes off him bit by bit, and they stood him up on his legs again" (101–2). After they humiliate him (which seems to be the main purpose of the exercise, as they are pleased to see that "his blustering spirit" has disappeared [101]), Badger takes him into the smoking room for a serious talking-to. The ensuing conversation is phrased in rather horrific terms that, if not describing real torture, at least sound like enhanced interrogation. First Rat and Mole hear "the long continuous drone of the Badger's voice," then "long-drawn sobs" from Toad. When they reappear, Toad is a broken fellow, unsteady, haggard, and drenched in tears, and Badger announces triumphantly that Toad has capitulated and told him what he wanted to hear. The coercion is revealed, however, when Toad, upon being ordered to repeat his confession before witnesses, instead renounces it, saying "O, yes, yes, in *there* [. . .] I'd have said anything in *there*" (102–3). Having failed to succumb to Badger's oratorical abuse, Toad is locked up in his bedroom under constant guard. Again, we see a disproportionate response to a problem; forcibly stripping, haranguing, and imprisoning is hardly a measured reaction to a new hobby.

Indeed, the astute reader must ask herself what the purpose of this "tough love" scene really is. Back in Badger's house, Rat remarks that "if he'd only employ a decent, steady, well-trained animal, pay him good wages, and leave everything to him, he'd get on all right" (61). Grahame doesn't call much attention to it, but in fact this is precisely what Toad does:

The Badger strode up the steps. "Take him inside," he said sternly to his companions. Then, as Toad was hustled through the door, struggling and protesting, he turned to the chauffeur in charge of the new motor-car.

"I'm afraid you won't be wanted to-day," he said. "Mr. Toad has changed his mind. He will not require the car. Please understand that this is final. You needn't wait." Then he followed the others inside and shut the door. (100)

If Toad has engaged a chauffeur—and the phrase "you won't be wanted to-day" suggests that the driver is permanent, rather than merely delivering the new car—the friends can hardly be stepping in to prevent further smashups. Badger's wintertime proclamation of "We'll *make* him be a sensible Toad!" (62) suddenly reads more like a schoolyard attempt to teach a fellow a lesson. Come early summer, the suspicion is confirmed when Badger fulminates,

> "At this very moment, perhaps, Toad is busily arraying himself in those
> singularly hideous habiliments so dear to him, which transform him from
> a (comparatively) good-looking Toad into an Object which throws any
> decent-minded animal that comes across it into a violent fit." (99)

Badger's complaint appears to be more sartorial than safety-related; he opens their conversation by stating that "Independence is all very well, but we animals never allow our friends to make fools of themselves beyond a certain limit" (101). At no point does he express any concern for Toad's safety, only that "you're getting us animals a bad name in the district" (101). Rather than saving Toad from himself, the animals are attempting to save their dignity and their reputations in the schoolyard that is the River Bank. If a chap can't be talked round, physical force will have to be brought to bear.

Of course, Toad's new hobby *is* ill-advised, and after escaping childish confinement under the eye of his friends, he finds himself incarcerated as an adult, for a very real crime and at the mercy of a grim gaoler. But this foray into adulthood does not last long: The gaoler's daughter sees him not as a criminal but as an animal, to be added to her menagerie of a canary, a squirrel, and several piebald mice. The fact that they converse at length is no bar to her ambition to train him to "eat from my hand, and sit up, and do all sorts of things" (134). For the modern reader, the prospect of a talking pet may summon up images of Koko, Washoe, and Alex the parrot, but in the context of 1908, the closest analogues to animals with a true capacity for language (rather than an ability to mimic) were human pets like Ishi, James Cook's captive Polynesian Omai, and the Huron that Samuel de Champlain named Sauvignon. The gaoler's daughter serves as a warning against seeking out the soft ministrations of the feminine hand: next thing you know, you'll be eating from it.

She is, in fact, the only character in *The Wind in the Willows* who is alert to the nuances of incarceration. Her concern for liberating Toad is based in a clear distinction between prison and cage: she "thought it a great shame that a poor little animal should be locked up in prison for what seemed to her a very trivial offence." She at least seems to grasp the insult implied by her efforts to train him, as she allows Toad to think that her interest is romantic rather than menagerial, "because she had the sense to see that Toad would be extremely offended" (137). Such a level of consideration is in marked contrast with the animals of the River Bank, who see Toad as a schoolboy who needs toughening up, not coddling.

Finally, the River-Bankers use their fellow creatures for labor—which frequently implies a form of incarceration, as in the case of the horse that they chase down to pull Toad's caravan. Like the threat of onion sauce, this exchange between animals is rather troubling:

> When they were quite ready, the now triumphant Toad led his companions to the paddock and set them to capture the old grey horse, who, without having been consulted, and to his own extreme annoyance, had been told off by Toad for the dustiest job in this dusty expedition. He frankly preferred the paddock, and took a deal of catching. (28)

In case the reader has missed the centrality of dialogue in their dealings with the horse, Grahame reminds us of it just before the caravan crash: "They were strolling along the high road easily, the Mole by the horse's head, talking to him, since the horse had complained that he was being frightfully left out of it, and nobody considered him in the least" (30). The horse is quite right: his desire to stay home has been overruled by their need for a draft animal, and he will not let them forget it. Only Mole—the junior member of the merry band—heeds his complaint. It is worth noting that not two but three animals resist going on the caravan adventure, but only the horse and the songbird are forced; Rat succumbs to persuasion, and unlike the other two, he is fully liberated by the crash.

The horse's complaints about what is essentially his assigned role in life get ignored, but class is more clearly forefronted in the other descriptions of servitude. In describing Toad Hall to the gaoler's daughter, Toad places particular emphasis on his domestic animals—"the pig-sties, and the stables, and the pigeon-house, and the hen-house; and [. . .] the dairy" (136). In a different animal, such a description might reflect suffering: just as he is "immured in a dank and noisome dungeon" (132), so the pigs, horses, pigeons, hens, and milk cows are immured in their respective holding pens back at home. But that is not Toad's way; instead he elides the animals entirely in order to concentrate on their houses, as jewels in the crown that is Toad Hall. The farm animals, despite the fact that every creature in *The Wind in the Willows* can speak, are just as hidden and spectral as the house servants, who are frequently implied but rarely seen. They become figures of nostalgia, evoking the aristocracy's anticipatory sense of loss; after World War I, the servant class will give way to wage earners.

In addition to farm animals and house servants, there are several scenes in which animals are treated as if they were servants, even though they are not. The two young hedgehogs visiting Badger behave in a much more servile fashion than one would expect of children who got lost on their way to school: they jump to their feet and bow when Mole and Rat enter the room, and Rat responds by telling them "You needn't 'sir' me quite so much"—not that they shouldn't "sir" him, but that they should be more moderate about it (and perhaps more in keeping with Rat's social standing). When Mole inquires about Badger's whereabouts, the older hedgehog replies as a servant: "The master's gone into his study, sir [. . .] and he said as how he was going to be particular busy this morning, and on no account was he to be disturbed" (63). Then, when Otter turns up and asks Mole to fry him some ham, Mole orders the hedgehogs to do it "and returned to his own breakfast" (67). At that point, Grahame makes the point that the hedgehogs are hungry again after their porridge breakfast (while Mole and Rat have had eggs and bacon), and he underscores it with Otter's teasing (but somewhat heartless) lie: having demolished all the fried ham himself, Otter, "winking at the Mole," says, "The sight of these greedy young hedgehogs stuffing themselves with fried ham makes me feel positively famished" (67). But instead of feeding the hungry lads, Badger sends them on their way, saying "You won't want any dinner today, I'll be bound" in a way that can only be described as unfeeling. They each receive a sixpence, and they depart "with much respectful swinging of caps and touching of forelocks," like good servants. Not only has Badger sent them away hungry, but he has packed them off into very deep snow (even if he has sent an invisible servant "to show you the way" [68]). The class distinction stands out here, for the hedge-hogs told Mole and Rat, "Terrible deep the snow is [. . .] No getting out for the likes of you gentlemen today" (63). Porridge, servility, and a hungry trudge through heavy snow are appropriate for hedgehogs, but for Mole, Rat, Otter, and Badger, it is bacon and eggs, service, and a cozy and companionable day by the fire.

Mole plays an interesting part in the class structure of Grahame's animal world, for he sometimes takes up the role of the servant himself. He sets out and clears up after the first glorious picnic with Rat, and when Otter turns up at Badger's, he says, "Here, Mole, fry me up some slices of ham, like the good little chap you are" (67). This last phrase is dismissive and pejorative in equal parts, to emphasize both Otter's natural sense of entitlement and Mole's position as junior to the other animals. Nor does Mole's social standing change much in the course of the novel. After the vanquishing of the Wild-Wooders, Badger—"his mouth full of chicken and trifle" (233)—commands him to see to it that the bedrooms are impeccably cleaned "before you sit down to your supper along of us."

Mole, however, is being treated less as a servant than as a supervisor; he has the hedgehogs do the actual frying up for Otter and then sits back down to his own meal, and in Toad Hall, he is given a squad of POW weasels to get the job done. In other words, Mole—not a member of nature's ruling class—is being trained by his friends to command others, and specifically as a mid-level functionary. In Toad Hall, this is particularly obvious, as Badger invites him to "give them a licking apiece, if it's any satisfaction to you" once the job is done. The fact that he does not is proof that he has learned how to balance command with mercy: as he says, "'And I didn't have to lick them, either,' he added. 'I thought, on the whole, they had had licking enough for one night, and the weasels, when I put the point to them, quite agreed with me, and said they wouldn't think of troubling me'" (233–34). Eton, Harrow, and Rugby had taken over from Haileybury[3] the responsibility of training the civil service by Grahame's day, and Mole fits neatly into this taxonomy of British colonial bureaucracy.

Culture Red in Tooth and Claw

In "Of School and the River," Kathryn V. Graham draws on the fact that the original audience for what was to become *The Wind in the Willows* was Kenneth Grahame's son Alastair to argue that the novel is a schoolboy's guide to getting on at an English public school—a sort of Mirror for (Little) Princes:[4]

> Though *The Wind in the Willows* serves admirably as a general guidebook to the ways of that interesting young animal the English schoolboy, its fictive and rhetorical strategies specifically reflect the particular anxieties and circumstances of its author and its addressee. In that sense, this obliquely cautionary and educational tale written by an initiate of the system is schoolboy lore customized to the meet the needs of a one-boy audience. (181)

Graham does not do a close reading of the novel and its characters, but each animal takes up his school role easily. Mole—visually impaired like Alastair Grahame—is the middle-class first-former of good sense but little experience, and during the course of the narrative, he learns both how to do and how to be done to (perhaps a defining characteristic of the middle class). Toad is his opposite, the rich boy of no sense who is hard at work squandering the family fortune on foolhardy schemes and thoughtless whims. Rat is the friendly mentor, wise in the ways of the world but still an easygoing mate. Otter is a good chap but high-handed, accustomed to bossing those of lower social class (as we see when he cuffs the rabbit to get information from him, plus another cuff for good measure). Badger is the gruff but kind-hearted senior prefect or fag-master, and the stoat-and-weasel contingent represents the bad kids, about whom the less said the better. Meanwhile, humans stand in for the adult authorities, from the headmaster/magistrate and his/the gaoler's kindly daughter to the matron/barge-women—whom you only have to deal with when you're in trouble.

Grahame's public school system effortlessly suggests itself as a microcosm of colonialism, the proving ground on which the members of the British Civil Service, from the executives at Whitehall to the minor functionaries on Tristan de Cunha, learn their appointed roles and how to perform them. The webbing of caste and class was woven into the very fabric of the post-East India Company civil service, with its division into Home, Diplomatic, Indian, and Colonial Services. In this reading, Grahame is a traditional Raj-era British imperialist, clinging tightly to a bucolic fiction supported and made possible by city workhouses and overseas plantations and factories—an Eden onto which the silhouette of the Indian subaltern cannot help but fall. Humphrey Carpenter's arcadian view of Grahame certainly nudges the reader in that direction, and we should not be surprised to find ourselves translating affection and longing for the English countryside into a narrative of class and imperialism.

But *The Wind in the Willows* brings home the point that the British public school isn't just a microcosm of the colonial system but a colony in and of itself, built by adults to subjugate children—those like-and-yet-not-like-us Others—with the goal of recovering and exporting their resources (to wit, their future abilities). The school, like the River Bank, is a marginal zone with its own social structure, populated and policed by these Others and subject to regulation by the outside world of adults. Badger does his best to control Toad but must in the end hand the job over to the police; likewise, Victorian schoolmasters delegated as much discipline as possible to the senior prefects, head boys, and fagmasters, but they remained the final dispensers of justice. Meanwhile, within the marginal community, each creature learns that happiness consists in taking one's natural and rightful place in society.

Empire always entails inhumane treatment, for however many gestures of diplomacy and persuasion accompany its beginnings, the cultural encounter is defined by physical power. Back in the imperial metropolis, the colonial subject is understood as a child or an animal, alternately and simultaneously. By encoding the failure of persuasion into the understanding of the ethnological Other, the colonizing power

makes force—and treating humans as something other than human—
the originary form of interaction. Grahame's narrative of social place
and power recognizes this as fact, but in repeatedly bringing our attention back to the linguistic exchanges between the animals precisely at
those moments of cruelty, he stops just short of condoning them. His is
an accommodating pragmatism designed to help young schoolboys and
other woodland creatures get on in life rather than change it. Sarah
Gilead says that most canonical children's literature disrupts the idyll it
constructs—and can't help doing so, given that it is written by adults,
with adult concerns. But I would argue that Grahame starts with the
raw material of the broken idyll—much like the abandoned civilization
of Badger's house—and builds from the rubble a new idyll, a postlapsar-
ian paradise in which force is a given and everyone settles himself into
his appointed place in the world.

Despite Grahame's well-documented love of the pleasures of Edwardian culture, the social view described above might seem more in keeping with Victorian notions of empire. Edward VII's reign, after all, was
the decade of dominion, when certain colonies became autonomous
polities, and others made strides toward independent rule.[5] But just as
childhood is the natural repository for all our urges toward nostalgia,
a time that is socially constructed as eternally happy and untroubled
(which intellectually even the most starry-eyed adult knows that it is
not), so too do schools preserve features, phenomena, and anomalies
long after the adult world has cast them off. Fagging persisted for centuries after the end of serfdom in England; skills that were long ago
dispensed with in adult life are still solemnly taught to children (e.g.,
penmanship and recorder playing). Schools, like childhood, become
colonies of memory: the place where we bury our former selves and
their metonymic artifacts, for ongoing excavation and exportation to
the mature metropolis, according to its needs.

Thus it is that children's literature is the first place that we, as adult
readers and scholars, look for remnants of ourselves. Every book is potentially the history of our ethical development. In "Utopian Hopes,"
Roderick McGillis sketches out a possible critical landscape of *The
Wind in the Willows* that consists of a conservative reading ("Home is
perfection"), a radical reading ("Home is a trap"), and what he calls a
visionary, or hybrid, reading, in which home is both heaven and hell.

I call this critical landscape "possible" because according to McGillis, there is no radical reading of *The Wind in the Willows*, no scholar who argues that the comfort of the River Bank and the camaraderie of its denizens are malign influences. Perhaps not (although Neil Philip's work on the Victorian mob and Tony Watkins's conception of home move some way in that direction), but Grahame's equation of River Bank, school, and colony acknowledges the inevitability of power, the importance of conformity, and the limits on individuality—all things not usually articulated in children's books. Children's literature is generally the most reliable source for lessons on resisting peer pressure, remaining optimistic (or even idealistic), and above all, being yourself; from "The Ant and the Grasshopper" to *Pollyanna* and *Harry Potter*, adults have written children's books in sheer contravention of the fact that the world demands conformity and negotiation. Children's literature, as written and understood by adults, is like John Berger's zoo in "Why We Look at Animals"—a monument to absence. The *Wind in the Willows*, however, with its sustained attention to the relationship between persuasion and force, argues for presence: the inescapability of inhumane behavior, the limits on individuality, and the need to navigate the waterways of power. If we don't recognize the argument as such and glory instead in the messing about with boats, friends, and good eats, that's all to the good. Badger would be happy—we have yielded to persuasion. No need to *make* us be sensible Toads.

Notes

I would like to acknowledge the help of Dara Regaignon, my colleague at Pomona College, whose feedback was invaluable in the writing of this essay.

1. *L'important n'est pas ce qu'on fait de nous mais ce que nous faisons nous-mêmes de ce qu'on a fait de nous.* Translation mine.

2. Mary Douglas is frequently cited here. She writes, "The contrast between man and not-man provides an analogy for the contrast between the member of the human community and the outsider" (289). She is cited in (among others) Steve Baker, *Picturing the Beast*. I owe Baker a debt of gratitude for propelling my thoughts about animal-human interactions, particularly his chapter "The Rhetoric of Animality." In addition, Baker's work pointed me in the direction of a number of scholars whom I might otherwise not have found.

3. The East Indian Company's training college, closed in 1854.

4. The Mirror for Princes (*Speculum Principi*) was a genre of royal advice book in the Middle Ages and Renaissance, often composed at the accession of a new monarch or following a traumatic military defeat. The most famous example is Niccolò Machiavelli's *The Prince*.

5. Australia, New Zealand, Newfoundland, and South Africa all became dominions under Edward VII. The Government of India Act was passed in 1906, the same year as the Denshawai Incident, an event that contributed to England's loss of Egypt.

Works Cited

Arbuthnot, May Hill. *Children and Books*. Rev. ed. Chicago: Scott, Foresman, 1957.

Baker, Steve. *Picturing the Beast: Animals, Identity and Representation*. Manchester: Manchester UP, 1993.

Berger, John. "Why Look at Animals?" *About Looking*. New York: Pantheon, 1980. 1–26.

Carpenter, Humphrey. *Secret Gardens: A Study of the Golden Age of Children's Literature*. Boston: Houghton Mifflin, 1985.

Cosslett, Tess. *Talking Animals in British Children's Fiction, 1786–1914*. London: Ashgate, 2006.

Douglas, Mary. *Implicit Meanings: Essays in Anthropology*. London: Routledge & Kegan Paul, 1975.

Gilead, Sarah. "The Undoing of Idyll in *The Wind in the Willows*." *Children's Literature* 16 (1988): 145–58.

Graham, Kathryn V. "Of School and the River: *The Wind in the Willows* and its Immediate Audience." *Children's Literature Association Quarterly* 23 (1998–1999): 181–86.

Grahame, Kenneth. *The Wind in the Willows*. London: Puffin, 2008.

Green, Peter. *Kenneth Grahame: A Biography*. Cleveland: World Publishing, 1959.

Lévi-Strauss, Claude. *Totemism*. Boston: Beacon, 1971.

McGillis, Roderick. "Utopian Hopes: Criticism beyond Itself." *Children's Literature Association Quarterly* 9 (1984): 184–86.

Neal, Arthur G. "Animism and Totemism in Popular Culture." *Journal of Popular Culture* 19 (1985): 15–24.

Noske, Barbara. *Humans and Other Animals: Beyond the Boundaries of Anthropology*. London: Pluto, 1989.

Philip, Neil. "*The Wind in the Willows*: The Vitality of a Classic." *Children and Their Books*. Ed. Gillian Avery and Julia Briggs. Oxford: Clarendon, 1989. 299–316.

Sartre, Jean-Paul. *Saint Genet, comédien et martyr*. Paris: Gallimard, 1952.

Shipley, Joseph T. *The Origins of English Words: A Discursive Dictionary of Indo-European Roots*. Baltimore: Johns Hopkins UP, 1984.

Sullivan, C. W., III. "'Chops, . . . Cheese, New Bread, Great Swills of Beer': Food and Home in Kenneth Grahame's *The Wind in the Willows*." *Journal of the Fantastic in the Arts* 15 (2005): 144–52.

Watkins, Tony. "Reconstructing the Homeland: Loss and Hope in the English Landscape." *Aspects and Issues in the History of Children's Literature*. Ed. Maria Nikolajeva. Westport, CT: Greenwood, 1995. 165–72.

Watts, Richard. "From Polite Language to Educated Language: the Re-emergence of an Ideology." *Alternate Histories of English*. Ed. Richard Watts and Peter Trudgill. London: Routledge, 2002. 155–72.

Willis, Lesley. "'A Sadder and a Wiser Rat/He Rose the Morrow Morn': Echoes of the Romantics in Kenneth Grahame's *The Wind in the Willows*." *Children's Literature Association Quarterly* 13 (1988): 108–11.

~

CHAPTER FIVE

A Contemporary Psychological Understanding of Mr. Toad and His Relationships in *The Wind in the Willows*

Jonathan Mattanah

Characters in novels exist in a paradoxical state. On the one hand, they are fixed objects, figments of an author's rich imagination, bound entirely by the temporal and spatial constraints of their literary medium. In this sense, they are not real. On the other hand, they are depicted by their authors as having thoughts and emotions (both those they express to others and private fantasies and feelings), experiencing satisfying and troubling relationships, and undergoing change and development over the course of their "lifetimes." In this sense, they are true, perhaps even more true than real people because they know how it all ends and sometimes even what their life has meant in the larger scheme of things. As David Richter notes in issuing cautions about the psychoanalytic interpretation of literary figures, fictional characters are "both more and less than real persons" (1109).

Because of their true-to-life form, literary characters have often been analyzed by psychologically informed critics as if they were real people or modeled on real people. In a period when the truisms of Freudianism are no longer taken as the gospel, however, practicing psychoanalysts and psychologists, as well as literary critics, are increasingly subjecting such analyses to pointed critique. Patrick Hogan points out that when applying the methods of clinical psychoanalysis to the analysis of a character in a text, one is on shaky ground because the character is not a real person and therefore does not have the same unconscious beliefs and desires as a patient in a clinical setting. In a similar vein, Richter points out that although some aspects of characters have a "mimetic" function, that is, they represent human action and motivation, other aspects of characters have only textual functions, such as "the revelation or concealment of information to an audience" (1109). Hogan concludes his essay by issuing a series of cautions to the literary analyst who wishes to pursue psychoanalytic literary criticism, suggesting that such criticism be extremely clear about the precise object of the analysis (whether it is the characters of the text, the author, or the audience), make full use of all scholarly tools available to literary psychoanalysis, and weigh carefully the evidence relevant to any claims made based on a psychoanalytic hypothesis.

My aim in the current essay is to provide a psychologically informed interpretation of the character of Mr. Toad from *The Wind in the Willows* that attends to many of the cautions raised by Hogan and other critics concerned by the overly simplistic application of psychoanalytic theory to the realm of literature. Providing a careful, empirically grounded psychological analysis of a literary character in a novel can lead to valuable insights. First, such an analysis can provide a concise picture of a complex human experience, allowing the reader to comprehend that experience within the "life" struggle of a fictitious character. In the case of Toad, I believe Grahame provided not only a rich account of the trials and tribulations of a person suffering from a narcissistic personality disorder, but also a snapshot of how the friends of such a person might respond to him, both appropriately and inappropriately. Tracing that account in this novel provides clinically rich material for practicing mental health professionals and anyone else who has an interest in these kinds of phenomena. Second, psychological analysis of literary characters can often address inconsistencies in a character's behavior and help resolve ambiguities in the text itself. Viewing Toad from the particular psychological approach I introduce in this paper helps the reader understand his frequently erratic behavior and may justify his alteration by the novel's end. Whether Toad has truly changed as a person, as the text suggests he has, is one of the major unresolved issues in this novel. Hence, the psychological analysis in this paper helps advance an understanding of Toad as a character within the text of *The Wind in the Willows*.

In fact, Mr. Toad has been the subject of considerable psychological analysis by other literary critics. Because of his characteristic excesses, his constant boasting, his addiction to motorcars, and his extreme mood fluctuations, Toad has typically been viewed by such critics as pathological. Andrew McBride makes a cogent argument for describing Toad's addiction to motorcars as meeting almost all of the diagnostic criteria for the modern psychiatric concept of a "dependency syndrome" (135) as laid out in the latest version of the Diagnostic and Statistical Manual of Mental Disorders (DSM-IV).[1] He notes that Toad's "joy-riding" (129) is motivated by the pleasure associated with fast and reckless driving, rather than by the desire to steal, as is the case in many instances of joyriding addictive behavior. Along a similar line, Peter Green, one of Kenneth Grahame's biographers, suggests that Toad's excessive and pathological behaviors are "suggestive of an adult manic-depressive" (282). Toad's psychological problems have even been the subject of a fictional psychological adventure story, in which Toad receives counseling for an episode of depression (de Board).

Most other psychological interpretations of Toad's character have tended to rely upon a classical Freudian framework. Within this framework, Toad represents the "Id personified" (Green 282), the most primitive aspect of the personality that seeks immediate gratification of its instincts with little consideration for societal constraints. Toad's reckless pursuit of fun, childlike egocentrism, and love of danger and excitement confirm his id-like nature for Michael Steig, who describes Toad's desires as "chaotic and dangerous" (314–15). In a lighter tone, Nicholas Tucker sees Toad as the "children's Falstaff," "the spirit of personified Riot, a perpetual and irrepressible threat to the status quo both of their friends and of the rather stuffy society outside that condemns them so freely" (162).

From a Freudian perspective, Toad's id-like nature is in need of reform by a stern, authoritative superego. For many critics, Toad's superego is embodied in the character of Badger, the stern father figure of the novel, who protects the other animals and even "paternally" pats them on the head (see Gaarden 44). As Lois Kuznets so aptly puts it,

"Badger is the main reforming force in Toad's life, a super-ego who has not yet been internalized" (emphasis in original, 125).

However, a classical psychoanalytic account of Toad, I would argue, does not do justice to his character, nor to the complexity of his interactions with his friends as the novel progresses. Instead of relying on the classical id/ego/superego triad, I would like to deploy a more modern psychoanalytic approach to understanding Toad, one that describes his psychological distress in depth and examines how other characters help him manage it. From a self psychology psychoanalytic perspective, Toad can fruitfully be viewed as suffering from a narcissistic personality disorder. Freud introduced the concept of narcissism in his classic essay "On Narcissism," in which he characterized it as a self-oriented drive in competition with object-oriented libidinal drives. For Freud, individuals with a narcissistic personality disorder have taken themselves as the primary love-object because of an overly strong narcissistic drive and perhaps an underdeveloped libidinal drive.

In the 1950s, Heinz Kohut[2] provided a different way of understanding narcissism and how it does or does not develop into a disorder. Rather than seeing it as a drive, Kohut described narcissistic expressions in young children as normal, healthy, and potentially valuable aspects of self-development, reflecting the young child's natural tendency to show off and wish to be admired by caretaking others. As part of that narcissistic tendency, children also wish to idealize their parents and receive soothing comfort from them, which helps shore up their sense of self through identification with a soothing and admired caretaker. In early childhood, caretakers should provide some admiration (Kohut called it "mirroring") and soothing for the child's narcissistic tendencies while at the same time setting appropriate limits around that narcissism. Over time, the child will learn to moderate his or her narcissistic tendencies; for a healthy child, narcissism will transform into self-esteem. If, on the other hand, the child fails to be admired and soothed by caretakers, or caretakers give free rein to the child's narcissism and fail to set any realistic boundaries around it, the child is at risk for developing a narcissistic personality disorder as he or she grows and develops.

According to the DSM-IV, individuals with a narcissistic personality disorder suffer from a pervasive condition in which they have a grandiose sense of their self-importance and constantly seek admiration from others. In addition, such individuals may be preoccupied with "fantasies of success, power, brilliance, or ideal love, they are frequently entitled, can be interpersonally exploitative, and tend to lack empathy with others" (661). In an insightful psychological analysis of Toad's personality, Mark West has made the claim that Toad suffers from a narcissistic personality disorder. He suggests that "Grahame's portrayal of Toad could almost be a case illustration of this particular psychological problem" (47). West highlights a number of features of Toad's narcissistic disorder that are consistent with the DSM-IV definition. First, Toad has largely superficial and one-sided relationships with his friends; he will invite them over but then insist on talking the entire time about himself. Second, West notes that Toad is unable to accept criticism from his friends and explains that because narcissists view themselves as superior to others, no one has the right to criticize them. Ultimately, West concludes that even if Toad is correctly viewed as having a narcissistic personality disorder, he is still a loveable character and we should not reject him because of his problems, especially since he has such a longing for friendship and admiration.

I wish to advance West's arguments by exploring in greater depth what lies beneath Toad's surface narcissistic boasting and grandiosity. According to Kohut, a person with a narcissistic personality disorder has a poorly developed sense of self and displays grandiose, exhibitionist features as a way to cover over his or her sense of inadequacy. Narcissists seek the admiration and soothing from their friends that they failed to receive from their parents and have not learned to provide for themselves; when they do not receive it, they frequently get depressed and despondent.

A number of passages from *The Wind in the Willows* highlight Toad's strong needs for admiration and soothing companionship from his friends. When we first meet Toad in the "Open Road" chapter, his boastfulness and conceit are immediately apparent. He is described by Rat as "both boastful and conceited" (Grahame, *Wind* 39) and when Mole comments on the "delights" of Toad Hall, Toad immediately responds, "Finest house on the whole river . . . Or anywhere else, for that matter" (41). Just beneath this bragging, however, one senses Toad's strong need for companionship and admiration from others. In responding to Mole's request to visit Toad, Rat tells him, "It's never the wrong time to call on Toad. Early or late he's always the same fellow . . . Always glad to see you, always sorry when you go!" (38). After dancing up and down when Mole and Rat show up for their visit, Toad says, "I was just going to send a boat down the river for you, Ratty, . . . *I want you badly*—both of you" (40; my emphasis). Later, when convincing them to accompany him on his trip, Toad says, "I can't possibly manage without you" (43). In these early passages, Toad shows his graciousness as a host to his new friend, Mole, but also demonstrates his underlying yearning for companionship and admiration.

Toad's desire for companionship and a listening ear is apparent as the novel progresses. Toad is constantly talking throughout the novel and hoping that others will listen. In the "Open Road" chapter, Toad talks largely "at" Rat, and Rat listens without paying much attention to him. In chapter 8, the gaoler's daughter listens patiently to Toad's endless chatter and exaggerated boasts. Another passage highlights Toad's need for companionship and discomfort with being alone. After Toad jumps from the train at the instructions of the conductor, he spends a cold night in the woods and wakes up the next day happy to be free. But he is alone in the woods and made uncomfortable and distressed by the silence. The narrator comments that Toad is looking "anxiously for company" and for "something that could talk" (201). Toad's constant need for admiration and soothing companionship reflects a weakened sense of self that does not allow for self-soothing.

It is apparent throughout the novel that Toad has an undeveloped and unstable sense of self, consistent with Kohut's description of individuals with narcissistic personality disorders. The first reference to Toad is made by Otter, who says of him, "Such a good fellow, too. But no stability—especially in a boat!" (29). In describing himself, Toad generally focuses on his outward appearance and the impression that he makes on others. He frequently refers to himself in the third person, as in this passage when he is bemoaning his imprisonment: "This is the end of the career of Toad . . . the popular and handsome Toad, the rich and hospitable Toad, the Toad so free and careless and debonair!" (154). When Toad says that he "live[s] for others! That's my motto in life" (44), he seems completely disingenuous, given his pervasive self-centeredness. However, if these words are taken to mean that Toad cannot survive without others, then he is describing himself correctly. Toad needs others to help define who he is; he values himself based on how others evaluate and react to him.

Kuznets also notes Toad's lack of a sense of self when examining each of the animals' homes and how each comes to love his home, or experience topophilia (literally, "love of place"). She sees the novel structured as a series of topophilic crises in which each character has to come to an appreciation for the true qualities of his home, partially through travels away from home, as is the case with Mole, Rat, and Toad. Toad's topophilic crisis is the most complex and takes most of the novel to resolve. At first, he has little appreciation for the comforts of his home and represents, as Kuznets says, a kind of "topophobia," a desire to be any place other than where he is currently. Toad's lack of stability is symbolized through the description of his home offered by Badger in chapter 4. When discussing the value of underground existence with Mole, Badger says,

> "I say nothing against Toad Hall; quite the best house in these parts, *as* a house. But supposing a fire breaks out–where's Toad? Supposing tiles are blown off, or walls sink or crack, or windows get broken—where's Toad? Supposing the rooms are draughty—I *hate* a draught myself—where's Toad?" (88)

Kuznets argues that the homes of each character reflect their psychological state. Thus, when Badger describes Toad's home as extremely vulnerable to the natural elements, I suggest that he is metaphorically describing Toad as a character who is not grounded, who is at the whim of his emotional states, and who therefore lacks inner stability or sense of self.

Thus, it seems fair to conclude that Toad's character reflects both the overt, bombastic traits of a narcissistic personality disorder and the vulnerable characteristics that lie beneath the surface. A further understanding of Grahame's mindset in developing Toad's narcissistic character can be gained by noting some similarities between Toad and Grahame's own son, Alastair, as Alastair is described by Grahame's biographers, Peter Green and Alison Prince. According to Green, a similarity between Toad and Alastair was initially noted by a family friend, Constance Smedley, who encouraged Grahame to turn his bedtime stories to Alastair into a novel. While visiting the Grahames, Smedley overheard Grahame telling Alastair the story, and she noted that "Alastair's own tendency to exult in his exploits was gently satirized in Mr. Toad" (qtd. in Green 269). Green records further that Grahame himself, in a letter congratulating Ms. Smedley on her engagement, remarked on a similarity between Toad and Alastair. Grahame writes " . . . as for Mouse I dare not tell him, for he cannot keep a secret [cf. Toad and the secret passage] and would run out tomorrow to tell all the pigs and cows" (qtd. in Green 295). Alison Prince, in a more recent biography, speculates that Alastair was the major source for Grahame's invention of Toad and elaborates on a number of characteristics of Alastair that appear in Toad's character.

As Prince describes him, Alastair was an entitled and conceited child, who was aggressive and hostile toward other children and cared little about the consequences of his actions. Prince mentions a telling incident described by Grahame in a letter to his wife in which the three-year-old Alastair slapped a helpless little girl with much disdain. Prince remarks with dismay that Grahame felt he could do nothing to correct the boy's behavior. Much like Toad, Alastair was also fascinated by motorcars and was a daredevil around them. Prince records that Alastair devised a game of lying down in front of approaching motorcars, tempting them to run him over (193). At a slightly older age, Alastair became extremely sensitive to the sadness in the world, saying to his father, "There's nothin' but crying in *this world*, is there daddy?" (201; italics in original). Prince writes about Alastair's need to escape to a fantasy world where he could "romp" freely, "with no need to be sensible or clever" (188). She remarks of Alastair's precocity that "there is every sign that he was pert rather than brilliant, and that he had inherited his mother's romantic tendency to self-enhancement, complete with her fears of being exposed as less than exceptional" (211).

In sum, Prince paints a picture of a child who, on the surface, was arrogant, entitled, lacking in empathy for other children, and haughtily dismissive of others. Underneath, he was extremely vulnerable, had little sense of himself, and felt constantly pressured to become somebody that he could not become. From this description, it appears that Alastair was developing signs of a narcissistic personality disorder with prominent grandiose symptoms masking a brittle, vulnerable self. Consistent with Kohut's ideas about the origins of narcissistic personality problems, Alastair grew up with a mother who idealized him but, according to Prince, was frequently physically absent during his early childhood and thus limited in her responsiveness to her son's needs. Alastair's father, on the other hand, was totally unable to set limits around Alastair's narcissistic tendencies. In other words, instead of receiving appropriate soothing and mirroring combined with important limits around unbridled narcissism, Alastair was largely indulged by his parents with few limits set on his excessive behavior. Prince suggests that perhaps Grahame created the character of Toad to express his concern for his son heading "with arrogance and vulnerability into the world" (227), and created the other, older animal characters to rescue and protect him. In one of the letters Grahame wrote to Alastair recounting Toad's adventures (letters that later served as the basis for the book), Grahame warns Alastair about Toad's behavior. He says, "This was the sort of stuff he [Toad] sang, the conceited animal. But his pride was soon to have a fall. Let it be a lesson to us, not be so puffed up & conceited as the proud Toad" (*Dearest Mouse* 69).

According to Prince, Grahame was concerned with how to rescue Alastair from his dangerous tendencies toward excessive pride and arrogance. Through the character of Toad, he explored not only the consequences of such excesses, but also whether and how a character with such tendencies could be helped to change his behavior. Indeed, one of the major unresolved issues about *The Wind in the Willows* is whether Toad *has* been changed or reformed by the end of the novel or not. After the banquet scene, in which Toad appears humbly before his admiring friends, the narrator famously comments that "He was indeed an altered Toad!" (271). But in the scenes leading up to this moment, Toad continues to scheme about ways in which he can narcissistically brag about himself at the banquet, with stories and songs about his grand exploits. Only when his friends deny him this final scene of boasting does Toad retreat to his bedroom, sing a song of praise to himself, and then emerge, seemingly more humble and able to soak up his friends' admiration of him without saying much. Given the last-minute nature of Toad's "alteration," many critics have doubted its sincerity, finding the end of the novel unconvincing. As William Robson puts it, "the real challenge to the author was to make us believe in a chastened Toad. But he cannot do it" (102).

From a classical psychoanalytic perspective, it is doubtful that Toad can be changed. He represents the id, the chaotic part of the personality that must always be reckoned with but that cannot be fully vanquished. From a self psychology perspective, however, individuals are capable of modifying their narcissistic tendencies, even in adulthood, given a nurturing and empathic environment. Is there evidence from the novel that Toad is provided this kind of environment?

In the early part of the novel, Rat and Badger, whom critics have characterized as the parental, caretaking figures in the novel,[3] are not particularly tolerant of Toad's characteristic excesses. While Rat at times indulges Toad, Badger seeks to control him using punitive, forceful measures. In chapter 11, however, a chapter I see as a critical turning point in the novel, Rat, Badger, and Mole are more empathic toward Toad while still being firm and providing Toad useful ideas about how he might change. A careful exploration of the changing nature of his friends' responses to him helps to highlight the manner in which Toad may have been altered by the novel's end.

In the beginning of the novel, Rat seems exasperated and judgmental of Toad, not particularly fond of his antics. Rat explains to Mole how Toad quickly tires of one activity and moves on to the next. In what reads like a mildly exasperated tone he says, "Last year it was houseboating, and we all had to go and stay with him in his houseboat, and pretend we liked it" (29). This is echoed slightly later in the scene in which Rat pretends to be listening to Toad talk while actually having little interest in what Toad has to say. After the disastrous encounter with the motorcar, Rat becomes completely frustrated with Toad's dumbstruck reaction and says "savagely" to Mole, "O *bother* Toad, I've done with him" (53; italics in original). Rat's reaction to Toad is understandable here, given Toad's complete lack of concern for his friends' well-being and unwillingness to help salvage the remains of the caravan after the accident. However, Rat does not display the same exasperation with Mole in similar circumstances. For instance, when Mole grabs the oars of the boat away from Rat, or wanders off into the Wild Wood by himself, Rat nurtures Mole and forgives his childlike excesses. But with Toad, Rat is impatient and frustrated.

Rat's frustration with Toad may be softening somewhat by chapter 4 of the novel. Badger inquires about Toad's behavior and Rat and Mole discuss in great detail Toad's smashes and accidents and his insistence on driving himself rather than employ a "decent, steady, well-trained animal" (80). Mole adds that Toad has been in the hospital three times and has had to pay fines, which, according to Mole is "simply awful to think of" (80). The paying of fines is particularly awful for Mole and Rat because it reflects on the bad reputation Toad is causing for the animals of the River Bank. Badger reacts by saying that when the winter is over, "we'll take Toad seriously in hand. We'll stand no nonsense whatever. We'll bring him back to reason, by force if need. We'll *make* him be a sensible Toad" (81, italics in original).

This discussion between Rat, Badger, and Mole foreshadows the critical scene in chapter 6 when Badger, with the aid of Rat and Mole, decides to "take Toad in hand." Badger announces to his friends that "The hour of Toad!" (118) has come, and Mole excitedly chimes in, "*We'll* teach him to be a sensible Toad" (118). Even Rat is stirred by this missionary zeal and says "We'll convert him! He'll be the most converted Toad that ever was before we've done with him" (119). The three friends proceed to Toad Hall, dismiss Toad's latest car and its driver, and forcibly remove Toad's racing car garments. Badger then explains clearly the nature of the concerns he has with Toad's behavior:

> You knew it would come to this, sooner or later Toad. You've disregarded all the warnings we've given you, you've gone on squandering the money your father left you, and you're getting us animals a bad name in the district by your furious driving and your smashes and your rows with the police. Independence is all very well, but we animals never allow our friends to make fools of themselves beyond a certain limit; and that limit you've reached. (122)

Clearly, Badger's primary concern is the way in which Toad's behavior reflects badly on the other animals, the damage Toad has done to the reputation of the "decent" animals in the neighborhood. Toad resists Badger's speeches and says he is not sorry for the glory he experienced while driving. Both Michael Mendelson (134) and William Robson (99) have noted that Toad at this moment is appropriately defying autocratic, paternal authority and standing up for a certain amount of independence and freedom. But both also see Toad taking this freedom too far in his subsequent misguided adventures. I agree with Robson and Mendelson that Badger's heavy-handed authoritarian methods of converting Toad are extreme. However, their extremeness is only half the problem. Badger's tactics also show a complete lack of empathy for Toad's situation. Self psychologists would suggest that in order to help a person with a narcissistic personality disorder change, one must use great empathy to understand the person's situation and then provide reasons why he or she might want to change for his or her own benefit. In this scene, by contrast, Badger focuses almost entirely on his own need to maintain a good reputation for himself and his fellow animals in the neighborhood, a factor that may have little bearing on Toad's considerations when he engages in his reckless driving.

Rat's interaction with Toad, although similarly misguided, is the direct opposite of Badger's in this scene. He immediately recognizes that Badger's heavy-handed reform tactics are not going to work, and he becomes indulgent of Toad's antics as the scene progresses. When Toad enacts a quasi-suicidal gesture, Rat believes it and rushes off to get help for Toad, allowing Toad to escape. Interestingly, Rat and Badger act like disagreeing parents here, Badger the stern, unsympathetic father figure and Rat the overly indulgent mother figure. But this splitting of parental roles does not help Toad. Instead, it allows Toad to take advantage of Rat's weakness and escape, now launched on his most dangerous, narcissistic adventure.

After escaping his home, occupied by an angry Badger and a chastised Rat, Toad ventures on a madcap journey filled with misadventures and moments of tremendous conceit and despair, escaping one danger only to face another immediately afterward. Some of his adventures parallel Mole's adventures in earlier chapters. For instance, like Mole, Toad finds himself in the Wild Wood and spends the night in a tree hollow. But, unlike Mole, Toad is radically alone during these experiences, with no supportive animals to help him out. Consequently, Toad does not learn much about himself or how to moderate his narcissism during this time.

At the end of these adventures, Toad ends up in the river and floats along until he arrives at Rat's waterside home. Toad's recognition of Rat is described using almost precisely the same language as that used in chapter 1 when Mole first encounters Rat. The text describes both Toad and Mole seeing "A brown little face, with whiskers. Grave and round, with neat ears and silky hair. It was the water Rat!" (224; see also 20). As Mendelson points out, the parallelism seems deliberate here. Just as Mole is helped on a journey of self-discovery by Rat starting in chapter one, Rat and Badger and Mole are now going to help Toad discover important aspects of himself in chapter 11.

Importantly, the title of the chapter is symbolic of its contents. "Like Summer Tempests Came His Tears" is the only chapter in the novel that directly quotes a literary source, and it is certainly an unusual title, compared with the straightforward ones of the other chapters. The quotation is from Tennyson's poem, *The Princess*, specifically from the fifth interlude contained within the poem. This interlude tells the story of a woman receiving the dead body of her warrior husband. She will not cry as her maidens tell stories of her husband's greatness or uncover his face. The maidens are concerned about this, saying, "she must weep or she will die" (184). Finally, when the nurse brings the couple's child to sit upon her knees, the woman cries, and the quoted line appears: "like summer tempests came her tears-/'Sweet my child, I live for thee'" (184). The genuineness of the tears, only brought forth by a strong sense of what the woman has lost and what she now will have to do on her own, seems relevant to Toad's situation here. Toad's "tears" are more genuine in this chapter and not simply manipulative as in earlier chapters. Toad's companions, like the nameless woman's friends, impress upon him what he has lost and help him understand what he must do to continue his life with his friends. Perhaps Grahame means to imply that Toad is like the widow in her grief. Toad must mourn his childhood self of excessive and irresponsible behavior, like the widow must mourn her dead husband, in order to be able to live out his future more adult-like self, as the widow must care for her child and raise him to adulthood on her own.

Each of Toad's friends interacts with him in a new way in this chapter, helping him to alter his narcissistic tendencies. First, Rat is firm but empathic, a combination of responses not seen earlier. After Toad boasts at length about his adventures, Rat says to him,

Now, Toady, I don't want to give you pain, after all you've been through already; but seriously don't you see what an awful ass you've been making of yourself? . . . you have been handcuffed, imprisoned, starved, chased, terrified out of your life, . . . and ignominiously flung into the water . . . Where's the amusement in that? . . . And all because you must needs go and steal a motor-car. You know that you've never had anything but trouble from motor-cars from the moment you first set eyes on one. But if you *will* be mixed up with them . . . why *steal* them? Be a cripple, if you think it's exciting; . . . but why choose to be a convict? When are you going to be sensible, and think of your friends, and try to be a credit to them? (228; italics in the original)

In trying to point out to Toad the error of his ways, Rat emphasizes Toad's foolish behavior and the fact that he is losing friends in the process. He also suggests that Toad could continue driving motorcars, but not have to steal them. Unlike Badger's speeches earlier, Rat is directly addressing Toad's needs here, trying to motivate Toad to change by pointing out what Toad has lost from his actions and even providing compromises that will allow Toad to enjoy his pleasures without going to extremes. Toad breaks down twice in response to Rat's speeches to him, promises to change his behavior, and sheds "bitter tears" (236), a reference perhaps to the title of the chapter and its symbolic import. Although Toad keeps returning to his more boastful posture, especially in response to Mole's efforts to draw him out, it is possible as a reader to believe that Rat's imploring remarks, along with Badger's and Mole's efforts mentioned below, are beginning to have an effect on how Toad views himself and his relationship with his friends.

Badger's role in helping Toad alter his narcissistic tendencies is primarily a symbolic one, introducing Toad to an aspect of his home and possibly a part of himself that will help ground his unstable personality. In discussing how to retake Toad Hall, Badger introduces the underground passage with great fanfare. He calls it a "great secret" and says "impressively," "There—is—an underground—passage" that "leads right into the middle" of Toad Hall (241). Critics have noted the symbolic importance of this passage for Toad's development. Bonnie Gaarden connects the passage to a "birth" (52) for Toad, much like Mole's original emergence aboveground, and suggests that Toad is entering a new stage of life after his journey through the passage. Sarah

Gilead refers to Toad "traversing an underground passage (his own dark self)" (156) in order to do battle with weasels and stoats, symbols of his own aggressive/erotic drives, and ultimately tame himself and return to society.

Whereas Gilead's remarks reflect a classical psychoanalytic view of Toad overcoming his id-like nature through traveling the underground passage, the passage can also be understood from a self psychology perspective as providing "grounding" for Toad's unstable self. Badger highlights the psychological value of underground places in an earlier discussion with Mole about his home:

> Once well underground, you know exactly where you are. Nothing can happen to you, and nothing can get at you. You're entirely your own master, and you don't have to consult with anybody or mind what they say. Things go on all the same overhead. . . . When you want to, up you go, and there the things are, waiting for you. (87)

In other words, when you are underground you are a master of yourself, able to manage your own feelings without as much need for others. Interestingly, immediately following Badger's introduction of the underground passage to Toad, Toad has a dream about it:

> . . . he was alone in the secret passage, pushing onwards, but it twisted and turned round and shook itself, and sat up on its end; yet somehow, at the last, he found himself back in Toad Hall, safe and triumphant, with all his friends gathered round about him, earnestly assuring him that he really was a clever Toad. (244)

There are two notable differences between Toad's thoughts in this dream and his earlier thoughts about himself in relation to his friends. First, in the dream, Toad is struggling to navigate the underground passage rather than making his way through it easily. At earlier points in the novel, each time Toad succeeds in escaping from some danger, his reflections suggest that his escape was easy and fully expected, given his tremendous abilities. For example, when escaping from his bedroom after fooling Rat into sending for a doctor, Toad says, "Smart piece of work that! . . . Brain against brute force—and brain came out on the top—as it's bound to. Poor old Ratty! A worthy fellow, Ratty, with many good qualities, but very little intelligence, and absolutely no education. I must take him in hand one day, and see if I can make something of him" (131). Toad's dream-state acknowledgment of a struggle may reflect progress in his self-development. He is recognizing that a true sense of self-worth requires effort and hard work on his part rather than easily won victories that he is entitled to because of his greatness. Second, in the dream, Toad acknowledges the value of his friends "earnestly assuring" him that he "really" is a clever Toad. Toad is recognizing his need for admiration from his friends and realizing that they play an active role in providing that to him. At earlier points in the novel, Toad tends to sing songs of "self-praise" (130) as he does after stealing the horse from the barge-woman and trading it for money and food. Toad says to himself, "what a clever Toad I am! There is surely no animal equal to me for cleverness in the whole world! . . . Ho, ho, I am The Toad, the handsome, the popular, the successful Toad!" (214–15). While requiring reassurance that one is clever is certainly a narcissistic need, Toad's dream-state acknowledgment of it is progressive. Through recognizing the need, Toad may be able to internalize his friends' admiration more completely and consequently be able to tone down his own urge to brag.

Mole provides the last helpful response to Toad in this chapter. He seeks to draw Toad out, to genuinely and fully hear about Toad's adventures. The text says that "Mole drew his arm through Toad's, led him out into the open air . . . and made him tell him all the adventures from beginning to end, . . . The Mole was a good listener . . ." (250). Mole's genuine interest in Toad's adventure is contrasted clearly with Rat's perfunctory interest in Toad during their initial outing in the caravan. Toad and Rat are conversing, but the text tells us "at least Toad was talking and Rat was saying at intervals, 'Yes, precisely; and what did *you* say to *him?*'—and thinking all the time of something very different . . ." (48, italics in original). In chapter 11, Toad responds with great enthusiasm to Mole's invitation, telling exaggerated adventures, which are approved of, in their telling, by the narrator. The narrator says of Toad's stories that they "belonged more properly to the category of what-might-have-happened-had-I-only-thought-of-it-in-time-instead-of-ten-minutes-afterwards. Those are always the best and raciest adventures; and why should they not be truly ours, as much as the somewhat inadequate things that really come off?" (250). By telling exaggerated stories, Toad is satisfying his narcissistic need to show off without having to enact that need through excessive and dangerous behaviors. This movement from action to imagination is progressive from a self psychological perspective and foreshadows the last alteration of Toad in the final bedroom scene.

In the final chapter, Toad plans to tell his stories at a joyful banquet attended by all his friends in the neighborhood. Badger, Rat, and Mole catch on to Toad's plans and firmly warn Toad against giving any speeches during the celebration. Badger and Rat work together to explain to Toad that it is for his own good that he should end his boasting and conceit. Rat puts it sensitively: "It's for your own good, Toady, you know you *must* turn over a new leaf sooner or later, and now seems a splendid time to begin, a sort of turning-point in your career. Please don't think that saying all this doesn't hurt me more than it hurts you" (266).

Toad accepts his friends' comments and retires, somewhat sadly, to his bedroom to prepare for the banquet. Rather than rearrange the chairs in his room into the shape of a car and enact a wild, driving escapade, as he had done in the earlier bedroom scene of chapter 6 (125–26), Toad demonstrates his psychological growth by using imagination rather than enactment to soothe his injured pride. He conceives of the idea of singing a song of his own greatness in front of an imaginary audience. He carefully arranges the chairs in a semicircle to create the impression of an audience and, "letting himself go" (268), sings an exaggerated, boastful song about his triumphant return to Toad Hall. The narrator says that after Toad sings his song loudly, twice, he "heaved a deep sigh; a long, long, long sigh" (269). Toad then joins the banquet and accepts humbly the praise heaped on him by all the animals for having fought to reclaim Toad Hall.

Kuznets highlights this bedroom scene as a key moment in which Toad learns to appreciate his home as a place where he can express himself creatively. Toad has resolved his topophilic crisis within the confines of the most intimate room of his large and cavernous home. It is appropriate that his appreciation should begin in a bedroom, a room generally associated with comfort and safety for children. But Toad's song of self-praise can also be read as a form of self-soothing that he is able to do imaginatively rather than in front of his friends. He is learning to integrate the mirroring and soothing functions of others into himself, a step toward psychological health and away from pathological narcissism, according to self psychologists.

Contrary to some critical viewpoints, there are psychological and textual reasons to argue that Toad *is* "altered" by the end of the novel. He has developed some capacity for self-soothing and thus may be able to give up his constant need for admiration from others. Gaarden has suggested that "altered" is a more appropriate term than "reformed" to describe Toad's changes. "Reformed" implies that Toad has been bad and now will be good and is the term used by his friends when they first seek to restrain him in chapter 6. "Altered" suggests that Toad can integrate some new ways of thinking and acting into his growing understanding of himself.

Although some critics agree that Toad may have been altered by the end of the novel, others do not. West, like Robson cited above, argues that because Toad cannot accept criticism, his reform at the end of the novel is disingenuous. To support his argument, West cites a fascinating statement made by Grahame himself about Toad's reform: "Toad never reformed; he was by nature incapable of it. But the subject is a painful one to pursue" (*My Dearest Mouse* 190).

Why was the subject a "painful one to pursue"? I have found no biographer or critic who has been able to explain why Grahame added those words. However, if one believes that Grahame had Alastair in mind when speaking these words about Toad, perhaps the pain reflects his growing awareness of his inability to "reform" Alastair. As we know from Green's and Prince's biographies, Alastair went on to develop a deeply troubled personality, withdrawing from peers, and living largely in a fantasy world in which he alternately overvalued and devalued himself. Tragically, Alastair eventually committed suicide in a dramatic way by allowing himself to be run over by a train.[4]

Linking Toad to what is known about Alastair and his fate lends a tragic quality to a character who has been viewed primarily as a comic and subversive force in Grahame's idyllic world. Indeed, as seen from the outside, Toad is farcical, amusing, and overblown, but hardly a character to be taken seriously or one with whom the reader has much empathy. Steig describes the Toad sections of the book as "low comedy, amusing but viewed from a distance" (315). Rather than maintain that distance, I have attempted to understand Toad's internal experience of himself, what he most desires from his friends, and how his friends' increasingly empathic responses to him help him to grow and develop. I suggest that, although Grahame himself might not have fully believed in Toad's capacity to change, he developed a deeply insightful story about the trials and tribulations of a character with narcissistic excesses who finds grounding in his home through the compassionate care of his wise friends.

Notes

1. The DSM-IV is the fourth edition of the official compendium of mental disorders compiled by the American Psychiatric Association (APA), last revised and published in 1994. In the late 1970s, the APA undertook an extensive revision of the manual and decided upon an atheoretical approach to classification of mental disorders based primarily on patterning of symptoms. This approach yielded superior agreement among mental health professionals in the identification of mental disorders but largely ignored the issue of whether these mental disorders accurately characterize those suffering with mental distress. As stated by Allen Frances, chairperson of the Task Force for the DSM-IV, "DSM-IV is . . . inherently limited by its status as a descriptive system. It is not based on a deep understanding of mental disorders because in most cases we lack that understanding" (5).

My own view is that the DSM is primarily useful as a familiar way (at least by those in the mental health profession) of identifying clinical phenomena that may be the focus of analysis in a particular piece of literary or social scientific scholarship. It is incumbent upon the scholar, however, to go beyond the DSM identifier and clearly define the phenomena being studied, making links to theoretical conceptualizations of the phenomena when possible, as I have sought to do in this essay about narcissism. The values and limits of the DSM in diagnosing mental disorders have been debated extensively by mental health professionals. For one example, see Herb Kutchins and Stuart Kirk, "DSM-IV: Does Bigger and Newer Mean Better" (May 1995) and Allen Frances and Michael First, "DSM-IV: Its Value and Limitations" (June 1995).

2. Kohut and his students have written extensively on the basic ideas of self psychology. Kohut's texts include *The Analysis of the Self* (1971) and *The Restoration of the Self* (1977). A useful introduction to the theory can be found in Marshall Silverstein's *Disorders of the Self: A Personality-Guided Approach* (2007). Kohut, in turn, was influenced heavily by the many British object-

relations psychoanalytic theorists active during the 1920s and 1930s. These theorists, including Melanie Klein, Edward Fairbairn, and Donald Winnicott, all argued that psychoanalytic theory needed to move away from a focus on drives and more toward a focus on needs expressed by the child in early development, and how parents respond to those needs. A thorough introduction to object-relations theories and how they differ from classical psychoanalysis can be found in Greenberg and Mitchell's *Object Relations in Psychoanalytic Theory* (1983).

3. Bonnie Gaarden has examined the "inner family" of *The Wind in the Willows*, arguing that Rat functions as a type of mother figure, Badger as the father figure, Mole as the good, developing child, and Toad as the "rawly unsocialized" bad child. Her analysis provides a rich discussion of how the characters enact their various family roles in the novel but does not fully address the quality of "parenting" that Toad receives from his friends.

4. See Green for a convincing argument that Alastair's death was indeed a suicide and not an "accident," as it was originally recorded (327–28).

Works Cited

American Psychiatric Association. *Diagnostic and Statistical Manual of Mental Disorders*. 4th ed. Washington: American Psychiatric Association, 1994.

de Board, Robert. *Counseling for Toads: A Psychological Adventure*. London: Routledge, 1998.

Frances, Allen, and Michael First. "DSM-IV: Its Value and Limitations." *Harvard Mental Health Letter* 11 (1995): 4–7.

Freud, Sigmund. *On Narcissism: An Introduction*. 1914. Ed. Peter Gay. New York: Norton, 1989. 545–62.

Gaarden, Bonnie. "The Inner Family of *The Wind in the Willows*." *Children's Literature* 22 (1994): 43–58.

Gilead, Sarah. "The Undoing of Idyll in *The Wind in the Willows*." *Children's Literature* 16 (1988): 145–58.

Grahame, Kenneth. *My Dearest Mouse: "The Wind in the Willows" Letters*. Ed. Marilyn Watts. London: Pavilion, 1988.

———. *The Wind in the Willows*. 1908. New York: St. Martin's Griffin, 1994.

Green, Peter. *Kenneth Grahame: A Biography*. Cleveland: World, 1959.

Greenberg, Jay, and Stephen Mitchell. *Object Relations in Psychoanalytic Theory*. Cambridge, MA: Harvard UP, 1983.

Hogan, Patrick. "What's Wrong with the Psychoanalysis of Literature?" *Children's Literature* 18 (1990): 135–40.

Kohut, Heinz. *The Analysis of the Self: A Systematic Approach to the Psychoanalytic Treatment of Narcissistic Personality Disorders*. New York: International Universities Press, 1971.

———. *The Restoration of the Self*. New York: International Universities Press, 1977.

Kutchins, Herb, and Stuart Kirk. "DSM-IV: Does Bigger and Newer Mean Better?" *Harvard Mental Health Letter* 11 (1995): 4–7.

Kuznets, Lois R. "Toad Hall Revisited." *Children's Literature* 7 (1978): 115–28.

McBride, Andrew J. "Toad's Syndrome: Addiction to Joy Riding." *Addiction Research* 8.2 (2000): 129–39.

Mendelson, Michael. "*The Wind in the Willows* and the Plotting of Contrast." *Children's Literature* 16 (1988): 127–44.

Prince, Alison. *Kenneth Grahame: An Innocent in the Wild Wood*. London: Allison & Busby, 1994.

Richter, David. *The Critical Tradition: Classic Texts and Contemporary Trends*. Boston: Bedford/St. Martin's, 2007.

Robson, William W. "On *The Wind in the Willows*." *Hebrew University Studies in Literature* 9 (1981): 76–106.

Silverstein, Marshall. *Disorders of the Self: A Personality-Guided Approach*. Washington: American Psychological Association, 2007.

Steig, Michael. "At the Back of *The Wind in the Willows*: An Experiment in Biographical and Autobiographical Interpretation." *Victorian Studies* 24 (1981): 303–23.

Tennyson, Alfred. *Tennyson's Poetry*. Ed. Robert Hill. New York: Norton, 1999.

Tucker, Nicholas. "The Children's Falstaff." *Suitable for Children? Controversies in Children's Literature*. Ed. Nicholas Tucker. Berkeley: U of California P, 1976. 160–64.

West, Mark. "Narcissism in *The Wind in the Willows*." *Psychoanalytic Responses to Children's Literature*. By Lucy Rollin and Mark West. Jefferson, NC: McFarland, 1999. 45–51.

PART II

REPRESENTATIONS OF
THE EDWARDIAN AGE

~

CHAPTER SIX

"Animal-Etiquette" and Edwardian Manners in Kenneth Grahame's *The Wind in the Willows*

Karen A. Keely

Kenneth Grahame's *The Wind in the Willows* famously begins as Mole, fed up with his spring cleaning labors, answers the call of spring and leaves his underground den. "Something up above was calling to him imperiously" (1), and with apparently little choice in the matter, Mole obeys the imperious command, the voice of instinct that stirs up feelings and guides actions in the animal kingdom. Throughout the novel, Mole will regularly heed the call of instinct, harkening to scents, sensations, and an inborn knowledge of how the world works and how he should work within it.

At the same time, however, Mole boldly breaks with his animal nature in departing from the underground world that is natural for his species, the burrows in which he feels most alert and lively. "[N]aturally an underground animal by birth and breeding" (69), Mole climbs into a new world, a River Bank full of sights and sounds and animals that are all strange and wonderful to him. Instinct will not be enough to guide him through this new world, for instinct alone would soon send him back underground.

As Mole makes his way into the new social arena of the River Bank, he must rely not only on instinct but also on what the novel repeatedly calls "animal-etiquette" as a guide for negotiating the relationships he begins to form there.[1] This etiquette, informed by but not limited to instinct, allows for Mole's smooth introduction into this new world and facilitates the friendships that he develops there. Indeed, thanks to this facilitation, these relationships quickly become intimate enough that Mole and his new friends can move beyond the observation of formalities with which they began and into that comfortable realm beyond the finest points of etiquette. Such comfort is only possible, however, because Mole's new world, despite the variety of species to be found in it, is relatively homogenous. In such a homosocial, economically privileged world, etiquette distinguishes "outsider" from "insider," functioning to maintain the community's boundaries. For those who win insider status, one of the prizes is, ironically, to be considerably free of the very rules of etiquette that initially marked privileged status.

Fortunately for Mole as he negotiates his introduction into this bounded community, the rules of conduct are well-codified in the world of the River Bank, much as they were in the greater Victorian and Edwardian England in which Kenneth Grahame, its creator, lived. The vast array of etiquette manuals published during the nineteenth century, with their descriptions of how to act toward whom and in what circumstances, thus serves as a helpful lens through which to read Grahame's novel and the relationships of the characters therein. Etiquette writers detailed how to greet acquaintances, how to serve oneself at dinner, how to pay formal calls, and even how to steer one's craft politely when boating. On this last point, Mrs. Humphry, writing in *Manners for Men* in 1897, insists that "the courtesies of the river may be summed up as similar to those on land" (54). In the world of the River Bank, Mole and his new animal friends rely on both their instinct and their knowledge of social custom to navigate these courtesies of river and land.

The animal characters in *The Wind in the Willows* are heirs to an Anglo-European tradition of prescriptive writing about manners that began in the medieval period with texts such as Desiderius Erasmus's *De Civilitate Morum Puerilium* (*On Civility in Children*, 1530, translated into English two years later) and Baldassare Castiglione's *Il Cortegiano* (*The Book of the Courtier*, 1528, translated into English in 1561). Castiglione's work in particular helped to found the genre of the courtesy manual, which remained popular through the eighteenth century.

Courtesy literature was directed at the upper classes and covered all facets of the ideal life, from appropriate dress and table manners to morals, attitudes, and social and personal values. In the nineteenth century, these conduct books evolved into a new genre, the etiquette manual, which was aimed at those in the rising middle class who were hoping to rise still further. By the nineteenth century, books of etiquette concentrated on teaching specific patterns of manners and left aside most questions of morality and values (Curtin 17–39; Wouters 19–30).

In her study of women's manners during the Victorian period, sociologist Leonore Davidoff warns that etiquette books are a record of idealized prescriptions for behavior rather than of how real people actually behaved (17–19). But historian Michael Curtin argues that, unlike the authors of earlier courtesy books,

> nineteenth-century etiquette writers were much less concerned with ideals and reforms than they were with providing an accurate portrait of the manners of their day. . . . [I]n most cases, the advice of etiquette writers could be easily followed and was not a distant goal which could only be approximated. In etiquette the "best models" were more in the nature of a common custom or a statistical norm of fashionable Society and not, as in traditional courtesy literature, an abstract concept like fortitude or a revered hero like Alexander. (4–5)

The nearly complete concurrence of advice given by Victorian etiquette manuals further suggests that these texts are descriptive as well as prescriptive of widespread behaviors (Curtin 52). Moreover, etiquette manuals' advice remained remarkably constant over time; consistent principles underlay accepted behavior despite the changing populations and social norms. As Curtin argues, "In essentials, an etiquette book purchased in the 1830s would still have been useful eighty years later, and indeed some etiquette books were reissued virtually unchanged as long as fifty years after their initial publication" (10). In the words of the anonymous author of the 1896 *Social Observances*, "The customs in force in society—in other words, the rules and observances—vary but slightly in the course of each year" (202).[2] In this essay, I will therefore rely on books of etiquette advice as a source for accepted standards of polite middle- and upper-class English behavior and will quote freely from Victorian as well as Edwardian conduct books as equally applicable for a reading of *The Wind in the Willows*.[3]

The etiquette manual was inextricably bound with matters of class. As Curtin notes, Victorian etiquette books were written for a middle-class audience hoping to emulate their social superiors, that is, "those who having achieved a solid financial base were ready to emulate some of the less substantial elements of aristocratic lifestyle" (41). According to historian Andrew St. George, Victorian "[m]anners were social control which kept others out, confined them to their place; and manners—in the form of refined, honed etiquette—were social emulation assiduously pursued" (xvii). Etiquette authors were often explicit in their purpose of helping the middle classes to rise; Mrs. Delano, for example, directs her 1914 "social guide" to "those people whom unkind circumstances have prevented from taking their place in the social World during their early years, and who, having at length been favoured by fortune, feel some natural diffidence in making their first entry" (qtd. in Curtin 42).[4] For these new entrants into the social world, etiquette manuals provided instructions as to the delicate matters of making introductions and paying formal calls, of driving carriages and taking public transportation, of dining at luncheons and teas and formal dinners and balls, of marrying and mourning.

Mrs. Delano's description of a neophyte entering the "social World" characterizes Mole well, explaining his reliance on animal-etiquette in his early River Bank days. Having lived his life in an underground world that was "plain and simple—. . . narrow, even," he climbs up to the surface on that fine spring day and embraces life on "the larger stage" (Grahame 103). But he does not immediately know the script for that stage, and as Mrs. Delano predicts, he "feel[s] some natural diffidence in making [his] first entry" into the River Bank world. His awareness of and education in etiquette play a crucial role in his early days on the River Bank, and he is generally socially adept as long as he bears in mind "animal-etiquette," the social customs of the middle and upper classes in the animal kingdom. For example, when Rat skirts away from telling him about the Wild Wood, Mole does not press the issue because he "knew well that it is quite against animal-etiquette to dwell on possible trouble ahead, or even to allude to it" (11). Similarly, when Otter disappears mid-sentence to catch and eat a mayfly, Mole is startled but quickly "recollected that animal-etiquette forbade any sort of comment on the sudden disappearance of one's friends at any moment, for any reason or no reason whatever" (17). That these two references both occur in the first chapter, as Mole feels his way as a stranger in a strange land, makes clear the role of formalized systems of manners in making one's first forays into a new social context. As Curtin notes, "for those in unfamiliar circumstances and uncertain how to act, etiquette provided a ready standard for regulating the externals of conduct and hopefully clearing the way for something more than polite and distant civility" (8–9). Showing fairly good manners as he meets various characters on the River Bank, Mole is indeed quickly ushered into friendships in which he need not think so explicitly about etiquette, having internalized the mores of the new social context as well as moved into an intimacy that rises above carefully scripted manners. As the 1896 *Social Observances* notes, good friends and relatives do not have to follow the strictest rules of etiquette with one another because they "are outside punctilio [that is, the finest points of etiquette], and . . . they have little to fear of being *de trop*. . . . Such misgivings and phases of feeling are only experienced by those who do not feel at home at the house where they visit" (6).

Introduction is a necessary first step before strangers can become acquaintances who may someday become friends "outside punctilio," and the formal introduction is thus of primary importance in etiquette. Victorian and Edwardian introductions functioned as social gatekeeping, in which the unworthy could be prevented from making the acquaintance of their social superiors. During introductions, the introducer's role was, in the words of *Routledge's Manual of Etiquette*, "to certify to each the respectability of the other" (qtd. in Curtin 131).[5] Etiquette manuals were full of warnings to introduce acquaintances with caution; as *Modern Etiquette in Public and Private* admonishes men, "care and judgment must be exercised, and the person introducing incurs additional responsibility" (42). M. E. W. Sherwood, the American author of *Manners and Social Usages*, similarly urges women to be careful about introductions:

Introducing should not be indiscriminately done either at home or in society by any lady, however kind-hearted. Her own position must be maintained, and that may demand a certain loyalty to her own set. She must be careful how she lets loose on society an undesirable or aggressive man, for instance, or a great bore, or a vulgar, irritating woman. . . . Unsolicited introductions are bad for both persons. (30)

Ideally one would obtain the prior permission of both parties before performing an introduction. With or without such permission, the format of the introduction did not vary; the "inferior is introduced to the superior" (*Modern Etiquette in Public and Private* 41–42). Social status was an inextricable component of introductions, and thus Mole's introduction to the other animals in *The Wind in the Willows* sheds light on the main characters' relative class standings.

There is great disagreement in the critical discussion of the characters' economic and social statuses, in large part because Grahame is inconsistent in his presentation of their class markers. All of the main characters "speak a standard middle-class English with characteristic idioms of the period" (Hunt 107–8), but there clearly are status differences among them. Mole is usually cast as a lower-middle-class clerk type, but Toad is sometimes seen as landed country gentleman and sometimes as *nouveau riche*. Assessment of Rat's status ranges from a comfortably middle-class man to a wealthy gentleman of leisure, and Badger has been seen as both a notable squire and the old family retainer of such a squire. Otter is usually depicted as either middle or upper class.[6]

Despite Grahame's discrepancies in depicting the animals' class markers, we can reach some conclusions about the characters' relative statuses by looking at their manners toward one another. Mole is, by virtue of his straitened means and his newness to the River Bank, at the bottom of the class hierarchy among the major characters, but he ranks above rabbits, hedgehogs, and other animals who are more clearly among the working classes.[7] When Mole is introduced to the established inhabitants of the River Bank, we see class etiquette at work. Whether Toad is landed gentry or *nouveau riche*, whether Otter is very rich or only comfortably well off, they are all higher than Mole in status, and he must be appropriately modest and decorous as he meets each of them. Obeying the class hierarchy explicit in etiquette manuals allows Mole an entrée into this society; once he has been accepted into this closed world because of his appropriate performance of etiquette, he can move into a friendship in which such etiquette is less important.

Mole's first and eventually dearest friend is Rat, and the latter's higher social status is apparent from his initiating both their first greetings and then their social intercourse:

> Then the two animals stood and regarded each other cautiously.
> "Hullo, Mole!" said the Water Rat.
> "Hullo, Rat!" said the Mole.
> "Would you like to come over?" inquired the Rat presently. (6)

In this exchange, Mole is following well Mrs. Humphry's advice, in her 1897 *Manners for Men*, to indicate by his manner that he is eager for such social interaction:

> Male acquaintances always wait for acknowledgment on the part of . . . those men who are their superiors in age or position. But this does not mean that they are shyly to look away from them and to ignore them. On the contrary, they must show clearly by their manner that they are on the look-out for some sign of recognition and are ready to reply to it. (13)

In inviting Mole over so quickly (after a pause, but before other words are spoken), Rat indicates that he is willing to pursue a relationship beyond the introduction and sets a tone of familiarity for the new relationship, a step that is his prerogative as the higher-status party who decides when and in what way to acknowledge his social inferior. Mole may misread this informality, for his next conversational move is a brief descent into rudeness, responding to Rat's invitation with a less than gracious reply: "'Oh, it's all very well to *talk*,' said the Mole rather pettishly, he being new to a river and riverside life and its ways" (6, emphasis in original). This "newness" is most obviously responsible for his ignorance about boats and how one can possibly visit a new acquaintance who is on the other side of the river, but it also causes him to misstep in his first social interaction of the River Bank. Perhaps in reaction, his next actions in the scene—stepping into and inquiring about Rat's boat—are taken "gingerly" and "shyly" (6) as he recovers his equanimity in this new social world.

Mole makes no such gaffes in his next introduction; he makes Otter's acquaintance at a picnic in a scene that, to any Edwardian well-versed in etiquette, makes the status difference between the two clear. The intimacy of Otter and Rat's friendship is obvious in the jocular mock-insulting tone of their initial exchange, one notably *sans* the formal greeting that would be required between mere acquaintances: "'Greedy beggars!' [Otter] observed, making for the provender. 'Why didn't you invite me, Ratty?'" (14). This type of jovial rudeness is typical of, for example, P. G. Wodehouse's upper-class bachelor characters of the same era. Rat then presents his new acquaintance:

> "By the way—my friend Mr. Mole."
> "Proud, I'm sure," said the Otter, and the two animals were friends forthwith. (14)

Peter Hunt argues that "Grahame simply evades the difficult problems of interclass communication," particularly in this initial scene between Mole and Otter (104), but in fact this introduction makes dramatically clear how much higher Otter's class status is than Mole's. Mrs. Humphry is explicit in her etiquette advice that the first name mentioned in an introduction should be that of the lower-status party: "In introducing two men to each other the name of the inferior is mentioned first. By the inferior I mean the younger, the less important, or of lower rank" (*Manners for Men* 15). Rat thus initiates the new relationship by naming "Mr. Mole" for Otter's benefit and does not even take the usual second step of naming Otter for Mole's benefit. Of course, in a world in which species and name are identical, Mole has already identified the new picnic guest as "the Otter" (14), much as Otter presumably knows that the unknown mole is Mole before Rat makes the introduction. Politeness, however, would dictate that Rat identify both parties by name rather than relying on their ability to identify species, so the absence of the second half of the introduction implies that Otter is apparently of high enough status that his identity can be presumed known to all underlings, even those brand new to the river world.

Toad, of course, is even more explicitly of higher status than Mole, and although he is "both boastful and conceited," he is also "good-natured, and so affectionate" (25), qualities apparent in his making Mole's acquaintance. The moment that Mole and Ratty appear at Toad

Hall, Toad immediately welcomes Mole into his social circle, "[shaking] the paws of both of them warmly, never waiting for an introduction to the Mole" (27). Again, the species-as-name equation would make such an introduction pragmatically unnecessary although still socially expected, but it is Toad's right as the social superior to establish the terms of the acquaintance. He is the only one of the gathered characters, for example, who may initiate a handshake (Humphry, *Manners for Men* 13–14; Devereux 19–20) and acknowledge another without benefit of formal introduction. Mole does not presume on this initial greeting (perhaps having learned his lesson from his first meeting with Rat), and his first contribution to the conversation is appropriately to make "some civil remark about Toad's 'delightful residence'" (28). Toad responds in standard Toad fashion—"Finest house on the whole river . . . Or anywhere else, for that matter" (28)—and then blushes when Rat nudges Mole to indicate that Toad is here living up to Rat's earlier characterization of him as "boastful and conceited" (25). Mole is initiated through this exchange into an intimate camaraderie in which chaffing companionship is possible despite class differences. He is moving beyond punctilio.

Mole's final introduction, to Badger, is long delayed, for Badger epitomizes the "English reserve" that was of some concern to several etiquette writers, who warned that proper etiquette was disappearing in the modern age as people became less willing to make social overtures (see, e.g., *Social Observances* 20–28 and Sherwood 354–56; also Curtin 128–30, 145). Badger so dislikes "Company" that he rudely refuses an introduction during Mole's first picnic (15). This is Badger's right as a social superior, and Mole does not seem offended but rather eagerly anticipates an eventual meeting. Rat tells Mole that there is no point in issuing an invitation to Badger, for he "hates Society, and invitations, and dinner, and all that sort of thing" (43). Mole then wants them to "call on" Badger, but Ratty becomes alarmed and discourages Mole from such presumption: "O, I'm sure he wouldn't like that at *all*. . . . He's so very shy, he'd be sure to be offended. I've never even ventured to call on him at his home myself, though I know him so well" (43–44, emphasis in original). It is thus extraordinary behavior on Mole's part that winter to attempt a formal call on Badger before they have been introduced (46). Indeed, it is so outrageously rude that it is difficult to imagine the usually polite Mole's acting this way, unless Badger's social status is lower than the squire role that is often assumed for him by critics. If the two animals are closer in status, Mole's rudeness is less extreme and perhaps more believable. After an introduction, an Edwardian social superior made the formal first call to signify his or her willingness to continue and deepen the relationship (Curtin 137–40), and of course in the case of Badger and Mole, no actual introduction has yet been made. Given the more relaxed manners allowable in the smaller societies of the countryside, as opposed to formal London society, Badger could have initiated the relationship even without an introduction: "In the country there was much less worry about the regular maintenance of calls because all the old-time residents knew each other by virtue of proximity. The question only arose for new arrivals, and for them the rule was that older residents, led by the highest ranking family, paid the first call, even without prior introduction" (Curtin 142). Mole, however, although a "new arrival," takes it upon himself to make a formal call without introduction, and his unpleasant Wild Wood adventure thus has the unintended effect of smoothing over what would otherwise have been rude behavior; under the exigent circumstances of a snowstorm and physical danger, no more introduction is needed than Rat's calling through the locked door, "O, Badger, . . . let us in, please. It's me, Rat, and my friend Mole, and we've lost our way in the snow" (63). Badger and Mole can thus embark on an increasingly friendly relationship without Mole's having blundered at the beginning of their acquaintance.

Once Mole has been welcomed into the River Bank community, he begins to worry less about etiquette, for, as noted by *Manner and Tone of Good Society*, "The rules of etiquette, though stringent as regards intimate acquaintances, have little or no application as regards intimate friends; friendship *over-rules* etiquette, and in a manner usurps its place" (qtd. in Curtin 8, emphasis in original).[8] When Mole and Ratty and Badger share a late-night meal in Badger's home on the night of the snow storm, for example, they indulge in

> that regrettable sort of conversation that results from talking with your mouth full. The Badger did not mind that sort of thing at all, nor did he take any notice of elbows on the table, or everybody speaking at once.

As he did not go into Society himself, he had got an idea that these things belonged to the things that didn't really matter. (We know of course that he was wrong, and took too narrow a view; because they do matter very much, though it would take too long to explain why.) (66)

Grahame's narration here is humorous, of course, in assuming an impotent adult authority, sure that etiquette is important but unable to explain to the readers' or characters' satisfaction what that importance is. Readers, however, will already have noted by this point in the novel that without the introductions made possible by animal-etiquette, the characters could not have achieved the familiarity in which manners can cease to be so important.

Even within this community beyond punctilio, however, there is some call for etiquette, for manners make day-to-day interactions more pleasant. It is in such everyday exchanges that Grahame recasts some forms of instinctual animal behavior as appropriate "manners." For example, the animal behavior of hibernation elicits socially appropriate responses that minimize distinctions among species. On a cold winter's night, Badger, Rat, and Mole have agreed that they must join forces to prevent Toad's further self-destruction with motorcars, but then Badger turns to his friends:

"Now look here!" he said at last, rather severely; "of course you know I can't do anything *now?*"

His two friends assented, quite understanding his point. No animal, according to the rules of animal-etiquette, is ever expected to do anything strenuous, or heroic, or even moderately active during the off-season of winter. All are sleepy—some actually asleep. (69)

The widespread fact of animal hibernation in the winter does not mean that the characters actually speak of it. Instead, they all practice the Edwardian form of polite evasion of overly personal topics to avoid mentioning sleep, as when one young hedgehog tells Mole the next morning that Badger is unavailable, for "The master's gone into his study, sir, . . . and he said as how he was going to be particular busy this morning, and on no account was he to be disturbed" (71); Mole immediately understands with no offense that Badger has proffered a polite cover story to mask the fact of his sleeping all morning. Animal-etiquette thus shares with human etiquette an avoidance of socially recognizing the body's needs. Sociologist Norbert Elias has argued influentially that the rise of courtesy books and early etiquette manuals were features of the centuries-long "civilizing process" through which Europeans' bodies have been brought under the control of the *habitus* of learned social patterns regulating the way they speak, interact with others, eat, have sex, and engage in other bodily functions. The result of such extended regulation has been to increase the feelings of shame and repugnance with which people view the body and its functions and to mask those functions through systems of social etiquette developed over time (Elias 42–47), hence the conversational side-stepping of the fact of hibernation.

Animal-etiquette is not, however, simply Edwardian manners and repression mapped onto the animal world, for in some important respects the novel's characters act in opposition to human manners, and in these instances the differences are clearly due to instinct. For example, etiquette manuals in the period were insistent on the importance of walking side-by-side down the street, with men "always remaining on the kerb side of any lady they may be accompanying" (Humphry, *Manners for Men* 12). But the River-Bankers do not follow their advice, behavior that the narrator feels compelled to explain: "Animals when in company walk in a proper and sensible manner, in single file, instead of sprawling all across the road and being of no use or support to each other in case of sudden trouble or danger" (106). Grahame has here superimposed instinct onto Edwardian etiquette, but in both cases, the underlying principle is the same: securing the safety of the more vulnerable members of society.

Grahame initially seems to place the highest value on instinct in the chapter "Dulce Domum," but even that discussion concludes with an emphasis on the value of etiquette. The chapter begins with the homing instinct that Rat and Mole share, "that small inquiring something which all animals carry inside them, saying unmistakably, 'Yes, quite right; this leads home!'" (82). That instinct then becomes "a faint sort of electric thrill that was passing down [Mole's] body" (91), telling him that his original home, the underground burrow of Mole End, is near. The narrator's voice, in a rare moment of acknowledging the distance between the human readers and the animal characters, takes on a wistful tone in noting how far people have moved from these animal instincts:

We others, who have long lost the more subtle of the physical senses, have not even proper terms to express an animal's intercommunications with his surroundings, living or otherwise, and have only the word "smell," for instance, to include the whole range of delicate thrills which murmur in the nose of the animal night and day, summoning, warning, inciting, repelling. (85–86)

Given Elias's argument that etiquette has helped to separate us from our animal selves, to hide bodily functions under layers of manners, instinct and etiquette might well be seen as opposing forces. If Grahame had insisted on animal-etiquette-as-instinct, therefore, we might have read in this equation an argument against the oppression of Edwardian manners, as a call for unleashed animal bodies.

This is not, however, the argument that Grahame makes, for throughout the novel he admires instinct only insofar as it coheres with personal and social control. For example, "instinct" is used damningly to refer to Toad's destructive obsession with automobiles; when he steals the motorcar from the inn, "he sped he knew not whither, fulfilling his instincts, living his hour, reckless of what might come to him" (121). Even the "Dulce Domum" episode, with its narrative wistfulness for lost animal instinct, quickly becomes a scene about the importance of showing hospitality, a central subject in etiquette manuals. Mole despairs more than once that evening that he cannot offer his guests, first Ratty and then the field mouse carolers, good cheer in the form of food and drink. It is Rat—who, after all, has apparently absorbed higher middle-class etiquette from his youth rather than coming to it later as Mole has—who can spring into action, thanks to his greater financial resources and his confidence in commandeering the lower classes to achieve his hospitable ends (in this case, giving money to a young caroler and sending him out to the store to buy supplies). Animal-etiquette here clearly calls for more than instinct; instinct brings Mole home, but it is the social training inherent in etiquette that makes that home hospitable.

Hospitality in the novel is thus decidedly class-based. Mole may be, in the River Bank society, low in class status, but clearly his below-ground status is somewhat higher in that he feels it incumbent upon himself to show *noblesse oblige* to the field mouse carolers. Indeed, one of the significances of etiquette in the novel, as well as in Edwardian society more broadly, is that it distinguishes the working classes from the middle and upper strata of society. Badger may have the notion that manners "belonged to the things that didn't really matter" (66), but that is because Badger's kitchen table is in that scene a middle-class, homosocial gathering place, a space outside formal etiquette by virtue of its homogeneity. It is worth noting that the young hedgehogs who appear in Badger's kitchen the next morning are aware that manners matter very much when there is a distinct difference in status, for they "ducked their heads respectfully" and "touch[ed] . . . their forelocks," as befits lower-class youth in the presence of their social betters (70, 75). The former behavior might be a sign of respect due to any elder, but the latter is the mark of deference due to the gentry by the working people. Rat may kindly tell them that "You needn't 'sir' me quite so much," but they stay firmly within the realm of proper etiquette, knowing better than to presume with "you gentlemen" (71).

The class basis of etiquette becomes even more apparent only two chapters later when Toad for the first time experiences the different social standards of the working classes. As he leaves the courthouse on his way to jail, the assembled crowd "assailed him with jeers, carrots, and popular catch-words; . . . [the crowd included] hooting school children, their innocent faces lit up with the pleasure they ever derive from the sight of a gentleman in difficulties" (124). Toad soon learns that working-class rudeness is not reserved only for the upper classes but is a regular part of intra-class behavior as well, although the tone of such encounters is marked not by hostility but by raillery. While he is dressing as a washerwoman, the gaoler's daughter tries to prepare him for his new role as a working-class woman: "if any one says anything to you, as they probably will, being but men, you can chaff back a bit, of course, but remember you're a widow woman, quite alone in the world, with a character to lose" (150). As she predicts, Toad does experience the social misconduct directed at someone with neither class nor gender status to protect her, and this misconduct is clearly sexual in nature although rendered jokingly: Toad-as-washerwoman "rejected the pressing invitations from the last guardroom, and dodged the outspread arms of the last warder, pleading with simulated passion for just one farewell embrace" (151). Even once Toad leaves the rough environs of the prison, his assumed persona is faced with working-class rudeness, as when the fox "looked him up and down in a sarcastic sort of way, and said, 'Hullo, washerwoman! Half a pair of socks and a pillow-case short this week! Mind it doesn't occur again!' and swaggered off, sniggering" (163). In these circumstances, Toad "suited his retorts to his company and his supposed character, and did his best not to overstep the limits of good taste" (151), but his pride is wounded by this treatment that does not accord with proper respect due to the higher classes. As Mrs. Delano notes in her 1914 *Ways of Society*, in public arenas the working classes can be "most aggressive" in their manners regarding their social betters because they are "assured that those of their own class present will support them"; at the same time, "This sort of people are quite callous as to their [own] class" (qtd. in Curtin 162).[9] In many respects the raillery Toad-as-washerwoman experiences echoes that of the main animal characters' chaffing of one another, with the difference that the latter is the joking of friends beyond punctilio, while the former is humor outside of middle- and upper-class etiquette altogether.

Toad experiences this rudeness while temporarily inhabiting a working-class space as an upper-class gentleman in disguise where he does not belong. We also see an opposite form of such class disguise and role-playing in the grand manor house of the River Bank, where the clearest examples of class-based etiquette and hospitality occur. Near the end of the novel, Toad Hall is the site of a banquet two nights in a row, the first held by the weasels to celebrate their seizing of the Hall and the second hosted by Toad to celebrate his return to his ancestral seat. A large social gathering demands closer attention to etiquette than the intimate affairs usually held by the River-Bankers.

The weasels' banquet, as described by the irritated stoats left on duty to guard the Hall, includes "feasting and toasts and songs and all sorts of fun" (236), and it is clearly a large and boisterous affair, one that is socially inclusive in that ferrets are welcome guests and yet maintains some sense of hierarchy in that the stoats are left outside as guards. As the four friends make their secret way into Toad Hall, they hear "the stamping of little feet on the floor, and the clinking of little glasses as little fists pounded on the table" and calls of "Ooo-ray-oo-ray-oo-ray-ooray!" (241–42). This is clearly a "carousing" affair (242), but it seems to be following the lines of a gentlemen's dinner party, complete with an after-dinner speech by the Chief Weasel, interspersed with strong reactions from his audience:

> "Well, I do not propose to detain you much longer"—(great applause)— "but before I resume my seat" (renewed cheering)—"I should like to say one word about our kind host, Mr. Toad. We all know Toad!"—(great laughter)—"*Good* Toad, *modest* Toad, *honest* Toad!" (shrieks of merriment). (242, emphasis in original)

Although the weasels are clearly outsiders, Wild-Wooders rather than River-Bankers, Humphrey Carpenter notes that they hardly "behave like a working-class mob" during this banquet and that "the speech given by the Chief Weasel is not rabble-rousing by a mob leader but a typical piece of after-dinner oratory at a banquet" (165). At the same time, the speech is clearly a joke at Toad's expense (much as the banquet itself is at his literal expense), and so we might read this scene as the working classes' mocking of the rituals of their social superiors. As Tess Cosslett argues, the Chief Weasel may well be "*imitating* an upper-class speaker, in the same way that Toad is so easily able to impersonate a lower-class washerwoman"; class in the novel is a performance, complete with appropriate costume and setting (178–79, emphasis in original). The dialogue of that performance is the language of Edwardian etiquette, the manuals of which function as scripts for exactly this class-based playacting. The Chief Weasel is interrupted by the attacking foursome just as he is launching into the next phase of his performance, "a little song . . . which I have composed on the subject of Toad" (242), one that begins on a similar note to the songs Toad composes about himself.

Such similarity between Toad's own style of entertaining and that of the weasels often gives rise to the assumption that Toad is *nouveau riche*, relatively new to the world of etiquette. His attempts to entertain in the style of the Chief Weasel are promptly quashed by Badger, however, who may practice informality among friends in domestic privacy but who knows that proper etiquette is required among gentlemen when gathered for a more public event. The banquet itself is clearly Toad's social obligation as the resident of the local manor, and it is Badger, who usually does not care for Society, who insists on adhering to a fine point of animal-etiquette in immediately staging the event: "we really ought to have a Banquet at once, to celebrate this affair. It's expected of you—in fact, it's the rule" (249). And Toad, once browbeaten into accepting the idea, envisions an event much like the weasels' banquet, including speeches and songs performed by the host. But he is stymied in this attempt by Rat, who had earlier chivvied Toad about his failure to live up to his role in society, to perform class adeptly: "When are you going to be sensible, and think of your friends, and try and be a credit to them? Do you suppose it's any pleasure for me, for instance, to hear animals saying, as I go about, that I'm the chap that keeps company with gaol-birds?" (216). Rat now reprimands Toad that his plans for banquet entertainments are not the stuff of proper etiquette:

"[Y]ou know that your songs are all conceit and boasting and vanity; and your speeches are all self-praise and—and—well, and gross exaggeration and—and"

"And gas," put in the Badger, in his common way. (253)

Badger may have used "common" language among friends, but it is Toad who has been preparing to act like a common rather than gentlemanly host, like a Chief Weasel rather than Toad of Toad Hall. Rat's criticism suggests that failure to conform to proper etiquette could lead not just to personal embarrassment, but also to a more calamitous breakdown of class boundaries.

Etiquette saves Toad from this poor performance and his friends from their embarrassment; at the banquet, Toad is clearly not reformed but does at least "alter" (257), discovering the more subtle amusement to be had in performing etiquette to the hilt. During the banquet he adopts proper deference—in response to personal praise, "Toad only smiled faintly and murmured, 'Not at all!' Or, sometimes, for a change, 'On the contrary!'" (256)—and enjoys the response that this unexpected conformity to social convention causes among his guests:

Toad felt, as he moved from one guest to the other, making his modest responses, that he was an object of absorbing interest to everyone. . . . There was much talking and laughter and chaff among the animals, but through it all Toad . . . looked down his nose and murmured pleasant nothings to the animals on either side of him [at the dinner table]. At intervals he stole a glance at the Badger and the Rat, and always when he looked they were staring at each other with their mouths open; and this gave him the greatest satisfaction. (257)

Toad's enjoyment at being noticed in a new way makes it clear that he has not changed in his desire to be the center of attention, so he is simply the old Toad in a new role, but this is the role that is expected for a host. He has temporarily adopted what the 1881 *Glass of Fashion* identifies as the proper attitude of the "talker who talks not to display his wit or accomplishment, but to promote the comfort of the company in which he finds himself" (qtd. in Curtin 181).[10]

Moreover, in talking quietly only with his immediate neighbors at the table rather than leaning or raising his voice to converse with those further away, Toad is fulfilling the higher decorum demanded at an Edwardian dinner party at which ladies are present, a puzzling performance given that no women appear at the banquet. Toad's formality is clearly a change of pace for this homosocial world; the male guests are obviously used to a more freewheeling single-sex atmosphere and feel some constraint with Toad's new etiquette. Indeed, "[s]ome of the younger and livelier animals, as the evening wore on, got whispering to each other that things were not so amusing as they used to be in the good old days." And yet Toad, "by pressing delicacies on his guests, by topical small-talk, and by earnest inquiries after members of their families not yet old enough to appear at social functions, managed to convey to them that this dinner was being run on strictly conventional lines" (257).

By the late Victorian and Edwardian eras, such "conventional lines" were for the most part the purview of middle- and upper-class women. Men had dominated the genre of courtesy books in the eighteenth century, but as courtesy books were succeeded by etiquette manuals focused on the rising middle class, women increasingly replaced men as arbiters of etiquette, both writing and reading books about manners and determining what and who was socially acceptable (Curtin 209–15, 301–2; Wouters 27; Davidoff 16). Jorge Arditi has argued that the shift from ethics-based courtesy manuals of the eighteenth century and earlier to the class-based etiquette manuals of the nineteenth century provided an opportunity for women's voices to be heard through their own authorship of manners books, a shift he ties to the larger movement of agitation for the rights of women (*passim*, esp. 422). Nineteenth-century women thus became authorities on the etiquette of both women and men, and their gender in some ways became synonymous with etiquette itself. Indeed, "some etiquette writers claimed that 'society' and therefore 'etiquette' existed only in groups and situations in which both ladies and gentlemen were present" (Curtin 262–61); in those situations, "It must always be borne in mind that the assumption of woman's social superiority lies at the root of these rules of conduct" (Humphry, *Manners for Men* 16). For example, Mrs. Humphry's 1897 gendered pair of etiquette manuals, *Manners for Women* and *Manners for Men*, both emphasize gender relations and the proper treatment of women by men. *Manners for Women* begins with a chapter on "The Girl in Society," whereas *Manners for Men* begins with "Woman's Ideal Man"; even in a book for men about men, a woman's perspective dominates the discussion.

The absence of "ladies," therefore, is crucial to a reading of etiquette in *The Wind in the Willows*. Certainly many critics have remarked upon the male homosocial world of the novel, and I find it particularly interesting that all of the women who do appear briefly in the novel are decidedly working class and thus outside the realm of etiquette. The gaoler's daughter and the barge-woman are clearly below the middle-class and have no desire to emulate their social "betters," while the only female animals are the "mother weasels" seen on the very last pages of the novel, pointing out the gentry to their children. Mrs. Otter is never explicitly mentioned and exists only by implication. With no ladies present, etiquette itself takes a very different form. As the 1893 *Modern Etiquette in Public and Private* argues, "Etiquette is not to be learnt from association with men; it is woman who creates society. Just as the height of a stage of civilization can always be measured by the amount of deference which is paid to women, so the culture of a particular man can be gauged by his manner when in company with ladies" (37). But in the homosocial civilization of the River Bank, no such culture or stage of civilization can be gauged. There is, as we have noted, a decided etiquette in the animal world, but it functions mostly as a gatekeeping device to keep out the rabble (and the rabbits) and monitor the entrance of newcomers; within the middle- and upper-class social world of the River Bank, a more relaxed version of this etiquette facilitates smooth interaction among animals. The punctilio that is performed by Toad at his banquet is clearly out of the ordinary and seems not to be maintained beyond that one event. The novel closes with a decidedly masculine portrait of the four friends, characterized as fierce and "terrible fighter[s]" by the mother weasels (258), and this martial and virile aspect decidedly undoes any overemphasis on etiquette that Toad may have displayed at his dinner party. The homosocial world, shocked momentarily by the advent of formal manners that might indicate the presence of ladies, has been restored.

For Grahame, animal-etiquette functions as instinct-*cum*-self-restraint, yet the male homosocial world he offers in the novel indicates his idealization of a social world in which restraint is less necessary, etiquette of less importance, because no women are present. Grahame's own unhappy marriage has often been noted (see, e.g., Carpenter 151–53), and it is easy to imagine that he might well prefer a bachelor existence in which formal calls could be dispensed with, in which one might put one's elbows on the table without fear of reprimand, and in which class hierarchies remain but are not complicated by gender. Authors of conduct books recognized that the formality they insisted upon was only necessary because of gendered relationships, and that "[p]redominantly masculine activities like hunting and shooting were not usually matters of etiquette, except for occasions like the Hunt Breakfast when ladies were also active participants" (Curtin 210). As *Social Observances* notes, "Man is gregarious, and likes the company of his fellows" (235), and the company of fellows was least complicated when all of those fellows were male. Grahame famously said of his novel that part of its youthful charm lay in the fact that it was "free of problems, clean of the clash of sex" (Chalmers 145), including the ongoing opportunities for missteps or "problems" between men and women. Avoidance of such missteps was a central concern of etiquette manuals, a concern that proves largely irrelevant in this homosocial society.

The absence of such a "clash of sex" allows for the possibility of minimizing formal etiquette, giving Grahame's characters the chance to throw off some but not all of their social restraint. Grahame's bastion of bachelorhood, his pastoral paradise, is a male world that is polite but not overly formal, respectful but not rigid in its etiquette;

manners in *The Wind in the Willows* fulfill the vital function of ensuring that only the right animals enter River Bank society, but once inside that society, manners are decidedly relaxed. Animal-etiquette, with its combined force of instinct and Edwardian convention, remains important insofar as it smoothes over potentially awkward moments between friends, but having treated one another with the respect due to their relative social stations, Mole, Rat, Toad, Badger, and Otter are now free to talk with their mouths full and put their elbows on the table in tranquillity.

Notes

I am grateful to colleagues Liz Gray and Kevin C. Groppe for their thoughtful responses to drafts of this essay.

1. In the novel's first mention of "animal-etiquette," the phrase is hyphenated, so I have maintained this punctuation throughout, although Grahame himself is inconsistent in his hyphenation or lack thereof.

2. Many etiquette manuals, such as *Social Observances*, were published anonymously by "A lady" or "A member of the aristocracy" or "A gentleman." The fact that etiquette manuals continued to be published and purchased so widely despite the congruence of advice therein is surprising until we remember the repetition to be found in advice books in our own time.

3. Michael Curtin's 1987 *Propriety and Position: A Study of Victorian Manners* remains the best source of information on English Victorian and Edwardian etiquette manuals, many of which are extant only in personal and university special collections throughout England and the United States. Several of the primary sources used in this essay are quoted from Curtin's work, always with attribution, and Curtin's bibliography of primary sources (305–11) is a helpful resource. Also useful are Alain Montandon and Jacques Carré's "A Short Bibliography of Conduct-Books Published in Britain (1500–1993)" and Cas Wouters's extensive bibliography of late nineteenth- and twentieth-century manners books of four nations (England, the United States, the Netherlands, and Germany) in *Informalization: Manners and Emotions since 1890* (251–56).

4. Mrs. Danvers Delano, *The Ways of Society: A Social Guide* (London: Laurie, 1914), viii.

5. *Routledge's Manual of Etiquette* (London: Routledge, [1875?]), 1.

6. Peter Hunt helpfully summarizes the variety of these speculations about the characters' social standings, noting that English critics tend to have dif-

ferent assessments of the characters than do those outside of the English class system (Hunt 54–55, 57–59, 66, 69).

7. In a later reflection on the animal characters, Grahame remarked indirectly upon their respective class statuses, noting whimsically that Mole was

> evidently in rather poor circumstances, as incomes go nowadays, [but he] could probably have afforded some outside assistance say twice a week or so. . . . He probably then had a Char-Mouse in for a few hours and her dinner on certain days. . . . [H]owever narrow poor Mole's means may have been, it is evident that Rat was comfortably off—indeed, I strongly suspect him of a butler-rat and cook-housekeeper. Toad Hall, again, must have been simply crawling with idle servants, eating their heads off. (qtd. in Chalmers 61–63)

This reflection was in answer to a query from Professor G. T. Hill of London University, who wanted to know who had cleaned up the white-washing detritus after Mole's sudden departure from Mole End, for when Mole returns in the chapter "Dulce Domum" he is faced with no evidence of his abandoned task (Chalmers 61–63).

8. *Manner and Tone of Good Society; Or Solecisms to Be Avoided*, 3rd ed. (London: Warne, [1876?]), 7.

9. Mrs. Danvers Delano, *The Ways of Society: A Social Guide* (London: Laurie, 1914), 126.

10. *The Glass of Fashion: A Universal Handbook of Social Etiquette and Home Culture for Ladies and Gentlemen. With Copious and Practical Hints upon the Manners and Ceremonies of Every Relation in Life, at Home, in Society, and at Court* (London: Hogg, 1881), 190.

Works Cited

Arditi, Jorge. "The Feminization of Etiquette Literature: Foucault, Mechanisms of Social Change, and the Paradoxes of Empowerment." *Sociological Perspectives* 39 (1996): 417–34.

Carpenter, Humphrey. *Secret Gardens: A Study of the Golden Age of Children's Literature*. Boston: Houghton Mifflin, 1985.

Chalmers, Patrick R. *Kenneth Grahame: Life, Letters and Unpublished Work*. London: Methuen, 1933.

Cosslett, Tess. *Talking Animals in British Children's Fiction, 1786–1914*. Aldershot and Burlington: Ashgate, 2006.

Curtin, Michael. *Propriety and Position: A Study of Victorian Manners*. New York: Garland, 1987.

Davidoff, Leonore. *The Best Circles: Society, Etiquette, and the Season*. London: Croom Helm, 1973.

Devereux, G. R. M. *A Book of Edwardian Etiquette*. London: George Allen & Unwin, 1983. Rpt. of *Etiquette for Women: A Book of Modern Modes and Manners*. London: C. Arthur Pearson, 1902.

Elias, Norbert. *The Civilizing Process: The History of Manners and State Formation and Civilization*. 1939. Trans. Edmund Jephcott. Oxford: Blackwell, 1994.

Grahame, Kenneth. *The Wind in the Willows*. London: Methuen, 1908. New York: Simon & Schuster, 1989.

Humphry, Mrs. C. E. *Manners for Men*. London: Bowden, 1897. Devon: Webb & Bower, 1979.

———. *Manners for Women*. London: Bowden, 1897. Devon: Webb & Bower, 1979.

Hunt, Peter. *The Wind in the Willows: A Fragmented Arcadia*. New York: Twayne, 1994.

Modern Etiquette in Public and Private. Rev. ed. London: Frederick Warne, 1893.

Montandon, Alain, and Jacques Carré. "A Short Bibliography of Conduct-Books Published in Britain (1500–1993)." *The Crisis of Courtesy: Studies in the Conduct-Book in Britain, 1600–1900*. Ed. Jacques Carré. Leiden, The Netherlands: E. J. Brill, 1994. 183–93.

St. George, Andrew. *The Descent of Manners: Etiquette, Rules & the Victorians*. London: Chatto & Windus, 1993.

[Sherwood, M. E. W. (Mary Elizabeth Wilson).] *Manners and Social Usages*. Rev. ed. New York and London: Harper, [1918?].

Social Observances: A Series of Essays on Practical Etiquette. London: Frederick Warne, 1896.

Wouters, Cas. *Informalization: Manners and Emotions since 1890*. Los Angeles: SAGE Publications, 2007.

CHAPTER SEVEN

~

Locating Englishness within the Commodity Culture of the Early Twentieth Century in *The Wind in the Willows*

Ymitri Mathison

In *The Fall and Rise of the Stately Home*, a study of how the English aristocratic country house came to be accepted as the quintessential symbol of English identity, Peter Mandler suggests that Kenneth Grahame's *The Wind in the Willows* is "perhaps the most famous of all hymns to the Old English countryside" (180). Mandler points to a traditional vision of Englishness in the novel, a vision that focuses on "the English love of domesticity, of the countryside, of hierarchy, continuity and tradition" (1). While Mandler attributes an idyllic and "amazing fantasy of the organic community" to Grahame's Englishness (180), Peter Green emphasizes the novel's anti-industrial stance through its protest against an ever-encroaching urbanism and evocation of nostalgia for a "lost rural innocence" (243).

The novel posits an idyllic and pastoral vision of Englishness past that is fixed and timeless. Postcolonial theorist Robert J. C. Young argues, however, that a reputation for fixity in Englishness is a mask, one used to hide the ways in which Englishness was, and is, "continually being contested" (2) by non-English groups, such as the working class and the "minorities" of Britain: the Scots, Welsh, and the Irish. This essay will focus on a construction of Englishness that emerged in the early twentieth century in reaction to what was often viewed as a threat to Englishness in the period: Britishness. Analyzing Kenneth Grahame's novel in the context of conflicts between these constructions of national identities in the late nineteenth and early twentieth centuries, I will argue, opens up a more historically specific way of understanding the novel's underlying tensions. In this chapter, I focus on the difficulties of defining Britishness and Englishness at a time when both identities achieved fluidity in society and were becoming culturally hybridized. As a result, the upper and middle classes needed to distinguish Englishness more sharply from Britishness, an identity that threatened to become the ubiquitous identity of the nation and empire. Grahame's text took refuge in the middle and upper classes' common heritage of the idea of the gentleman and a romanticized pastoralism privileging the rural over the urban. Both of these visions paid homage to an English, rather than a British, sense of racial pride. *The Wind in the Willows* testifies to the importance of the rural landscape for defining national identity, as well as the difficulties of sustaining the identity of Englishness for the middle class and the gentry in an urban, capitalistic, consumer-oriented, and imperialized society.

Linda Colley argues that the concept of "Britishness" emerged during the eighteenth century as an oppositional identity, as England, Scotland, Wales, and Ireland united in the face of multiple wars with France (1). By the 1750s, "English" and "England" had given way to "British" and "Great Britain" not only in official documents, but also in everyday language (Colley 13). With the long peace of the nineteenth century, however, the terms of opposition once again began to change, with Britishness, ironically, now the oppositional term set against the more highly valued construction of "Englishness." By the turn of the twentieth century, Britain's status on the world stage stemmed from its imperial power: it controlled nearly one quarter of the globe. Claiming a British identity, then, allowed one to take pride in Britain's preeminent position in the development of modern industry, as well as its territorial and cultural dominance throughout the world. Britishness, thus, came to represent the nationalism of the militarist and commercial cultures of the empire. As Patrick Brantlinger observes, "For most Victorians, whether they lived early or late in the queen's reign, the British were inherently, by 'blood,' a conquering, governing, and civilizing 'race'" (21).

In actual discourse, however, Englishness was not always so sharply delineated from Britishness, particularly when class boundaries were crossed. Many from the middle class frequently used the wealth acquired through "British" industrial and imperial enterprise to buy their ways into the "English" landed gentry class. These cross-class movements often led, ironically, to an embrace of the identity of Englishness, with its ethos of gentility and the noblesse oblige tradition, while the more commercial, imperial identities associated with Britishness were deemphasized or even rejected.

Since the exclusive identity of Englishness was not always sharply delineated from the more inclusive identity of Britishness during the Victorian period, both frequently coalesced into each other. The middle class straddled the identities of both Britishness and Englishness. The lower end of the middle class represented the Britishness of individuals moving from lower or working class into middle class while the upper middle class incorporated the culture, habits, and mannerisms of the upper class's Englishness into itself. Simultaneously, members of the upper class who became involved in the British aspects of the nation (aristocrats who owned factories, gentry who drew income from colonial plantations, nobles whose younger sons served in the imperial army) found themselves adopting aspects of British identity. Consequently, Britishness became manifested in Englishness, forming culturally hybrid identities, rather than both being distinct identities separated by class. Britishness also created layers of identities because it was the overarching identity of the nation-state and further complicated the upper and middle classes' exclusive identity of Englishness. Since their members partook of both identities, strands of Englishness and Britishness could not always be unraveled from the larger knot.

Some members of the gentry class, however, felt threatened by these shifting and hybridizing national identities, and became invested in maintaining Englishness as a separate identity and in protecting the purported purity of Englishness against the contamination of Britishness. To do this, they began to construct a vision of "true" Englishness as a Wordsworthian pastoral. According to Alun Howkins, while English culture had contained a "ruralist strain" for much of its history, the period from 1880 to the interwar years produced a historically specific vision of rural England and the Englishness one could find there (63). This vision arose in response to gentry-class fears that the migration from the country to the city during the Victorian period had led to a "racial degeneration" of formerly solid English stock (66). All commentators of the period, whether Liberal, Labour, Conservative, or Socialist, shared the assumption that "[i]n contrast to the towns, and London in particular, the country and country people were seen as the essence of England, uncontaminated by racial degeneration and the false values of cosmopolitan urban life" (69).

By the late nineteenth century, then, many in the middle and upper classes invested the rural landscape with English racial pride. Englishness was embodied through the cult of national heritage and the country manor house, giving it a timeless sense of privileged aristocratic grandeur. It was a nostalgic form of feudalism that seemed at first glance to be at odds with the increasing mass urbanism, industrialization, and consumerism. However, the upper class's investiture of the rural landscape and the country house with English racial pride, and hence with Englishness, soon developed into a form of commodification and consumerism. Ironically, what were supposedly fixed and unchanging symbols of an exclusive, privileged Englishness were packaged for middle-class consumption; taking a vacation trip to the English rural landscape, or a holiday jaunt that included a tour of a famed English country estate (complete with gift shop), the British middle class could purchase Englishness. Allowing the middle class to buy into the identity of Englishness tarnished Englishness's exclusivity and brought to the forefront its increasing hybridity with Britishness. As Raymond Williams suggests, the consumption of Englishness formed a significant aspect of the national psyche in the period:

> From about 1880 . . . [t]here was also a marked development of the idea of England as "home," in that special sense in which "home" is a memory and an ideal. Some of the images of this "home" are of central London: the powerful, the prestigious and the consuming capital. But many are of an idea of rural England: its green peace contrasted with the tropical or arid places of actual work; its sense of belonging, of community, idealised by contrast with the tensions of colonial rule and the isolated alien settlement. (281)

English rural landscape and "its green peace" as a mourned utopian space no longer subject to change, growth, and decay became commodified as a static landscape within the national imagination.

Firmly situated as they are in a rural arcadian English landscape, Mole's adventures can be read as the story of his assimilation into Englishness. Of Grahame's four main characters, it is the gentle Mole, whose class identity links him more closely to British identity than to English, who presents the clearest threat to the representation of Englishness that Grahame's text works to construct. But by rooting itself in the private sphere of domesticity, Mole's search for adventure disavows the Britishness of the British empire. The novel's opening chapter parodies the call for adventure in boys' adventure fiction, which imagines the world as Britain's ever-expanding territories. In the opening chapter, Mole does not cross an ocean to journey to unknown territories; instead, he leaves his home, rebelling against a mundane household activity, spring cleaning his house on a beautiful spring day. Such a task implies his lower-middle-class status, his poverty, and thus his Britishness, since he cannot afford to hire a maid. As he gambols through the meadow, he is freed from all restraints and from his lower-middle-class status. However, he conceives of himself as being solidly middle class when he sneers at the rabbits at the toll hedge and invokes the middle class's contempt and belief in the lower classes' inherent respect for them: "He [the elderly rabbit] was bowled over in an instant by the impatient and contemptuous Mole" (Grahame 2). This scene suggests the middle-class imperative of reinforcing its hierarchical superiority toward the demographically working class majority, which they feared would one day overwhelm them as a class culturally, politically, and economically.[1] At the beginning of the novel, Mole leaves behind the Britishness of his underground "lowly little house" when he "scraped and scratched and scrabbled and scrooged" (2) his way into the sunshine, a meadow, and the outer world of the River Bank. His entrance into the rural landscape, then, is the first step in his reinvention of himself as English.

The map that Rat draws of the River Bank for Mole defines the inner circle of the exclusive society of Englishness; it is a self-contained, utopian rural world that becomes a space for order against the disorder of the world, a space for the communal reaffirmation of identity, and a space for the emplacement of the self. Ian Baucom argues "For the subjects of both nation and empire, the task of 'locating' English identity became ever more complex as England struggled to define the relationship between the national 'here' and the imperial 'there'" (37). By placing the "national here" within an idealized rural and country house landscape, the upper and middle classes located their moral center within the traditional boundaries of England and thereby attempted to establish the exclusivity of Englishness. An intrinsic part of the rural landscape of the River Bank, the Rat embodies Englishness through his belief in the superiority of the rural culture. He lives in a state of willful denial of the large world outside of the River Bank and refuses to admit his dependence on it. He suggests to Mole that the Wide World "doesn't matter, either to you or me. I've never been there, and I'm never going, nor you either. . . . Here's our backwater at last" (Grahame 6). When he symbolically aims his boat away from the urban industrialized world, his anti-industrial stance reconstructs the map of England as an arcadian rural landscape having a parallel existence within the urban industrialized British world of the empire. Ironically, however, his action simultaneously emphasizes the impossibility of fixing divisions between Englishness and Britishness because they are artificial and cannot be sustained. When Rat commands Mole not to go to the Wide World and then argues that it "doesn't matter, either to you or me" (6), it is almost as if he is making a last stand, trying to ensure a determined insularity against industrialization and the basic tenets of the empire that had flowered in the last century, a Britishness built on travel and adventure.

John David Moore argues that The Wind in the Willows is a "book with a map, an enclosed space whose boundaries are significant. Within its borders we find an inner sanctum, a piece of countryside that for the most part is as domesticated as the homes of Rat, Mole, or Badger" (46). Even though the landscape in the novel can be literally mapped, the "inner sanctum" of the countryside is not merely an identity-preserving place; it is also an identity-conferring club. Only the inner sanctum's inhabitants, such as Badger, can confer the identity of Englishness through acceptance. Mole seems to recognize Badger's role in the River Bank hierarchy; focalizing through Mole, the narrator notes "[Badger] seemed, by all accounts, to be such an important personage, and, though rarely visible, to make his unseen influence felt by everybody about the place" (Grahame 23). In spite of Mole's requests to be introduced to this "important personage," Rat demurs, believing that he cannot presume upon Badger's friendship due to Badger's higher status in society: "I've never even ventured to call on him at his own home myself, though I know him so well" (23). When Mole decides to meet the Badger on his own, Rat finds a cold and scared Mole in the Wild Wood hiding in the hollow of a tree, and explains why he had warned Mole against venturing there alone before:

> We river-bankers, we hardly ever come here by ourselves. If we have to come, we come in couples, at least; then we're generally all right. Besides, there are a hundred things one has to know, which we understand all about and you don't, as yet. I mean pass-words, and signs, and sayings which have power and effect, and plants you can carry in your pocket, and verses you repeat, and dodges and tricks you practice. (28–29)

Rat implies that Mole lacks the status and mannerisms of Englishness to reach the inner sanctum of the rural gentry, the Badger's home, his reason for venturing into the Wild Wood.

Mole needs Rat's patronage in this closed rural world because Englishness, the customs and manners of a gentleman, can only be achieved by learning its "pass-words, and signs, and sayings . . . and dodges and tricks." Spoofing to some extent the arcane manners and customs of the upper classes, Grahame suggests that the treasure to be discovered in this rural arcadia is ultimately the social status of an English gentleman. Both Rat and Mole are respectfully granted the title of gentleman when they are greeted by two young lower-class hedgehogs in Badger's kitchen in the morning. One of the hedgehogs informs Rat that the snow is so deep that there is "[n]o getting out for the likes of you gentlemen today" (39). The hedgehog implies that Rat and Mole's higher class status permits them the luxury and privilege of staying indoors without having to go to work. During the nineteenth century, the concept of the gentleman was modified by the middle class to fit a changing modern world. Christine Berberich suggests "the idea of the gentleman was developed into an 'invented tradition': based on the mediaeval cult of the knight, it was adapted and modified to fit contemporary needs" (21).[2] Aristocratic ideals of chivalry and gentility were combined with middle-class puritanical morals and values. Englishness, then, embodied both of these seemingly contradictory ideals and, as a result, did not have to be based upon birth, but rather could be performative, further reinforcing its increasing hybridity. Mole has the potential to acquire the identity of Englishness by learning how to perform it. He achieves acceptance into the exclusive River Bank society through the patronage of his friend Rat, who introduces him to his wide acquaintances, such as the Otter. But he also becomes accepted by conforming to English gentlemanly manners and performing Englishness correctly. The novel carefully points to the Mole's knowledge of "animal-etiquette." For example, at the beginning of the novel, when the Otter suddenly disappears in the midst of telling his story about Toad, he recollects the importance of not commenting upon such disappearances. Grahame also suggests that Mole grows more facile with etiquette as the novel progresses, consolidating the Englishness of his identity.

It is not only how one treats others, but also how one spends one's time, that performatively demonstrates Englishness. Mole and Rat's common English cultural heritage is measured by their leisure activities. When Rat teaches Mole to row a boat, he demonstrates to him how the countryside is part of his patrimony, a patrimony that includes such intangible commodities as the exclusionary code of gentility, respect from the lower classes, and identification with England's historic architecture. Mole is baptized into his patrimony—an idyllic rural life composed of such leisure events as composing poetry in the evenings, boating, and picnicking—when he enters the rural space of the River Bank.

During the Edwardian period, such rural spaces became a refuge within the collective geography of the imagination for the middle and upper classes, a refuge against the onslaughts of the industrialized imperialized world. To Britain's servants of the empire, leaving England involved not only leaving behind family and friends, but more importantly, leaving behind an English rural space that preserved the exclusive cultural identity of Englishness. As J. S. Bratton notes,

> The tension between Old England, its beauty and cultivated fertility, its security, its beloved associations with family or sweetheart left behind, and the new lands of promise, which are exciting, but also hard and masculine, dangerously unfamiliar, lawless and lonely, is a deep structural polarity in the fiction of the second half of the nineteenth century. (87)

Within the self-insulated world of the River Bank, a Wordsworthian pastoral innocence is purposefully cultivated, commodified, and fetishized, so that Mole's idyllic life with Rat is a commodity desired by the middle class in their search for an idyllic rural utopian life and a newly emerging construction of Englishness. The middle and upper classes believed that despite the rise of its great cities since the eighteenth century, England was at heart an idyllically rural nation. On a domestic level, the home embodied the idyllic rural life that Ford Madox Ford called "the spirit of the home of ancient peace" (50).[3] It was a dynamic Anglo-Saxon spirit that combined the conquering and military culture of Britishness and the empire with the identity of Englishness. Mole discovers just such a spirit when he hears exciting, adventurous stories "about weirs, and sudden floods, and leaping pike, and steamers that [fling] hard bottles" (Grahame 11), but he also feels the spirit's sense of serenity when he lays "his head on his pillow [in the Rat's best bedroom] in great peace and contentment" (11).

The core identity of Englishness is based on guarding its ideals, such as the idea of the gentleman and the ethos of gentility, from the terrifying industrialized world. Maintaining such ideals had become increasingly difficult due to the reduction of rural space as cities encroached into the countryside in the form of suburbs. Tony Watkins argues that by the Edwardian period, the countryside was no longer seen "as a place of work but redefined as an Arcadia of rural leisure" (35) for weekend getaways and holidays. The map of such a rural world is becoming smaller, as Rat ruefully explains to Mole: "The bank is so crowded nowadays that many people are moving away altogether" (Grahame 5). This reduction of rural space has, in turn, made untouched rural space a valuable commodity, no different from any other consumer item. Even as the "national here" of Englishness is celebrated through Rat and Mole's leisure activities, it exists uneasily with the "imperial there" of Britishness that produces all the commodities the middle and upper classes very hungrily consume. For their impromptu picnic, Rat's large wicker basket is filled with "coldtonguecoldhamcoldbeefpickledgherkinsaladfrenchrolls-cresssandwichespottedmeatgingerbeerlemonadesodawater—" (4). In spite of its goods being based upon the industrial world, home and its comforts are framed within an idealized arcadia that conceals consumerism within a façade of discursive innocence.

When Mole and Rat are visited by young caroling field-mice in the Mole's former home, the scene demonstrates the confluence of the landscape and architecture as possessing a bucolic form of Englishness that can push back against the wider world of empire and industrialization. A yearly tradition, the caroling preserves the common heritage of the rural English landscape against the devaluation of the self by industrialized machine culture. The middle and upper classes' proprietary obligation to their lower-class tenants lends morality to the landscape in which affiliation between the various houses of the area are held together by obligation, hierarchy, and authority. Englishness, then, is the currency between groups of people and is defined by the many unwritten rules that order society. Knowledge of such rules is literally an economic and cultural asset. When the field-mice come to his house, Mole takes on the obligations of the lord of the manor by giving them dinner because his is the last house.[4] The value of Englishness is predicated upon the country house culture in which both the upper and lower classes are tightly bound to a seigneurial relationship that was quickly disappearing due to the rise of modernity's mass democracy. Since his neighbors appear not to be aware he had suddenly left his home months ago, Mole is in the awkward position of not being able to fulfill the obligations of the English host due to his empty larder. With the help of Rat, he manages to perform his role. But then he crosses class boundaries when he talks familiarly with the field-mice: "As they ate, they talked of old times, and the field-mice gave [the Mole] the local gossip up to date" (Grahame 58). This incident emphasizes how identities are performative rather than birth-based, as Mole performs the role of the English lord of the manor but then backslides into his former lower middle-class status by gossiping with the field-mice.

When Rat sends one of the caroling field-mice to the grocery store to buy prepackaged food, the value of commodities brings to the forefront congeries of goods exported from distant places and the consumer's willful amnesia of where these items were produced: "Fresh, mind!—no, a pound of that will do—see you get Buggins's, for I won't have any other" (56). The Rat's insistence on a certain brand exemplifies how consumerism has become intrinsically part of the rural culture in spite of the upper and middle classes' attempts to keep the industrialized world at bay. Discussing the increasing commodification of culture in the nineteenth century, Thomas Richards argues that "At the most basic level, capitalism had always turned everything it touched into a commodity, into an object of exchange" (195). The commodity as a literal currency of exchange destabilizes what was considered to be a sacred obligation between the lord of the manor and his tenants—a paternalistic and seigneurial relationship that has traditionally harkened back generations. However, the inherent authority of the identity of Englishness is not disrupted because Rat and Mole do fulfill their obligations. In spite of the encroaching industrialized world, rural English culture is maintained through ritualized events.

Living with Rat, Mole is part of the leisured middle class, enjoying the life of a gentleman with no pecuniary concerns. However, place of belonging, the domestic space of the home, reinforces normative class divisions of Englishness from Britishness. When Mole returns to his house unexpectedly, he sees his house as he believes Rat would see it, and he is ashamed of his poverty and the lower-middle-class status that his house represents. His class status testifies to the ambiguity created by industrialization that allowed for the blurring of class divisions, and hence the hybridization of Englishness. Comparing his home to the other three animals' homes, he implies his lower-middle-class status and, significantly, his guilt at having abandoned his home: "'I know it's a shabby, dingy little place,' he sobbed forth at last, brokenly: 'not like—your cosy quarters—or Toad's beautiful hall—or Badger's great house—but it was my own little house—and I was fond of it—and I went away and forgot all about it—and then I smelt it suddenly . . .'" (Grahame 50). Mole's guilt reflects the ambivalence felt by members of the middle class who enjoyed the fruits of industrialization even as they privileged the rural lifestyle.

The relationship between the self and domestic space as an identity-determining site privileges not just Englishness but also the national identity of Britishness. Both identities are not just hybridized into each other, with each less than the other. Instead, the two identities can exist in a dialectical relationship, one in which both contradictory identities, Englishness and Britishness, can coexist without diminishing one another. Since he had worked for a living, Mole appreciates his house as a private sanctuary against the exigencies of the world: "Shabby indeed, and small and poorly furnished, and yet his, the home he had made for himself, the home he had been so happy to get back to after his day's work" (48). The novel acknowledges Mole's Britishness or lower-middle-class history and tentatively attempts to resolve his status of being between Britishness and Englishness. Before he falls asleep, Mole feels at peace with his identity, and he realizes that his home through memory and remembrance will continue to be a space for security, comfort, and love: "The upper world was all too strong, it called to him still, even down there, and he knew he must return to the larger stage. But it was good to think he had this place to come back to, this place which was all his own" (58). Mole's pride in his humble roots or acceptance of his Britishness ironically emplaces him more firmly within the rural middle class and the identity of Englishness that his British roots would seem to call into question.

Mole's unconscious search for a new and better home places him within the national imagination of Britishness in which subjectivity is defined by access to cheap, mass-produced commodities and an easy disposal culture, which in turn begets a culture based on mourning for an idealized past. His modest cataloguing of his furniture and bric-a-brac suggests the importance of desire created by the commodity culture. Giving Rat a tour of his house, Mole earnestly explains how "that was a wonderful find and a bargain, and this other thing was bought out of laborious savings and a certain amount of 'going without'" (54). His small home reflects both the upward mobility of the masses and the ambivalence generated in the upper and middle classes by the commodity culture, a culture in which their monopoly of consumer goods was overturned by the creation of more affordable goods for the masses through mass production.

Mole's house is not the only structure that demonstrates tensions and ambiguities between Englishness and Britishness in Grahame's novel. We can also trace such tensions in the depiction of the more famous residence of the River Bank—Toad Hall—and its renowned inhabitant, Mr. Toad. As a commodity, the country manor house displays the material progress of the nation, with the house valued for embodying its residents' common heritage of Englishness. However, the house also represents the instability of Englishness due to the taint of industrialization in its social cartography. From the seventeenth century, the "gentry were drawn not only from families with strong landed ties but increasingly from city merchants, lawyers, and financiers and other members of the expanding commercial class" (Clemenson 11). Because of the many large fortunes created by the empire and industrialization during the Victorian period, by the early twentieth century the upper class could not absorb the nouveau riche, entrepreneurs from the lower or middle classes who had amassed their wealth through industry or from the empire. The upper class saw their identity of Englishness hybridized into Britishness and fetishized as a commodity through an important symbol of their identity, the country manor house. This devaluation is embodied by Toad, who belongs to the landed gentry class due to his ownership of Toad Hall. Toad's father may have made the wealth that allowed him to buy Toad Hall since Badger implies he was not born there. Toad's father "discovered [the underground] passage . . . that was done hundreds of years before he ever came to live there" (132). This type of information is generally inherited through the generations, and Toad's father ensures that Toad will inherit it through Badger. When Toad boasts about his house and his possessions, it suggests his kinship with the vulgar behavior of the nouveau riche even though he is at least second generation in terms of ownership of the house: "'Finest house on the whole river,' cried Toad boisterously. 'Or anywhere else, for that matter'" (14). His almost constant need to advertise his wealth and position to anyone he meets suggests that a late Victorian discourse concerning identity was fashioned from a circulation of commodities, not the aristocratic ethos of Englishness, which valued obligation and duty as its primary beliefs.

The cult of the stately country house was an attempt by the landed elite to reestablish a hierarchical feudal system at a time of mass production, consumerism, and loss of elitism due to increasing numbers of nouveau riche. David Cannadine suggests the "veneration" and preservation of the country house was a new phenomenon begun in the late Victorian period. He argues that the "main reason why so many great mansions were demolished from the Tudor to the Victorian period was so that their owners might move with the times, and thus put up new and improved versions instead" (99). The possessor of the country estate renovated the house to keep up with the times, but he also had the sacred obligation to pass it down to his heir since "an heir to a settled estate was in essence an hereditary trustee or limited owner, during his lifetime serving as the guardian of the family patrimony in order to pass it on intact to the next generation" (Clemenson 15).[5] The landed gentry class's affiliation through generational continuity and authority consolidated its identity of Englishness as being exclusive, and its members had a sacred obligation to preserve the culture of the rural countryside. Ownership of a country home estate involved an almost paternal trust and obligation to the estate's tenants and to the people of the countryside. Probably part of either the lesser landed gentry or the yeoman class,[6] Toad classifies himself as "A Typical English Squire" (145) in an address he plans to give at the banquet to reestablish his return. He believes that ownership of his country house, Toad Hall, has conferred on him his station and identity of Englishness without any duties and obligations. His façade of Englishness has multiple cracks in it and exemplifies his cultural hybridity through his belief that his wealth allows him to display himself as a spectacle to his guests at the banquet. Toad plans to give a series of speeches and songs focusing on his recent adventures while his friends try to protect him from the consequences of his clownish and self-aggrandizing actions, which would reduce him to the level of low-class unrefined nouveau-riche boor. Badger discusses this problem with Rat: "This good fellow [Toad] has got to live here, and hold his own, and be respected. Would you have him a common laughing-stock, mocked and jeered at by stoats and weasels?" (147). Toad's belief that his gentry class status will protect him from his reckless behavior has consequences not only to his status in society but to his house. Unlike Mole, who continues to have pride in his humble home, Toad's pride in his home is based on his ability to indulge in his fads rather than ensuring the next generation will inherit his estate. For example, Badger chastises Toad for jeopardizing his inheritance, Toad Hall: "You've gone on squandering the money your father left you" (Grahame 61).

Toad believes his home gives him an entré to the highest reaches of landed society: "'Toad Hall,' said the Toad proudly, 'is an eligible self-contained gentleman's residence, very unique; dating in part from the fourteenth century, but replete with every modern convenience. Up-to-date sanitation . . .'" (83). Toad's catalog of his house emphasizes not only his wealth and income, but also his ability to modernize it with "Up-to-date sanitation" (83), which points to his nouveau riche status through his belief of the house as a commodity. He values the age of his house for the prestige it confers upon him, but through the renovations to it, he emphasizes his wealth without regard to preserving the history of the house. Toad does not realize that the identity of Englishness is ultimately conferred and reinforced by the community and that the country house acts as an object of exchange in this relationship. While several critics have pointed to psychological reasons for Toad's lack of knowledge of the secret passage in his house, such lack of knowledge can also be read as his lack of investment in a construction of Englishness that links master to manor.

In contrast to Mole, whose rise in status is due to his modest and quiet manners, Toad advertises his vulgarity and arrogance. He believes his home gives him access to the privileges of the landed elite until he is thrown into jail for stealing a motorcar and labeled by the chairman of the Bench of Magistrates as an "incorrigible rogue and hardened ruffian" (68), so the full force of the law can come down on him. He is judged and punished by the Wide World not just for the theft of a car, but for his disaffiliation with the identity of Englishness. His punishment is a temporary banishment into the lower class, as he must flee the law disguised as a lowly washerwoman. Because he does not fulfill his English seigneurial role, Toad's home can no longer serve as his currency in the marketplace of privilege. His actions that deny his seigneurial relationship with the countryside embody the hybridization of Englishness and degeneration of the rural country house culture caused by increasing numbers of British entrepreneurs buying these great houses.

Toad's wealth and gentry status allow him to flit from one fad to another, such as boating, caravanning, and motoring, as he plays the role of the aristocratic gentleman. His travel in his luxuriously outfitted caravan is a movement away from the democratization of travel—affordable and convenient mass transportation, such as railway trains—a democratization that in turn led the middle and upper classes to fetishize domesticity and valorize travel for pleasure, with both valued as embodying Englishness. Tony Watkins suggests that tourism of the countryside or tours of country homes was a search for "that 'real England' [that] co-exist[ed] with an actual England that is far from ideal; the real is 'hidden away'" (35) and can be discovered by traveling to it. Rat, very much a homebody, is persuaded by Toad and Mole to embark on a trip in Toad's gypsy caravan. Toad paints a glowing picture of travel as embodying freedom from responsibility and an exploration of the Wide World even though they are never planning on leaving England: "The open road, the dusty highway . . . The whole world before you, and a horizon that's always changing" (Grahame 15). On their first night, Toad wishes his companions good night and adds, "This is the real life for a gentleman!" (17). His self-congratulatory comment reinvents the survival lifestyle of the poor, camping, as a middle-class leisure activity, privileging the rural over the urban as an antidote for the democratization of Britishness. Tourism permitted the upper and middle classes to romanticize the lifestyle of the rural poor as a Wordsworthian ideal and to consume it from a distance. Even before the car accident, Toad becomes tired of roughing it on the road and the "simplicity of the primitive life" (18) in spite of his luxuriously fitted caravan. However, he later receives a dose of reality; when running away from the law, he is hungry and cannot buy food. He encounters a gypsy whose caravan is his home, a meeting that reinforces how he had earlier ignorantly amused himself with his recreational caravan. Yet despite Toad's supposed poverty, he does have an asset, his stolen horse, which he sells for money and a commodity he had traditionally taken for granted, breakfast. The stew he buys probably consists of illegally poached game: "partridge, and pheasants, and chickens, and hares, and rabbits, and pea-hens, and guinea-fowls" (116). Toad's movement, from playing at being "poor" to actually having to barter for his breakfast, suggests that the democratization of wealth due to industrialization and imperialism means that the identity of Englishness can also be lost due to loss of wealth.

After being jailed for stealing a car (and cheeking a policeman), Toad is reduced to the status of a lower-class hardened criminal, the life of English gentlemanly privilege no longer his. His sense of identity is erased as he imagines languishing in jail until "people who were proud to say they knew me, have forgotten the very name of Toad" (81). But Toad's memories of his life before his arrest suggest that it is the British, rather than English, identity that he laments losing, a privilege linked to the ability to purchase: "the outer world of sunshine and well-metalled high roads where he had lately been so happy, disporting himself as if he had *bought up every road in England*" (81, emphasis added). Ironically, even as some form of wealth was a necessary attribute for the identity of Englishness, the enormous fortunes of captains of industry reduced them to Britishness through their vulgar display of wealth even as the wealth gave them the lifestyle of Englishness. Toad, to some extent, lives this lifestyle through his apparent bottomless wealth.

Likewise, Toad is restored to himself and his patrimony through a commodity: the buttered toast the gaoler's daughter brings him. Commodities register not only degrees of wealth and status, but also culture; in the toast scene, a middle-class morning ritual is fetishized and becomes a consuming spectacle:

> The smell of that buttered toast simply talked to Toad, and with no uncertain voice; talked of warm kitchens, of breakfasts on bright frosty mornings, of cosy parlour firesides on winter evenings, when one's ramble was over and slippered feet were propped on the fender; and the purring of contented cats, and the twitter of sleepy canaries. (83)

Home, as symbolized by the buttered toast, is an antidote to an increasingly mechanized, urban, chaotic world. Within the actual claustrophobic physical space of a jail or prison-house, an everyday comfort food, buttered toast, evokes a utopian world of childhood so the self can be preserved within the memory of the nation's moral center of propriety, order, and comfort. The images of the kitchen, fireplace, and the cat that the toast evokes in Toad capture an idealized, pastoral narrative of childhood that is strangely devoid of parents and family but becomes an adult refuge of domesticity.

Like Mole, Toad demonstrates that Englishness is always performative, even if the person in question is "to the manor born"; Toad, like Mole, must be taught the correct lifestyle and obligations of the lord of the manor by his friends. At the banquet he is ordered to give by Badger after he is restored to his house, Toad correctly performs the part of an aristocratic, and *English*, gentleman. "[B]y topical small-talk, and by earnest inquiries after members of their families not yet old enough to appear at social functions, [he] managed to convey to [his guests] that this dinner was being run on strictly conventional lines" (Grahame 149). Through his performance, Toad takes on the seigneurial role of the lord of the manor, which suggests that the identity of Englishness for the English upper class may be intrinsic to birth. Having sown his wild oats, he is now ready to fulfill his patriotic duty of administering his English heritage.

Unlike Toad and Mole, who must learn correct English behavior, Badger embodies it from the start. As "a member of the old aristocracy" with "the authority that birth and breeding have conferred upon him," the Badger's "vast tunnelled dwelling . . . gives him access to any part of the landscape—the great country house and its estates dominating the villagers" (Carpenter 164). Unlike Toad's centrally located country house, Badger's house is notably difficult to find, its large size deceptively hidden underground. Badger's unassuming home finds its mirror in his reticent and self-deprecating attitude; both attest to the aristocracy/gentry's culture of understated elegance. His home's vast tunneling throughout the countryside and its many entrances suggest his vast influence as the lord of the manor, but the centrality of the kitchen and the hearth makes his home seem more like a comfortable farmhouse than the museum-like public spaces of a country manor house. His home does, however, reinscribe the hierarchies of Englishness through his largesse and his benevolence as a host through the comforts of his kitchen, his seigneurial status demonstrated by the countryside that looks to his paternalistic authority and patronage. When Rat and Mole are missing from their home, Otter tells them the countryside looks to the Badger's leadership: "But I knew that when people were in any fix they mostly went to Badger, or else Badger got to know of it somehow" (39). As the center of authority for the area and the titular lord of the manor, Badger has the sovereignty and benevolence of the English paterfamilias.

Badger's identity of "gentleman" is situated with an aura of refinement and located through an ethos of patriarchal authority. Unlike Toad, who is completely unaware of the underground passage in his home, Badger can easily conduct a tour of his home's labyrinthine passageways. Such passageways symbolically partake of all of England, so that Badger's Englishness, instead of being located within a particular geographical area, embodies and preserves the nation's collective memory. That his house is built under an ancient city makes it an identity-determining site and gives him a direct link to the past and to the pastoral utopian world. As David Lowenthal asserts, "To secure themselves against the evils of rampant change and the dangers posed by the new industrial order, Victorians took refuge in one or another past, pasts not so much preserved as extravagantly re-created in architecture, art, and literature" (*The Past Is a Foreign Country* 102). In spite of the Victorians' reinventing traditions through their cultural arts and making their English landscape into a "consummate artefact" (Lowenthal, "The Island Garden" 140), Badger points to the transience of humans and their cities with the animals, especially badgers, enduring after them: "People come—they stay for a while, they flourish, they build—and they go. . . . But we [badgers] remain" (43).

The natural paradisiacal world of nature that has come to define an Edwardian sense of Englishness will outlive the turmoils of modern society. Englishness ultimately is embodied in a Wordsworthian recollected arcadian world that is under siege from human industrialization and imperialism; the only defense available to the natural landscape appears to be evanescent and transitory snow castles valorizing the rural landscape as an oasis against human destruction. When the Otter comes to the Badger's house, his lyrical descriptions of the winter wonderland landscape as a castle minimize winter's threatening dangers: "Snow-castles and snow-caverns had sprung up from nowhere in the night—and snow bridges, terraces, ramparts—" (40). Secluded from the modern urban world and an oasis against the elements, Badger's house transforms the threatening outside world into a countervailing image of the English home embodying communal unity.

The Wind in the Willows testifies to the importance of the rural landscape in national memory and identity even as it grapples with the consequences of industrialization, imperialism, and modernity on the individual self. Recoiling from a modernity gone mad, the upper and middle classes created an idyllic rural arcadian landscape they could participate in as embodying the authentic England as opposed to the chaotic, urban, industrialized, and imperialized world that commodified the self. Englishness was represented by a mourned recollected utopian rural landscape and a way of life in danger of being destroyed due to industrialization. As the architectural symbol of this idyllic world, the country house and the rural landscape that surrounded it were invested as a refuge against the artifices of civilization and became a repudiation of modernization.

Notes

1. Middle-class fears of loss of political power due to working-class men gaining the right to vote after the Second Reform Act of 1867 exacerbated fears of being contaminated by working-class vices and criminality. Even as they tried to encourage workers to stay in their traditional homes in the rural countryside, the lure of industrialized cities that needed workers continued to encourage migration to the cities.

2. In her argument, Berberich points to Hobsbawn's concept of invented tradition—that traditions, rituals, and ceremonies were deliberately created, giving the present a sense of historical continuity. See Hobsbawn, pp. 1–14.

3. Ford goes on to suggest an intrinsically dialectical relationship between the Englishness represented by a mourned utopian rural world and the imperialized conquering heroes of Britishness: "Thus nowhere in the world, so much as in England, do you find the spirit of the home of ancient peace; nowhere in the occidental world will you find turf that so invites you to lie down and muse, sunshine so mellow and innocuous, shade so deep or rooks so tranquil in their voices . . . and these English rose-gardens and cathedral closes bred a race whose mission is, after all, to be the eternal frontiersmen of the world" (50–51).

4. Although Troy Boone argues that Mole belongs to the urban working class (89), Mole does not view himself that way, and Water Rat greets him and treats him as an equal belonging to the middle class.

5. *The Settled Land Act of 1882* granted "the tenant-for-life," the current owner, the "powers of dealing with the land 'by way of sale, exchange, lease and otherwise'" (Clemenson 16). In other words, it removed the burden of entailments on an estate that restricted the current owner from acting as he pleased with the property. Each previous owner through the legal act of entailment ensured that the next three future heirs could not sell the parts or the whole property. It insured that an estate could not be broken or divided among several heirs.

6. The 1873 *Return of Owners of Land* census classified yeoman as possessing estates of a hundred to a thousand acres and lesser gentry as owning estates of a thousand to three thousand acres (Clemenson 19).

Works Cited

Baucom, Ian. *Out of Place: Englishness, Empire, and the Locations of Identity.* Princeton: Princeton UP, 1999.

Berberich, Christine. *The Image of the English Gentleman in Twentieth-Century Literature.* Burlington: Ashgate, 2007.

Boone, Troy. "'Germs of Endearment': The Machinations of Edwardian Children's Fictions." *Children's Literature* 35 (2007): 80–101.

Brantlinger, Patrick. *Rule of Darkness: British Literature and Imperialism, 1830–1914.* Ithaca: Cornell UP, 1988.

Bratton, J. S. "Of England, Home, and Duty: The Image of England in Victorian and Edwardian Juvenile Fiction." *Imperialism and Popular Culture.* Ed. John M. MacKenzie. Manchester: Manchester UP, 1986. 73–93.

Cannadine, David. *The Pleasures of the Past.* New York: Norton, 1989.

Carpenter, Humphrey. *Secret Gardens: A Study of the Golden Age of Children's Literature.* Boston: Houghton, 1985.

Clemenson, Heather A. *English Country Houses and Landed Estates.* London: Croom Helm, 1982.

Colley, Linda. *Britons: Forging the Nation 1707–1837.* New Haven: Yale UP, 1992.

Ford (Heuffer), Ford Madox. *The Spirit of the People: An Analysis of the English Mind.* London: Alston Rivers, 1907.

Grahame, Kenneth. *The Wind in the Willows.* 1908. Ed. Peter Green. Oxford: Oxford UP, 1983.

Green, Peter. *Kenneth Grahame 1859–1932: A Study of His Life, Work and Times.* London: John Murray, 1959.

Hemmings, Robert. "A Taste of Nostalgia: Children's Books from the Golden Age—Carroll, Grahame, and Milne." *Children's Literature* 35 (2007): 54–79.

Hobsbawn, Eric. "Introduction: Inventing Traditions." *The Invention of Tradition.* Ed. Eric Hobsbawn and Terence Ranger. Cambridge: Cambridge UP, 1983. 1–14.

Howkins, Alun. "The Discovery of Rural England." *Englishness: Politics and Culture 1880–1920.* Ed. Robert Colls and Philip Dodd. New York: Croom Helm, 1986. 62–88.

Lowenthal, David. "The Island Garden: English Landscape and British Identity." *History, Nationhood and the Question of Britain.* Ed. Helen Brocklehurst and Robert Phillips. New York: Palgrave, 2004. 137–48.

———. *The Past Is a Foreign Country.* Cambridge: Cambridge UP, 1985.

Mandler, Peter. *The Fall and Rise of the Stately Home.* New Haven: Yale UP, 1997.

Moore, John David. "Pottering about in the Garden: Kenneth Grahame's Version of the Pastoral in *The Wind in the Willows.*" *Journal of the Midwest Modern Language Association* 23 (1990): 45–60.

Richards, Thomas. *The Commodity Culture of Victorian England: Advertising and Spectacle, 1851–1914.* Stanford: Stanford UP, 1990.

Watkins, Tony. "'Making a Break for the Real England': The River-Bankers Revisited." *Children's Literature Association Quarterly* 9 (1984): 34–35.

Williams, Raymond. *The Country and the City*. London: Chatto & Windus, 1973.

Young, Robert J. C. *Colonial Desire: Hybridity in Theory, Culture and Race*. London: Routledge, 1995.

CHAPTER EIGHT

~

Animal Boys, Aspiring Aesthetes, and Differing Masculinities: Aestheticism Revealed in *The Wind in the Willows*

Wynn Yarbrough

The Wind in the Willows might be read as the grown-up Kenneth Grahame's fantasy of a secret society, an all-male Arcadia that, by his own words, could be magically "free of the clash of sex" (qtd. in Kuznets, *Kenneth Grahame* 13). The former banker and part-time writer initially began his classic novel as a series of bedtime stories for his son, Alastair, but the all-male society he created appealed to adults as well, suggesting that Grahame's fantasy of an all-male utopia was and is one shared by many other male readers. Feminist critics have rightly pointed out that despite Grahame's claim to the contrary, conflict between the sexes permeates his story (see Poss; Kuznets, "Father Nature"; Marshall). But while critics have called attention to the exclusion of the feminine from *The Wind in the Willows*, few have focused on the construction of masculinity in Grahame's touchstone text.[1] Such a study, I would argue, reveals a more nuanced view of Grahame's gender politics. For Grahame's text, far from espousing a single normative masculinity, explores multiple constructions of the masculine, including one under great suspicion during the Edwardian age: masculine aestheticism.

Contingent to the study of masculinity in any text are the historical and sociopolitical circumstances at play during its time of construction. Consciously or unconsciously, Grahame wrote against the backdrop of what Susan Kingsley Kent has described as "masculinity under fire" (229). During the final decades of the nineteenth century and the opening decade of the twentieth, salvos against British masculinity erupted from multiple directions. Increases in city populations and concurrent fears that city living would weaken the health and sap the vigor of city dwellers sparked anxiety that the race of Englishmen was in a state of physical decline. Such fears seemed substantiated by the humiliating defeats the British army experienced at the hands of Dutch Afrikaner farmers in the Boer War of 1899 and the high rejection rate of would-be soldiers due to the inability of more than one third of applicants to pass a military physical. Fears of "race degeneration" loomed large in the face of such rebukes to the nation's sense of its virility and manhood (Kent 236–37). For example, Lord Baden Powell's scouting movement, with its emphasis on preparing boys to uphold Britain's imperial goals, began in 1908 in reaction to the embarrassments of the Boer War. Powell's movement drew from a wealth of Victorian masculinity myths, many popularized by children's writers like Stevenson, Haggard, and Kipling. But its impetus was born out of fear that the English race, particularly males, weren't ready to defend, lead, or expand the British Empire.

Intertwined with this martial insecurity was anxiety stemming from burgeoning political and social movements among women, which often advocated dramatically different relationships between the sexes than those promulgated by traditional Victorian masculinity. The Women's Social and Political Union, founded in 1903, five years before the publication of *The Wind in the Willows*, placed women's issues (suffrage, marriage rights, health rights) at the forefront of society. From the passage of the Married Women's Property acts of 1870 and 1882 (which freed women from restrictions to property and money when they were married) to Annie Besant's 1877 trial for promoting contraception as a means for women to control their reproductive freedom, early feminists had begun the march toward "new woman"-hood, disturbing not only the heteronormative picture of marriage and sex relations, but also the construction of a normative English masculinity in the process (Kent 248–53).

Working-class manliness proved another threat to middle-class Edwardian males. Newly enfranchised working-class males, and the trade unions that emerged to represent them, became more vocal during this period. Membership in unions increased through the end of the nineteenth century and well into the beginning of the twentieth, bringing not only slogans and rallies, but also activities that threatened the economic and political status quo: the women's match strike of 1888, the Great London Dock Strike of 1889, and strikes by railway workers, shipbuilders, and coal miners (1907–1908). No longer content to align themselves with liberal gentry MPs, workers sought a new kind of representation, one aligned more closely with a socialist agenda (Kent 233).

The most sensational challenge to normative masculinity, however, came in the form of the public's heightened awareness of male homosexuality. In 1885, the Criminal Law Amendment Act criminalized sexual activity between males. The Cleveland Street scandals (1889–1890), in which police uncovered a male brothel in Cleveland Street, revealed the buying and selling of sexual services of boys to aristocratic customers, rumored to include Prince Albert Victor. Oscar Wilde's trial for "gross indecency" (i.e., homosexuality) in 1895 may have been the most shocking and most stirring sociopolitical event of the end of the century. As Kent asserts, the prosecution of Oscar Wilde "trumpeted the existence of homosexuality among men throughout the nation, raising questions about how one might truly recognize manliness" (248). Wilde's trial also led to a change in the way English speakers used the word "effeminate"—from signifying men "who spent too much time in the company of women, who were captivated by women and their sensualizing effects" to signifying "men who had sex with other men" (248).

Such a shift called into suspicion another type of masculinity that had emerged during the Victorian period: aesthetic masculinity. The Aesthetic Movement was inherited, philosophically, from the Enlightenment, with its emphasis on freedom from authority, particularly the church. Influenced by both the Pre-Raphaelites and the French aesthetics (Théophile Gautier through the Symbolists, Mallarmé and Verlaine), artists and writers sought to express beauty in their art without the need to adhere to social, literary, artistic, or moral conventions. In British literature, writers were influenced by the Romantics, particularly Shelley and Keats. As Gene Bell-Villada contends in *Art for Art's Sake and Literary Life: How Politics and Markets Helped Shape the Ideology & Culture of Aestheticism: 1790–1990,*

> Within the full setting of Keats's total thought and the English poetics of his time . . ."Beauty is Truth, Truth Beauty" may best be construed as posing those two entities neither as distinct nor as identical, but as unitary concepts, as partners with a larger whole. From the globalizing perspective of Coleridge, Shelley and Keats, art and knowledge exist together, not in isolation, are one and indivisible, not separate or disconnected. (68)

English Romanticism encouraged intense subjectivity and individualism, which would find expression in the 1890s through writers known as Aesthetes and Decadents: Oscar Wilde, Arthur Symons, Ernest Dowson, and Lionel Johnson, to name a few.

English Aestheticism has its philosophical basis in the ideas of John Ruskin and Walter Pater. Ruskin's interest in decorative art and craftsmanship influenced a generation of artists and writers, such as Dante Gabriel Rossetti, Edward Burne-Jones, and William Holman Hunt. Pater's aesthetic credo, "To burn always with this hard gemlike flame" (152) and to seek the "poetic passion, the desire of beauty, the love of art for art's sake" (153) became the principal philosophies of one of his (and Ruskin's) most famous pupils, Oscar Wilde. Aesthetes had their champion in Wilde who, cribbing Pater, writes

> . . . the passion for beauty engendered by the decorative arts will be to them [the audience] more satisfying than any political or religious enthusiasm for humanity, any ecstasy or sorrow for love. For art comes to one professing primarily to give nothing but the highest quality to one's moments, and for those moments' sake . . . (qtd. in Lambourne 141).

Wilde's works, and those of other Aesthetic Movement proponents, focused on beauty, life imitating art, suggestion and sensuality, and intense visual and imagistic effect. Such writers sought to open up a space for male intellectual labor, and in particular, male artistic labor, in the realm of the masculine.

Literary aestheticism influenced many writers in the period, including the young Kenneth Grahame. During his early writing career, Grahame published in *The Yellow Book*, a journal famous for including work by prominent members of the Aesthetic Movement such as Aubrey Beardsley, W. B. Yeats, Ernest Dowson, and Arthur Symons. But Grahame decidedly distanced himself from *The Yellow Book* circle following

Wilde's trial. In fact, after Wilde's conviction, many writers and artists distanced themselves from Wilde and the excesses of the Aesthetic crowd. Lionel Lambourne, in *The Aesthetic Movement*, describes the popular reaction to Wilde and aestheticism:

> In the 1880s, even at its most affected, Aestheticism had only aroused feelings of amused irritation from its critics. But now, Wilde's flagrantly overt advocacy of the intimate connections between the "slim gilt souls" of true Aesthetes and "the love that dare not speak its name" aroused disgust. Philistinism flourished, and "revulsion" and "unhealthiness" became epithets often used to describe both Art Nouveau artifacts and the "decadent" literature of the *fin de siècle*. (225)

Wilde's conviction for "gross indecency" effectively ended the Aesthetic Movement, and the figure of the masculine aesthete quickly became a convenient scapegoat for the ruptures in the illusive picture of stability and normed masculinity that the empire sought to depict. But many of the central tenets of aestheticism had been internalized by writers of the period, including Kenneth Grahame. We can see Grahame's inheritance from the aesthetes in his stylistic devices, anti-industrialization sentiments, and aesthetic iconography. While Grahame, like many of his contemporaries, did not share the taste for decadence or sexual experimentation of the later Decadent writers, he did not turn away from the movement completely (Green 148–54). Reading *The Wind in the Willows* in this context, then, we can see that Grahame's work aims to recuperate aspects of aestheticism, particularly in terms of masculinity.

Analyzing constructions of masculinity in *The Wind in the Willows* reveals the clear presence of aesthetic themes, aesthetic characters, and aesthetic objects. In the course of his River Bank stories, I will argue, Grahame revives the spirit of aestheticism put under suspicion as a result of the Wilde trial. But when real crises emerge at the end of the novel, Grahame must tame such aesthetic impulses. How Grahame plots the novel—from open-ended Stevensonian adventure and rambling neo-paganism, to aesthetic flirtations and psychological epiphany, to group conscription and a war scene that reinscribes class-based rural hierarchies—demonstrates both the gender license available to Grahame as well as the constrictive reactions to such license, especially as gender is revealed by Grahame's aesthetic characterizations.

Grahame scripts gender performances that allow for a range of masculine identities: policeman, teen rebel, artisan/artist, father, and working-class individualist. There is no one mode of being masculine in this novel, but there are performances and processes that allow for various representations of masculinity. While Grahame does rehabilitate aestheticism as a mode of masculinity, performing as an aesthete, including entertaining same-sex intimate friendship, is only acceptable in particular contexts.

Philosophically, Eve Sedgwick, author of *Between Men: English Literature and Male Homosocial Desire* (1985) and *Epistemology of the Closet* (1990) and noted gender and queer studies theorist, provides a useful framework for considering Grahame's novel. Many of Sedgwick's binaries (Greek/Christian, Sentimental/Antisentimental, Direct/Vicarious, Art/Kitsch, Same/Different, Homo/Hetero, Abstraction/Figuration, Wholeness/Decadence, Voluntary/Addiction, and Health/Illness most prominently) are evident in Grahame's process of characterization (*Epistemology of the Closet*, 11). The beginning of the novel encourages, celebrates, and crafts aesthetic objects and performances as magical, mystical, joyous, and liberating. But this magical quality also becomes dangerous and powerful when characters "fly too close to the sun."

Grahame processes aestheticism out of the novel the way he processes the characters into a more heteronormative, class-based, hierarchal masculine society by the end of the story (the retaking of Toad Hall). Aestheticism is acceptable, but only as a minor aspect of identity firmly rooted in heteronormative, class-based, hierarchal masculinity. Grahame leads his characters on journeys where binaries have to be worked out and aestheticism becomes a minor, but essential part of the "affective or social force" (Sedgwick 2) that binds these characters to their unstable masculinity.

Grahame's own life included an extended bachelorhood, a disastrous marriage, and a deep tie to a childhood marked by initial trauma (death of mother, abandonment by father). This life, combined with the era's anxiety over sexual roles, gender possibilities, and the burgeoning women's suffragette movement, provides a context for the novel in which aesthetic identity exploration is, at first, liberating but, by novel's end, must ultimately be managed and controlled. And though controlled, gender remains unstable in this famous children's novel "free of the clash of sex."

The Mole Who Would Be Aesthete

Grahame's characterization of Mole reveals his ambivalences about aestheticism, but he scripts Mole's performances as potentially aesthetic, particularly in the beginning of the novel. Mole's rejection of the utilitarian (cleaning), and embrace of his physical senses in his rambling have all the hallmarks of the aesthete. While Mole does begin the story cleaning his house, "Spring . . . penetrate[es] . . . his dark and lowly little house with its spirit of divine discontent and longing" (9), this spirit of seasonal change, in this description, isn't a gentle reminder: Spring disrupts a commonplace existence seen lacking in inspiration and intensity; nothing short of a change in consciousness is what Mole undergoes.

After Mole escapes this most utilitarian of tasks, he bolts for the river. The narrator comments on Mole's escape in witty, aesthetic fashion: "After all, the best part of a holiday is perhaps not so much to be resting yourself, as to see all the other fellows busy working" (11). Work, and the value of work, both qualities we associate with Victorian utilitarianism, are scorned by the narrator in Mole's initial characterization. Grahame is careful to couch the idea around "holiday," though it smacks of class privilege. In the Victorian era, work and masculinity were intertwined and masculinity was judged by "accumulation and action, self-denial and foresight" (Livesey 109): a holiday would be the only permissible place for Mole to "break free." Mole's escape from the duty of housecleaning can be seen as childish, but it also resonates with the spirit of the aesthetic rejection of the workaday life.

But more indicative of the aesthetic movement, as represented by Wilde and the English aesthetes, is the sensuousness in Grahame's descriptions, especially descriptions of Nature. Nature is Mole's tutor, most specifically in the revelation of its beauty, but only as it is rendered in highly ornamental language. Aestheticism valued art for art's sake, or in this case, nature for art's sake. As Mole escapes the home, "soft breezes caressed his heated brow, and . . . the carol of happy birds fell on his dulled hearing almost like a shout" (10). Mole becomes intoxicated by the river's beauty: "All was a-shake and a-shiver—glints and gleams and sparkles, rustle and swirl, chatter and bubble. The Mole was bewitched, entranced, fascinated" (11). Grahame's descriptions accumulate through sensuous stimuli, word choice, syntax, and punctuation, an accumulation that targets sight and hearing. Mole doesn't just embrace the beauty of nature but, like an aesthete, becomes less manly and more vulnerable to the moment when beauty can offer him the aesthetic experience.

But aestheticism isn't merely concerned with effects generated by sound, color, paint, or word choice. Aestheticism has deep roots in the Enlightenment, and as it was expressed in France, a strong aversion to authoritarianism, especially that of the church. We see a glimpse of such antiauthoritarianism in Mole's refusal to heed the rabbit guards when he begins his rambling. He ignores the authority of the roads, particularly the "elderly rabbit" when he doesn't pay the toll on the "private road" (10). Flouting rules is not only condoned, but seemingly justified in the bliss generated by Mole's sensuous appreciation of nature. Stylistically, Grahame's depictions of Mole's initial epiphanies echo the writing of the French symbolists, whose influence on the Aesthetic Movement occurred indirectly, through Arthur Symons's championing of their work in *The Symbolist Movement in Literature* (1899). Bell-Villada asserts that "the French poets and their allies claimed beauty not as a first step toward anything at all but as a self-contained, all-sufficient, even solipsistic experience" (56). No authority is needed here and Mole's scenes are, literally, self-contained as Grahame removed any authority or companionship from this initial articulation of masculine aestheticism.

We might read Mole as a potential aesthete in his home decorative choices as well. Though aesthetic decoration was popularly signified by japanned woodwork, blue china, stained glass work on doors, and peacock feathers arranged on the walls, these were merely the consumerist images of decorative aestheticism found in *Punch* cartoons, in Wilde witticisms, and in lines of the Gilbert and Sullivan satire, *Patience*. In contrast, Grahame neither satirizes aesthetic design nor signifies commercially recognizable aestheticism in the descriptions of Mole's home.

Throughout the novel, Grahame frequently builds scenes through sensuality and description that are lush rather than minimal. This is the case with Mole's home as well. The domestic interior of Mole's home reveals an attention to artistic design that we don't find in the descriptions of the other three male characters' homes. Mole's house has "a small round pond containing goldfish, . . . surrounded by a cockleshell border. Out of the center of the pond rose a fanciful erection clothed in more cockleshells and topped by a large silvered glass ball . . ." (94). While this bric-a-brac is certainly phallic and suggestive, reminiscent of the verb choice earlier where Spring "penetrates" Mole's home (9), it does not evoke a traditional Victorian masculinity. Instead, it suggests an attention to décor aligned with that of aesthetic masculinity.

Significantly, the narrator describes the interior of Mole's home not at the start of the novel, but only when home and the return to home have become as important as the initial liberation scene. Underlying this conflict about home is Mole's larger conflict between differing constructions of masculinity he might adopt, for the décor within Mole's house points to multiple constructions of masculinity. The "sleeping-bunks in the walls" evoke a traditionally masculine life at sea (95); his "little wooden tables marked with rings that hinted at beer-mugs" (93), with its suggestion of Wilde's famous quote, "work is the curse of the drinking class," also hints at a working-class masculinity. But the "plaster statuary—Garibaldi, and the infant Samuel, and Queen Victoria" (94), as well as the pond and silver ball, point to an aesthetic masculinity seemingly in conflict with the masculinity that his table and sleeping bunks suggest. The conflict in Mole's decorating style points to a larger conflict in Mole: loyalty to masculine heteronormativity in conflict with the intoxicating pull of this new identity, that of the masculine aesthete. The emphases on color, shape, and the reflective glass ball that "reflect[s] everything all wrong . . . [with] a very pleasing effect" (94) parallels the initial sensations and their disorienting effects on Mole in the beginning of the novel.

While plaster statuary may be considered a middle-class interior design choice, Grahame crafts Mole's interior design after a house he had stayed in during his travels in Italy (Green 163). While Badger's home is born of practicality and Rat's house frequently floods and functions as a writer's studio, Mole's house and its mirror ball reflecting "everything all wrong" with "pleasing effect[s]" are modeled on autobiographical aesthetic pretensions: Mole's house is a home where identity is in flux. Mole's dichotomous representation in the novel parallels Grahame's own early adult life. For example, Grahame wrote for both the *National Observer*, under the conservative direction of W. E. Henley, and for *The Yellow Book*, under the more aesthetically minded Henry Harland and Aubrey Beardsley; while working for the Bank of England, Grahame, future secretary, became a member of the Shelley society and acted in its controversial production of *The Cenci*.

Mole's home hints at the conflict in identities that Grahame himself faced. It also demonstrates the Aesthetic creed of living with beauty in one's house for effect. Both Grahame and Mole flirt with aestheticism because it is liberating. For Grahame, aestheticism offered a way to disrupt a solid, middle-class bachelor lifestyle, to test the waters of publication after his father's death. Mole, too, launches into aesthetic, sensuous appreciation of his world after he rejects the utilitarian; not the banking life, but the equally mundane spring cleaning of his divided/conflicted home.

But, I contend, Grahame's embrace of aesthetic masculinity proves only a flirtation. Aesthetic identity is liberating, for both Mole and Grahame, but when it proves too dangerous, both recede or, at the very least, straddle a more middle-class, hegemonic identity. Herbert Sussman's comments about Pater apply equally to Grahame and his creation, Mole; all ultimately feel compelled to bow down to "the Victorian practice of controlling male sexuality within the body armor of gentlemanly reserve so as not to disrupt self and society. . . ." (202). Mole begins the novel without this gentlemanly reserve as Grahame forgets his former occupation and scripts aesthetic epiphanies for Mole, in terms of interactions with nature and the impressions on his senses.

"If You Are to Shine in the High Aesthetic Line": Rat as Aesthete

While Mole is only a potential aesthete, the second character that Grahame introduces has far more direct links to masculine aestheticism. Rat is a writer, composer, bachelor, and, eventually, companion to Mole. His aestheticism is individualistic and centers on the production of literary texts, predominantly songs and poems. Grahame's depiction of Rat draws on key elements of aestheticism as identified by George Landow: self-reflexive mockery, speaking in paradox, refuting middle-class bourgeois values, and flirting with epiphany. Rat's reflexivity and his defense of art for art's sake are visible when he disturbs some baby ducks while they are holding their breath underwater. Rat's play sends the ducks scattering, and he composes a song about them with the key line "Everyone for what he likes!" (28). Freedom and epiphany are bracketed together in Rat's imagining of what the ducks might say about his "Ducks' Ditty": "'*Why* can't fellows be allowed to do what they like *when* they like and *as* they like, instead of other fellows sitting on banks and watching them all the time and making remarks and poetry and things about them? What nonsense it all is!' That's what the ducks say" (29). Grahame manages to channel Wilde in the witty self-referential stance Rat takes, distancing himself from the bourgeois values of sentimentality while revealing the freedom Rat (and the ducks) so desire.

Mole, not yet adept at the facile declarations of the aesthete, mistakenly misreads Rat's assertion, thinking that Rat truly thinks his own production "nonsense." Rat immediately sets him right; his song is not nonsense, but art for art's sake, not for the ducks or any other audience. As Peter Green notes, this scene has a striking literary source: Oscar Wilde's short story, "The Devoted Friend," from *The Happy Prince and Other Tales* (1888). But Green does not explore the connections between the scene and the aestheticism of Wilde's story. In it, an old water-rat claims,

> I know nothing about the feelings of parents . . . I am not a family man. In fact, I have never been married, and I never intend to be. Love is all very well in its way, but friendship is much higher. Indeed, I know of nothing in the world that is either nobler or rarer than a devoted friendship. (341)

Both Grahame's Rat and Wilde's water-rat challenge the communality that the ducks represent. Both characters have no family and are thus freer to satirize heteronormativity (marriage and group behavior). Each water-rat makes an "Other" of the ducks and their group behavior: in both stories each stands outside the ducks' communal and, arguably, hegemonic organization, waxing poetic on individual choice (in Grahame's case) and on egotistical devotion (in Wilde's story). Grahame's Rat demonstrates, like Wilde's early creation, that bachelorhood can produce an aesthetic character whose responses to community and societal rules are subversive.

We might also consider the relationship that develops between Mole and Rat as indicative of both aestheticism and the changing nature of masculinity in the period. Bachelorhood had changed by the beginning of the twentieth century. As John Tosh remarks,

> Bachelorhood and club or college life might be not merely a refuge from domesticity, but an alternative emotional resource. Among the more literary, this aspiration was expressed in a self-conscious "Uranian" ideal—an attraction to younger men which was erotic in character though seldom given full sexual expression. (185)

Mole follows Rat in an exploration of the river and country environs as well as in their newfound companionship and looks to Rat as a mentor in many ways. This Uranianism is most evident in "The Open Road" chapter. Here, Toad is fixed on caravanning across the countryside with Rat and Mole in tow. As Toad falls asleep, we witness the intimacy of the relationship between the two new friends:

> The Mole reached out from under his blanket, felt for the Rat's paw in the darkness, and gave it a squeeze. "I'll do whatever you like, Ratty," he whispered. "Shall we run away tomorrow morning, quite early—very early—and go back to our dear old hole on the river?" (37)

While there is no direct erotic dimension to this scene, Grahame certainly depicts a male-male friendship as providing an "alternative emotional resource" for the two animals. Rat serves not only as Mole's guide throughout the first part of the novel but also as his emotional partner.

Rat, like Mole, also experiences individual aesthetic emotions, particularly in the form of aesthetic epiphany. Mole certainly has his moments, but Rat's epiphanies are more literary, more highly concentrated, and intensely psychological. When Rat meets Pan in the "Piper at the Gates of Dawn" chapter, he is "[r]apt, transported . . . possessed in all his sense by this new divine thing that caught up his helpless soul and swung and dangled it, a powerless but happy infant, in a strong sustaining grasp" (132). Similarly, when Rat is stopped from leaving the River Bank with the Sea Rat, he experiences a complete breakdown. He tries to explain his visions to Mole, but "how could he put into words what had mostly been suggestion? How recall . . . the haunting

sea voices . . . ?" (182). Both of these scenes depict Rat's aesthetic responses to external stimuli.

While Richard Gillin has assessed the influence of Keats, Wordsworth, and Shelley in various aesthetic utterances of Rat, an analysis of
the language used in these scenes also reveals a fundamental interest in
how Rat processes these intense artistic and psychological experiences
that connect his epiphanies to the aesthetic. In Grahame's description of
Rat's reactions to Pan and to the Sea Rat, Grahame alternates between
a gothic sensibility, psychological realism, and childish enthusiasm.
But the epiphanies, language, and concentrated scenes are indicative
of aesthetic literary techniques such as those found in Wilde's *The Picture of Dorian Gray* or *A House of Pomegranates*, both of which include
many instances of characters experiencing epiphanies in psychologically
complex language similar to the language used by Grahame in Mole
and Rat's transformative scenes. For example, when Rat listens to the
Sea Rat, Rat is "spell bound and quivering" (177), "compelled . . . body
and soul" (178), "paralyzed and staring" (180); when Mole tries to stop
Rat's sea journey, he "look[ed] into [Rat's] eyes and saw that they were
glazed and set and turned a streaked and shifting gray—not his friend's
eyes, but the eyes of some other animal" (181). While Rat recovers from
each incident, the dreams he undergoes and the language he uses to
describe them recall similar words from an 1869 *Art Journal* review of
the paintings of Edward Burne-Jones: "This art . . . belongs to the realm
of dreams, nightmares, and other phantasms of diseased imagination"
(qtd. in Lambourne 92). Rat recovers from his aesthetic epiphanies, but
we can see how Grahame reins in excess through the help of friendship.
Perhaps an aesthete doesn't need another aesthete, Grahame suggests,
but a companion. For it is noteworthy that unlike, say Wilde, Grahame's
two principal characters aren't merely loners with tastes for good conversation, bon mots, or selfish scandals.

Ancestry Makes the Man:
Toad and His Aesthetic Excesses

While Grahame's Rat has its literary antecedents in the writing of Oscar
Wilde, Toad is the character who most often comes to mind when critics
look for Wildean influences in Grahame's novel. As Green argues, Gra-

hame's depiction of the ebullient, flamboyant, rule-breaking Toad can be read as a reflection or transmutation of Wilde into animal form (166, 284). While Rat serves as a depiction of the positive potential of masculine aestheticism, Toad emerges as a negative model of the aesthete, one far closer to the model of the dangerous and denigrated Wilde.

A Wildean flouting of the rules is evident in Toad's behavior and adventures. Under the spell of mechanization and progress (in the motoring scenes), Toad invokes class privilege and license. His actions are as excessive as is his dialogue, but Toad knows he will be forgiven for his excesses and will have a housekeeper to make his food and servants to look after him when he returns from his escapades, the same way his semi-aesthetic posturing is ignored or endured. His leisure allows him to be excessive, and Grahame "swells" Toad in excess: the law only holds for Toad when he recklessly endangers others and violates Grahame's idyllic River Bank with the automobile.

Another less obvious aspect of Grahame's critique of the aesthete is through his depiction of clothing. Clothing and the Aesthetic Movement as tied to Wilde and the dandy become synonymous with a masculinity that is too effeminate and too ineffectual for Grahame. Wilde was famous for his knee breeches, hat, and velvet jackets. He knew that clothing becomes a prop in the overall scheme of the aesthete. Wilde once famously changed into a suit after learning an audience of knee-breeched and smoking jacketed undergraduates awaited him. The loose fitting, flowing jackets stood in opposition to the stiff coats and waistcoats of the Victorian age. In essence, loose clothing insured freer movement, which aesthetes argued would be less constrictive and healthier than the clothing norms of the Victorians; a healthy body was a beautiful body. Much of Wilde's fashion included a "retro" look, favoring the seventeenth- and eighteenth-century styles of dress. As Wilde wrote, "One should either be a work of art, or wear a work of art" ("Phrases" 572). Both before and after his trial, dandy or aesthetic dress was cause for concern for both men and women: men as too effeminate and women as too loose (symbolically as well as physically). Grahame condemns Toad for his costumes in the novel and supports the simple dress of Rat, Mole, and Badger, thus reinforcing the heternormative, middle-class norm.

Like Wilde, Grahame makes costume part of aesthetic play or exploration. But in the case of Toad, Grahame includes moments of costumed aesthetic performance only to criticize them. When Badger and friends come to "take Toad in hand," the narrator describes Toad's costume in detail: "Mr. Toad, arrayed in goggles, cap, gaiters, and enormous overcoat, came swaggering down the steps, drawing on his gauntleted gloves" (108). Recognizing how Toad's costume gives authority to his performance as a man of the road, Badger immediately orders Toad to "take those ridiculous things off" (109). Once Rat and Mole enforce Badger's order, the performance can no longer be sustained: "A good deal of his [Toad's] blustering spirit seemed to have evaporated with the removal of his fine panoply. Now . . . he was merely Toad, and no longer the Terror of the Highway . . ." (109). In a real sense, Toad's costume is part of his identity and his power. When he loses these, he becomes muted, censured by the hegemonic force (in this case, Grahame's pen) that seeks to have him consolidate his identity as the landed gentleman he was born as and not the aesthete he could become. But criticism of aestheticism was part and parcel of British literary aestheticism. As British aesthetes developed a look and demeanor that the public came to understand and recognize, so they became ripe for caricature. Gilbert and Sullivan, Max Beerbohm, and others mocked the pretentious dress and affected mannerisms of British aesthetes to great effect in their plays and cartoons.

Toad's behavior could surely have been a target of such satire, particularly his urban aesthete's attitude toward nature. Oscar Wilde famously dismissed nature, particularly as it had been co-opted by the Romantics, as overly sentimentalized. In Wilde's "The Decay of Lying," we learn the aesthete's take on nature: "At twilight nature becomes a wonderfully suggestive effect, and is not without loveliness, though perhaps its chief use is to illustrate quotations from the poets" (943). Toad waxes poetic about the countryside to Mole and Rat, but in a way far different from that of Rat or Mole. He focuses not on its beauty but on how it affects him and his own imaginative possibilities. Despite his poetic outbursts, Toad finds little pleasure in the actuality of camping; he sleeps in after the first night of caravanning and has to be forced to do the chores required of one living in the midst of nature. When the motorcar appears, enraptures Toad, and renders the cart inoperable, we begin to see Grahame's subtle critique of the aesthete's dismissal of nature and embrace of the urban. The city as it invades the country (in the form of the motorcar) is problematic for Grahame; the aesthete, as linked to urbanization, is problematic for Grahame as well. Instead of someone invested in nature, Toad proves to be a faddist, someone who picks up whimsical hobbies, clothing styles, artistic tastes, and outdoor activities associated with aesthetic performance rather than with lasting belief.

I resist categorizing Toad's adventures as aesthetic performances. These mini-adventures are interesting to examine in terms of gender performance (cross-dressing, misogyny, and class bias), but the adventures, particularly the mock-heroic language, evoke the picaresque tradition more than the aesthetic. Toad rambles only to be subverted at the end of the story to set up Grahame's rushed conclusion, which preserves the established social hierarchy in rural England at the turn of the century. The adventure in the aesthete's hands draws on the psychological or ornamental qualities of language, realizations, and development. Toad's adventures are zany rather than illustrative of aesthetic values. We might remember that when Milne adapted the story for the stage, he focused on Toad's adventures, titling the production, "Toad of Toad Hall."

However, there are elements of his performance that do seem to be born of the fin-de-siècle spirit. Toad's self-aggrandizement and self-celebration in song have aesthetic literary antecedents. As discussed earlier, parodies of aesthetes were so enshrined in the culture that Wilde's visit to America at the end of the nineteenth century was supported by Richard D'Oyly Carte, partner with Gilbert and Sullivan, to promote *Patience, or Bunthorne's Bride*, their satiric opera critiquing the aesthetic movement of the 1870s and 1880s. Grahame scripts Toad like Gilbert and Sullivan script Bunthorne: a self-reflexive parody of the aesthete. Toad, dropping his greatest hint of being based on Oscar Wilde, confesses "I've been told I ought to have a salon, whatever that may be" (226). Salons, while famous in Europe and England before Wilde, were places where ideas were exchanged. Another example of delicious self-referentiality is Toad's song, in the third person, as he celebrates his adventures: "The word has held great Heroes,/as history books have showed;/But never a name to go down to fame/Compared with that of Toad" (200–201). If we consider the mantra "Life should imitate art" (Wilde, "Decay" 943) as central to aesthetic thinking, then Toad's penchant for invented stories also qualifies him as a first-rate aesthete:

> . . . Toad, with no one to check his statements or to criticize in an un-friendly spirit, rather let himself go. Indeed, much that he related belonged more properly to the category of what-might-have-happened-had-I-only-thought-of-it-in-time-instead-of-ten-minutes-afterwards. Those are always the best and raciest adventures; and why should they not be truly ours as much as the somewhat inadequate things that really come off? (233)

Grahame grants Toad license in the beginning of the novel, adorning him with some of the more extravagant characteristics of the aesthete. His verbal performances recall Wilde directly and indirectly and invoke the spirit of aestheticism. But Toad's aesthetic performances soon become suspect, and must be tempered, as I will discuss later in this essay.

A Divide Revealed: Mole's Partial Embrace of Masculine Aestheticism

With two examples of masculine aestheticism before him, Mole embraces aestheticism in many instances of the story. For example, his clothing choice is more urban and aesthete-like than would be expected. Rat declares to Mole while on the river, "I like your clothes awfully, old chap. . . . I'm going to get a black velvet smoking suit myself some day. . . ." (15). Mole, thus, is clothed in one of the most memorable of aesthetic garments, the smoking jacket; Grahame relocates the aesthete's urban clothing to the countryside. Grahame brings that urban cliché, "clothes make the man," to the country and, further, to the children's novel, where masculinity has many jackets.

Though he may dress like an aesthete, Mole's embrace of aestheticism is limited. Rat and Mole may be companions, but Grahame is careful to show that while Rat is an aesthete, Mole has his doubts. After Rat composes his poem to the ducks ("Ducks' Ditty"), Mole's response is hardly that of the aesthete: "'I don't know that I think so *very* much of that little song, Rat,' observed the Mole cautiously. He was no poet himself and didn't care who knew it; and he had a candid nature" (29). Mole's reaction is an indication of the character type Grahame uses in the novel: Mole is obvious and less prone to artifice than Rat. Mole rejects Rat's song in a typical, bourgeois manner. As Tess Cosslett asserts, "Grahame's characters represent a particular social hierarchy. Badger is the Squire, Toad the aristocrat, though also with a hint of the *nouveau riche*, Rat the leisured upper-middle-class gentleman, Mole a shabby-genteel Pooterish clerk, or a grammar-school boy" (178). Cosslett's categorization would be consistent with the commercial and even academic characterization of the aesthete as urban, witty, and middle to upper class. Mole, in Grahame's scheme, can't possibly be an aesthete. He may have pretensions or fall under its spell, but (forgive the pun) he is more grounded and reflects the prejudices of his class (if we agree with Cosslett's identification). Mole is a companion to the aesthetic Rat, but his companionship doesn't mean he will completely embrace that identity.

We see a similar character differentiation in the chapter "The Piper at the Gates of Dawn." Rat's appreciation of the moonlit boat ride as they look for Portly is full of sensuous appreciation: "The merry bubble and joy, the thin, clear, happy call of the distant piping! Such music I never dreamed of, and the call in it is even stronger than the music is sweet! Row on, Mole, row! For the music and the call must be for us" (131). We can contrast this with Mole's reaction: "I hear nothing myself . . . but the wind playing in the reeds and rushes and osiers" (131–32). Rat exclaims, "'This the place of my song-dream, the place the music played to me' . . . as if in a trance" (134). Rat's response hints at the influence of the French Symbolists on English Aestheticism. Both Mallarmé and Verlaine looked to synthesize music and poetry in frequently unidentifiable landscapes. I am not saying that the Pan episode is an intertextual allusion to these poets; rather I am suggesting that the music, as it calls to Rat (and not Mole) helps to clearly mark their differences, as true aesthete and aesthete sympathizer. As Verlaine writes in his poem "Art poetique," "Music above all else,/And for this prefer the Uneven/More Vague and more soluble in air,/Without anything in it which weight or which poses" (qtd. in Chai 29). Verlaine's verse and Rat's experience are musical and aesthetic at the expense of reason and rationality: an effect rendered by Verlaine and experienced by Rat.

We can contrast Rat's response to Mole's. Although Mole feels a "great Awe," his awe makes him feel "wonderfully at peace and happy"; Rat's emotions are far more extreme: Rat is "cowed, stricken, and trembling violently" (134). Significantly, it is through the eyes of Mole, rather than Rat, that the reader sees Pan:

> [Mole] . . . raised his humble head; and then, in that utter clearness of the innocent dawn, while Nature, flushed with fullness of incredible color, seemed to hold her breath for the event, he looked in the very eyes of the Friend and Helper; saw the backward sweep of the curved horns, gleaming in the growing daylight; . . . saw the rippling muscles on the arm that lay across the broad chest, the long supple hand still holding the pan-pipes. . . . All this he saw, for one moment, breathless and intense. . . . (134–35)

Grahame's Pan isn't the hedonistic deity of nature. As John David Moore suggests,

> [Pan] seems really to belong with Mole's collection of plaster garden statuary. This is a Pan made safe for a middle-class Arcadia, where instinct is equivalent to decorum and custom. As the genius of Grahame's suburban, sexless garden, Pan appears as a castrated Priapus. He is the god of nature certainly, but not nature red in tooth and claw. He is the Pan of the fin-de-siècle aesthetic paganism, though much tamer than anything in Beardsley or even Swinburne. As an aesthetic version of the goat god, this Pan finally does fit into the middle-class menagerie of well-dressed animals; the ideal Arcadian aesthete is not merely half man, half animal, but half animal, half aging dandy. (58)

Moore claims that Grahame is "aesthetic-light," in his portrayal of the Pan figure, but he does not mention that the Pan we see is the Pan that Mole sees. In contrast to Mole's description and emotional reaction, the sentiments expressed by Rat are anything but contained. Grahame uses Mole as the filter for Pan's presence because he isn't a convert to the aesthetic life: his intense moments of psychological epiphany have already been experienced. Grahame was all too aware of what happened when lines were crossed; a fully decadent Pan was too challenging to post-Wildean readers. Grahame also chooses to make Pan a natural presence rather than the aesthetic icon, perhaps to illustrate the disparate reactions from Mole and Rat.

Even as they collect themselves after their encounter with the god, the differences between Rat and Mole are striking: Rat lingers by the footprints while Mole hurries him to take the now recovered child Portly back to Otter and his wife. We see that Mole is as physically vulnerable to the aesthetic moment as is the more firmly entrenched aesthetic character, Rat. But surely he is less emotionally open to it, or at least less extreme in his emotional response. Grahame resurrects aestheticism in this scene, but Rat's emotional response suggests why Grahame chooses to have both characters washed by forgetfulness; the extreme emotion promised by a full embrace of aesthetic epiphanies proves too dangerous for Grahame to embrace wholeheartedly.

Perhaps most revealing of Mole's difference from Rat and Mole's rejection of the extremes of aesthetic epiphany is a scene at the end of the "Wayfarers All" chapter. The Sea Rat, invoking yet another emotional epiphany in Rat, suggests that Rat join him in traveling the world. Mole witnesses the problems with epiphanies gone too far: "Mole . . . placed himself in front of [Rat], and looking into his eyes saw that they were glazed and set and turned a streaked and shifting gray—not his friend's eyes, but the eyes of some other animal" (181). Grahame rejects not the epiphanies themselves, but rather aesthetic reactions to them that he finds extreme (i.e., Rat's sudden shifts in personality); such exaggerated responses to epiphanies suggest an underlying unbalance in character.

But Mole does not reject aestheticism altogether. English Aestheticism included a recognition that art and beauty, including literature, exist for their own sake. Mole may not write poetry, but he is a natural storyteller who doesn't imbue his story with heavy-handed morals or ethics:

> Casually, then, and with seeming indifference, the Mole turned his talk to the harvest that was being gathered in, the towering wagons and their straining teams, the growing ricks, and the large moon rising over bare acres dotted with sheaves. He talked of the reddening apples around, of the browning nuts, of jams and preserves and the distilling of cordials; till by easy stages such as these he reached midwinter, its hearty joys and its snug home life, and then he became simply lyrical. (183)

We see, again, two sides to Mole. He may certainly be influenced by aestheticism, particularly through his companion Rat, who has taught him the ways of the River in such lyrical language that Mole now draws on such language in his own story. But after the colors, shapes, moons, and various sundries of the harvest, Mole turns away from celebrating beauty to celebrating the sentimental and the home. His partial embrace of aestheticism, thus, is revealed as a more tempered approach to adventure, aesthetic inspiration, and alternative versions of domesticity than a full embrace of aestheticism would allow. He is, after all, trying to bring Rat back (home) from his "Wayfarers All" spell.

Again, Eve Sedgwick's work in *Between Men*, particularly her concept of male homosocial desire and the structural relations between men, is a useful paradigm when considering the relationship between Mole and Rat. Sedgwick illuminates René Discard's erotic triangles in her discussion of male-male bonds in heteronormative love triangles, but we might consider just such a geometry when we think of aestheticism and the bonding between Mole and Rat (Sedgwick 21). Mole "steals" Rat back from the Sea Rat, revealing both a desire and a bond more significant than the "imaginary" bond of the adventure story tradition represented by the Sea Rat. In other words, bonds of aesthetic homosociality trump antiquated modes of masculinity. And is it significant that Mole finishes his story and Grahame ends the chapter with Rat encouraged to start writing poetry again: Rat as aesthete, Mole as the aesthete's companion? One full aesthete in the room is enough, Grahame seems to suggest; if more than one man fully embraces aesthetic masculinity, then the threat of homosexuality cannot successfully be contained.

Aestheticism Taken in Hand:
Badger and the Heteronormative Force

Even Mole's partial embrace of aestheticism proves problematic when class threats emerge. Many critics have written about Toad's containment by the heteronormative Badger by novel's end. But Rat, too, comes in for his own denigration at Badger's hands. While Rat emerges as a positive masculine aesthete in an overall analysis of the story, even he must be tempered and constrained in the face of class warfare. Effeminacy is problematic, poets are potential problems: Enter the Badger.

As the novel progresses, aestheticism and performances imbued with characteristics of the Aesthetic Movement become suspect and have to be controlled—both Mole's identity and Toad's social position and home are at stake. Aestheticism becomes a victim of the "hermeneutics of suspicion" that surrounded Victorian ideas about codifying heteronormative masculinity (Adams 227). In light of Wilde's trial (and Grahame's temperament), Grahame censors aestheticism both through his plotting and through Badger's suspicion and judgments. Lois Kuznets sees Grahame's conversion as part of a wider reaction to the Wilde trial:

> After the trial and imprisonment of Oscar Wilde for homosexuality . . . Grahame moved away from this group [aesthetes] as did many others, since it [an art for art's sake posture] was obviously associated with a like "decadence" in the minds of the public at least. (*Kenneth Grahame* 10)

The novel begins in freedom and exploration of identities and personalities. But in the final two chapters, "Like Summer Tempests Came His Tears" and "The Return of Ulysses," Grahame reins in these initial explorations in aesthetic masculine identity.

Noticeable in the plotting of the novel is the absence of Badger from the beginning of the text. As Mole escapes his house, his flirtation with aestheticism or, at the very least, his companionship with the aesthete character in the novel, Rat, is given free rein. Badger is a corrective to both Mole's initial characterization and Rat's aestheticism.

Badger has been categorized as the squire figure in the novel (Cosslett 178) and he uses his authority to limit the influence of Rat, most particularly, on Mole. We first see this when Mole and Rat find Badger's house after they get lost in the Wild Wood. Badger buddies up to Mole and assumes a relationship with him: "When lunch is over . . . I'll take you all around this little place of mine. I can see you'll appreciate it. You understand what domestic architecture ought to be, you do" (78). Badger assumes that Mole will appreciate his excavated passageways of rooms and tunnels, that they will share the same taste in domestic architecture. Yet as we have seen, Mole's decorative interior (his choice of statuaries and that silver, reflective ball) suggests that while he may be a burrowing creature, he also has aesthetic inclinations. Badger's house demonstrates little appreciation for aesthetic décor; it is founded on provision and practicality, a utilitarian approach quite at odds with the aesthetic outlook. Mole's house, in contrast, reflects a character who is more imaginative, romantic, and given to dreaming and temptation. Badger enters the story as a potential mentor figure for Mole, a rival to the aesthetic mentor, Rat.

Badger attempts to replace Rat in a revision of the Uranian relationship, one in which the homoerotic relationship between Mole and Rat is replaced by a father/son bond. When Rat takes Mole under his wing, their mutual attraction illustrates what Grahame may have seen as the benefits of an all-male society and what young male students, like Oscar Wilde, inherited from the all male, homoerotic culture at Oxford. But it also suggests something less appealing to Grahame; as Naomi Wood asserts, innocence and pederasty were partners, philosophically, at Wilde's Oxford and in the late nineteenth century:

> Not only was classical imprimatur given to pederasty, but the epoch was already infatuated with the idea of childhood. Inheritors of a Wordsworthian Romantic tradition that privileged childhood over adulthood and innocence over experience, fin-de-siècle authors produced a newly sensual Romantic child through books directed toward children and about them, resulting in the "Golden Age of Children's Literature." (159)

I might add to Wood's assertion that it is this very innocence that gives license to the range of gender performances, including homosocial "chums." By introducing Badger as a corrective or alternate mentor figure, Grahame revises the Uranian ideal to allay the possible fears of his middle-class reading audience that a poet might be the sole influence on his principal character.

Badger also allays the fears of this audience through his regulation of Toad. As James Eli Adams remarks, "'Manliness' is exemplary of all gender norms in being always under pressure from the very social dynamics that authorize it, the changing consolidation of social authority through new varieties of suspicion, exclusion, and affirmation" (19). Badger functions in the novel as an embodiment of the pressure placed upon aesthetic masculinity in his use of "suspicion, exclusion, and affirmation." For example, he uses guilt and shame to remind Toad of his father (a minimal presence in the novel, but a significant one in constructing Toad's sense of masculinity). As Badger reveals the secret underground passage through which the characters will retake Toad Hall, he invokes Toad's father and the patriarchal relationship, placing himself in the role of surrogate father:

> My young friend [Toad] . . . your father, who was a worthy animal—a lot worthier than some others I know—was a particular friend of mine, and told me a great deal he wouldn't have dreamed of telling you. . . ."Don't let my son know about it," he said. "He's a good boy, but very light and volatile in character, and simply cannot hold his tongue. If he's ever in a real fix . . . you may tell him." (225–26)

Badger criticizes or compliments Toad (depending on his behavior and how that behavior conforms to the group norm), and polices Toad "under severe compulsion" to repay the barge-woman for her horse (253). Badger assumes the role of father to counter Toad's egotistical aestheticism (speeches, songs about retaking Toad Hall). He counters the Wildean character of Toad and restores him to his rural gentleman status through this constrictive, paternal influence.

But policing Toad isn't enough; during this time of class threat, Badger also feels compelled to check the aesthetic tendencies of even the less threatening Rat. One of Badger's heteronormative reactions to aestheticism is the rejection of language performances and those who use language outside of communication. For example, when Toad rashly tells the group they should "learn" the weasels and stoats about class order, Rat corrects his use of English. Badger defends Toad (a rarity in the novel): "What are you always nagging at Toad for? What's the matter with his English? It's the same what I use myself, and if it's good enough for me, it ought to be good enough for you!" (229). Badger censures Rat because he corrects Toad's vernacular language, shed of all ornament, for it has functioned in its communicative purpose. Rat's correction is linked to his use of language: he is suspect because he is a poet and these characters are preparing for a battle, an endeavor that demands a far different construction of the masculine. As Leo Braudy contends,

> War on the horizon [provoked] the need to purge the national body of those who were perceived as less than men or as men of the wrong kind. . . . [Such purging] picked up speed and urgency in the 1890s and as

the century turned. Pervading the atmosphere was a greater hostility to whatever was different. . . . (354)

In other words, Rat's correction of Toad's language is different from Badger's norm: Rat is perceived as the wrong kind, thus allowing Badger to attack Rat as an aesthete. It opens the door for censure of not only what is different, but what is perceived as dangerous: effeminate masculinity overly concerned with language and not dedicated to Badger's norm-centered call to arms to reestablish the hierarchy.

Judith Butler, reading Simone de Beauvoir, sees functionality in this type of censure: "presumptive heterosexuality . . . functions within discourse to communicate a threat . . ." (147). Rat's abilities with language are the threat, not language itself. Toad is brought under control by the group, barely, and his threat with language is nullified by the group when he is given, effectively, a gag order for the celebration party. It is worth remembering that he has to be sequestered, punished, and subdued several times at the end of the novel (sending out inflated invitations for the banquet, told not to give a speech, etc.), yet he still sings a song to himself before he has to face the banquet. Thus Toad's and Rat's use of language is a threat to a character like Badger and the presumptive heteronormativity that Badger represents.

Badger tempers the power of the aesthete in more direct speech at the end of the novel. When Badger sends Mole on reconnaissance (in front of the other characters), he effectively stereotypes Rat as a subversive artist: "I wouldn't trouble you [Mole, to fulfill this duty]. Only I know I can trust you to see a thing done, and I wish I could say the same of everyone I know. I'd send the Rat, if he wasn't a poet" (242). Badger effectively condemns the aesthete as ineffectual in warfare and, more seriously, unreliable. And in this rebuke, we see the spirit of the times. Green recalls W. F. Barry's article on neo-paganism in the *Quarterly Review* as an attack on "the effeminacy and hedonism which characterized neo-pagan behavior, attributing it to sixty years of peace, idleness, and over-education" (139). When critics speak of the crisis of masculinity at the end of the nineteenth century, we can see how an artistic and social movement (aestheticism), combined with the social and political unrest of the fin-de-siècle, became a natural scapegoat. It is no accident that the book ends with the class system restored rather than two men/boy/animals in front of Pan.

As a result of Badger's policing of both Toad and Rat, Mole changes over the last two chapters of the novel. He helps defend Toad Hall, unsuccessfully, with Badger while Toad is in prison/escaping, while Rat is left in his house, seemingly unfit for such activity (though we might remember the beginning of the novel where he has guns and cudgels in the Wild Wood, giving Mole comfort and security). In contrast to his denigration of Toad, Badger heaps praise on Mole for his reconnaissance and martial skills during the retaking of Toad Hall. And he separates Mole from Rat (or at least, from the masculinity Rat embodies) through his attacks on Rat's aesthetic actions and character. By novel's end, then, Mole's partial embrace of aesthetic masculinity is tempered even further, until a reader could be forgiven for forgetting that Mole's dalliance with aestheticism had even occurred.

Conclusion

In his study of masculinity and war, Braudy contends that

> throughout history the definitions of "man," "manly," and "masculinity" have shifted in response to the prevailing social and cultural demands. Ideals, aspirations, and assumptions, conscious or not, are as much part of reality as physiology—and often, the less understood they are, the stronger their influence. Instead of being a monolith, the mythical, patriarchal society in which men enjoyed total power was a constantly mutating background, sometimes crisscrossed with sweeping changes and counterchanges, sometimes dug into fixed positions with each square yard fought over ferociously. (xiii)

Kenneth Grahame demonstrates that gender wasn't as fixed as his middle-class, Edwardian audience might have imagined. In many ways, Mole and Rat can be seen following the biographical arc of Wordsworth and Coleridge: they begin in revolution and end in compromise. In terms of a monolithic view of gender as envisioned by the Victorians, Grahame avoids this gender battle, even indulging in freedom for his male characters, before capitulating in the end. Because the novel ends so suddenly, it is problematic to assume that this is Grahame's final stance on aesthetic masculinity, or that Badger's stance mirrors popular opinion surrounding aestheticism. Grahame's investment in aestheticism may be linked to the restraint that characterized Grahame's own life:

> The story [*Wind*] is also perhaps, at a deeper level, the cry of the repressed hedonist, who in his fantasy allows his instincts to run wild, only to demonstrate, as much to himself as to others, how vital it is that reckless self-expression be reined in. (Watts 182)

Aestheticism definitely has its place in *The Wind in the Willows*. We see its influence in the emotional and psychological moments that Mole and Rat enjoy and endure in their interactions with nature, and in the imagery that Grahame uses to describe the effects of these epiphanies on their senses. The antiauthoritarian scenes, particularly those at the beginning of the novel, echo the rebellious spirit of aestheticism. Grahame celebrates the aesthetic spirit—as long as it is exploratory and as long as it is contained. But the influence of the aesthete is constantly guarded against, particularly through the character of Badger.

Badger's resistance to Rat and Toad becomes a resistance not only to impulse and impetuosity but also to aestheticism: they are both specifically censored because of their aesthetic identification (Rat) or in fear of their aesthetic performance (Toad). Grahame resurrects aestheticism but, by novel's end, represents it as dubious and problematic when placed next to the imperative of maintaining social order. And historical context gives us reasons why Grahame plots his novel to match ambivalence about aestheticism. As William Greenslade argues,

> The late Victorian establishment and the propertied classes generally harboured anxieties about poverty and crime, about public health and national and imperial fitness, about decadent artists, "new women" and homosexuals. The loose assemblage of beliefs can be marked out as "degenerationism." . . . (2)

This degenerationism provokes Grahame to plot his novel so as to allow for what I will term "situational aestheticism": as long as the aestheticism doesn't interfere with the business and order of the country, men may do as they like. If we read against the ending of the novel, the reader can see a space for a different, non-normative type of masculinity in the Edwardian age. Because, after all, while the "friends stroll together in the Wild Wood" in the book's final pages, we can assume that, the threat of class uprising averted, Rat will still be allowed to be Rat, Mole and Rat will still live in a same-sex companionship at the end of the novel (Rat as poet, Mole as devoted friend), and Toad has not sung his "Last Little Song" but will wait for a lifting of the heteronormative code (253). World War I will, of course, leave Britain morally decimated, and the modernist movement will usurp and expand literary techniques and versions of masculinity. But we will always have this curious novel, *The Wind in the Willows*, in which boys/men/animals flirt with one literary context, aestheticism, in a liminal period of British history, the Edwardian age, in both liberating and constrictive ways.

Notes

1. For a discussion of masculinity in Grahame's "The Reluctant Dragon," see Schwab.

Works Cited

Adams, James Eli. *Dandies and Desert Saints: Styles of Victorian Masculinity.* Ithaca: Cornell UP, 1995.

Bell-Villada, Gene. *Art for Art's Sake and Literary Life: How Politics and Markets Helped Shape the Ideology & Culture of Aestheticism 1790–1990.* Lincoln: U of Nebraska P, 1996.

Braudy, Leo. *From Chivalry to Terrorism: War and the Changing Nature of Masculinity.* New York: Knopf, 2003.

Butler, Judith. *Gender Trouble.* London: Routledge, 1990.

Chai, Leon. *Aestheticism: The Religion of Art in Post-Romantic Literature.* New York: Columbia UP, 1990.

Cosslett, Tess. "Child's Place in Nature: Talking Animals in Victorian Children's Fiction." *Nineteenth-Century Contexts* 23 (2001): 475–95.

Gillin, Richard. "Romantic Echoes in the Willows." *Children's Literature* 16 (1988): 169–75.

Grahame, Kenneth. *The Wind in the Willows.* 1908. New York: Tempo Books, 1966.

Green, Peter. *Kenneth Grahame: 1859–1932: A Study of His Life, Work and Times.* London: John Murray, 1959.

Greenslade, William. *Degeneration, Culture and the Novel: 1880–1940*. Cambridge: Cambridge UP, 1994.

Kent, Susan Kingsley. *Gender and Power in Britain, 1640–1990*. London: Routledge, 1999.

Kuznets, Lois R. *Kenneth Grahame*. Boston: Hall, 1987.

———. "Kenneth Grahame and Father Nature, or Whither Blows *The Wind in the Willows*." *Children's Literature* 16 (1998): 175–85.

Lambourne, Lionel. *The Aesthetic Movement*. New York: Phaidon Press, 1996.

Landow, George. "Aesthetes and Decadents of the 1890s—Points of Departure." *The Victorian Web*. 17 Sept. 2002. Web. 22 Nov. 2008. http://www.victorianweb.org/decadence/decadence.html>.

Livesey, Ruth. *Socialism, Sex, and the Culture of Aestheticism in Britain, 1880–1914*. New York: Oxford UP, 2007.

Marshall, Cynthia. "Bodies and Pleasures in *The Wind in the Willows*." *Children's Literature* 22 (1994): 58–69.

Moore, John David. "Pottering about in the Garden: Kenneth Grahame's Version of the Pastoral in *The Wind in the Willows*." *The Journal of the Midwest Modern Language Association* (1990): 45–60.

Pater, Walter. *Renaissance: Studies in Art and Poetry*. Oxford: Oxford UP, 1998.

Poss, Geraldine. "An Epic in Arcadia: The Pastoral World of *The Wind in the Willows*." *Children's Literature* 4 (1975): 80–90.

Schwab, Sandra Martina. "What is a Man? The Refuting of the Chivalric Ideal at the Turn of the Century." *Beyond Arthurian Romances: The Reach of Victorian Medievalism*. Ed. Loretta M. Holloway and Jennifer A. Palmgren. New York: Palgrave MacMillan, 2005. 217–31.

Sedgwick, Eve Kosofsky. *Between Men: English Literature and Male Homosocial Desire*. New York: Columbia UP, 1985.

———. *Epistemology of the Closet*. Berkeley: University of California Press, 1990.

Sussman, Herbert. *Victorian Masculinities: Manhood and Masculine Poetics in Early Victorian Literature and Art*. Cambridge: Cambridge UP, 1995.

Tosh, John. *A Man's Place: Masculinity and the Middle Class Home in Victorian England*. New Haven: Yale UP, 1999.

Watts, Marilyn, ed. *My Dearest Mouse: The Wind in the Willows Letters by Kenneth Grahame*. London: Pavilion, 1988.

Wilde, Oscar. "The Decay of Lying." *The Collected Works of Oscar Wilde*. Hertfordshire: Wordsworth Editions, 1997. 919–43.

———. "The Devoted Friend." *The Collected Works of Oscar Wilde*. Hertfordshire: Wordsworth Editions, 1997. 339–49.

————. "Phrases and Philosophies for the Use of the Young." *Oscar Wilde: The Major Works*. Ed. Isobel Murray. Oxford: Oxford UP, 2000. 572–73.

Wood, Naomi. "Creating the Sensual Child: Paterian Aesthetics, Pederasty, and Oscar Wilde's Fairy Tales." *Marvels & Tales: Journal of Fairy-Tale Studies* 16 (2002): 156–70.

PART III

BEYOND THE TEXT

CHAPTER NINE

The Wind Blows to the East: On Chinese Translations of Kenneth Grahame's *The Wind in the Willows*

Shu-Fang Lai

Arthur Ransome's often-quoted negative review of Kenneth Grahame's *The Wind in the Willows* ends by saying, "[i]f we judge the book by its aim, it is a failure, like a speech to Hottentots made in Chinese. And yet, for the Chinese, if by any accident there should happen to be one or two of them among the audience, the speech might be quite a success" (Ransome 190). Writing in 1909, Ransome could not have imagined that one day not just one or two, but a great many Chinese-speaking readers young and old (including myself at seven years old), would read and enjoy Grahame's classic work. Since the 1970s, Grahame's story has developed a wide readership in Chinese-language countries such as China and Taiwan, where children today can enjoy the companionship of Mole, Rat, Badger, and Toad while growing up, and share the same wonder and love that children in the West have long had for Grahame's bucolic story. The present chapter investigates the introduction of Grahame's *The Wind in the Willows* to its Chinese readership in Taiwan, reviews its Chinese translations published in Taiwan, especially its serialization in the children's newspaper *Mandarin Daily News*, and analyzes how the work has gone through cultural and stylistic transformation in different translators' hands. This cross-cultural study recovers historical materials not noted before and shows the translators' reinterpretations of Grahame's book. It also places Grahame's novel in relation to the development of children's literature in a Chinese-speaking region.

Serialization in *Mandarin Daily News*

The first Chinese translation of *The Wind in the Willows*, by Chi-Ying Chu [朱琪英],[1] did not appear until 1959. Since that time, more than a dozen Chinese translations of the work have appeared, including adaptations and various illustrated editions in Chinese-language regions such as China, Taiwan, and Hong Kong. The most significant and successful in terms of popularity and literary value is the serial translated by Chien-Ming Chang [張劍鳴], which first appeared in 1973 in *Mandarin Daily News*, a newspaper specifically issued for children. Chang's translation, later published in two volumes in 1974 and as a single volume in 2001, has remained one of the most significant translations of Grahame's novel ever since. A brief introduction to the historical background of the newspaper may help us to see how Grahame's book was introduced to Taiwan at a time when many canonical works of Western children's literature were first translated into Chinese.

Mandarin Daily News was founded in 1948 by the Ministry of Education of the Chinese government, then led by the party of Kuomingtang (KMT). The triweekly state-owned paper was initiated for the purpose of promoting Mandarin Chinese, which had recently been chosen as the official language of the country. But in 1949, the Communists, led by Zedong Mao, took over mainland China, forcing the KMT government to retreat to Taiwan. *Mandarin Daily News* followed the government to the island. With a group of linguistic experts as board members, the paper began to publish daily in Taiwan, continuing its top-down educational mission of promoting the teaching of Mandarin.

Especially designed for children, *Mandarin Daily News* was the only newspaper that printed Chinese characters with corresponding phonetic symbols to provide readers with the correct Mandarin pronunciations. Its move to Taiwan was crucial to both the political and cultural development of the country during this period.[2] During the colonial years of Japan's occupation of Taiwan (1895–1945), Japanese culture had been forcefully implanted in the island, and in the late 1940s, the country was still under the influence of Japanese customs and practices. *Mandarin Daily News* became the best vehicle through which the newly arrived KMT government could solidify its rule over Taiwan. But while this tabloid-sized paper began with the goal of instilling Chinese culture, just as other papers published for adults did, it was not long before *Mandarin Daily News* began to feature information about other countries. Following the economic boom of the 1960s and 1970s, when the government greatly encouraged export trade, the people of Taiwan had a collective desire to learn more about the outside world and to have contact with the West. *Mandarin Daily News* was often our first encounter with Western culture. In this paper, many local writers first began to translate foreign literature for children (mostly from English to Chinese) and to publish a prodigious number of Western classics for children. It is worthwhile to note that Taiwan was still a rural country during the 1950s and 1960s, but some towns were rapidly developing with more and more factories founded to produce goods for the world. It was a time when the majority of Taiwanese people were beginning to receive compulsory education up to senior high school, and they valued hard work, education, and self-improvement. A medium like *Mandarin Daily News* was able to bridge the cultural gap between the island and the Western world.

Part of the newspaper's editorial policy was to publish translations of respected works of children's literature from other countries. In fact, before Grahame's story appeared, the paper had already published translations of Meindert De Jong's *The House of Sixty Fathers*, Ben Stahl's *Blackbeard's Ghost*, Booth Tarkington's *Seventeen*, Bertrand R. Brinley's *The Mad Scientists' Club*, and Marguerite Henry's *Black Gold*; after *The Wind in the Willows*, the paper featured translations of Stephen Fennimore's *Bush Holiday*, E. B. White's *Trumpet of the Swan*, Carol Ryrie Brink's *Baby Island*, and others. No doubt the paper has been a place for cultural exchange as well as a place where local translators and creative writers of children's literature have been cultivated.

Through its serialization in *Mandarin Daily News*, *The Wind in the Willows* was read in almost every classroom in most primary schools and many homes in Taiwan during the 1970s, shortly before "publishers of children's books began to mushroom" in the country during the 1980s (Desmet and Duh 1244) and before the computer took over the key role of facilitating interchange and intercourse between different cultures during the last two decades. This story, read in "teaspoons,"[3] has influenced readers of my generation and has become a great part of our collective memory of childhood.

According to Chien-Ming Chang [張劍鳴], the editor of *Mandarin Daily News* and the translator of the serial version that appeared in its pages, the first Chinese translation [楊柳風], done by Chi-Ying Chu [朱琪英, her real name, Chi-Ying Hsiue, 薛琪英] and published in Shanghai in 1936, was not a successful book. Though it boasted a preface by the famous poet Tso-Jen Chou [周作人], the text was an archaic translation, full of "foreignized" Chinese that is hard to follow. Ying's translation also left out much of Grahame's original story. For these reasons, this first translation never aroused public interest. In order to create a Chinese readership for Grahame's novel, Chang decided to translate the book himself based on "the best version with the best illustrations"—the unabridged edition by Charles Scribner's Sons to celebrate the fiftieth anniversary of the firm's publication of the book (Chang 9).

On September 6, 1973, a note addressed "To the Little Readers" appeared in the paper, telling of the forthcoming serialization of *The Wind in the Willows* "from tomorrow onwards." However, for the following three days, only the translator's preliminary words were printed, giving the historical and biographical background of the story. In his introductory account, Chang dwells on the origin of Grahame's novel. As is known, it was originally a bedtime story Grahame told his son Alastair over a period of more than two years, so the story has the intrinsic nature of a serial structure. The translator's division of the story into installments in a sense restores its original form. Nowhere else in the world has another serialization of the story been printed that enables child readers to come so close to Alastair's firsthand experience of such constant and intimate encounters with Grahame's anthropomorphized characters.

Finally, on September 10, 1973, installments of *The Wind in the Willows* began to appear in *Mandarin Daily News* and ran for a period of seven months (until June 3, 1974). Each day, the continuing story was printed either on the left- or the righthand side of the main page, often with a regular poem, a story, and sometimes a pictorial game. Some of the installments included reprints of the illustrations by E. H. Shepard. Chang's translation also included phonetic symbols for every word (standard for all writing in the paper). Such phonetic symbols enable those who have just started schooling but who are not yet fully literate to read the story themselves without difficulty.

The publication of *Wind* did not happen by coincidence. Before Grahame's *The Wind in the Willows* came out, *Mandarin Daily News* had been systematically introducing Western children's literature to its audience. It was a part of the paper's long-term project to introduce a series of foreign children's literature; Chang himself had already translated and published Rudyard Kipling's *Captains Courageous* in May 1965. In addition, he translated many other titles for children throughout his life, including Beverly Cleary's *Ribsy*, Donald J. Sobol's *Encyclopedia Brown Finds the Clues*, Lawrence Arthur's *Gold Stone*, Claire Huchet Bishop's *Twenty and Ten*, and Armstrong Sperry's *Call it Courage*. Though he had no formal literary education, only military training, he was long a champion of literature for children. As editor of *Mandarin Daily News*, a post he took on in 1961 after retiring from the army, Chang encouraged many authors of the younger generation to start writing for children; some of those writers later became academics in the fields of education and children's literature. Chang's translation of Grahame's story was the work that established his reputation in Taiwan as an outstanding translator in the field of children's literature. A close examination of the serial proves him both a great translator and a superb editor, one who not only brought out a beautiful and effective translation, but who also successfully adapted the story into serial form. Some of the installments are long and others are short, and there is no strict rule for how many installments make up each chapter. Normally a typical chapter is divided into an average of nineteen installments.[4]

Deciding how to arrange the installments for serialization took real skill. To begin with, Chang was careful in deciding where an installment should begin and end. For example, the first installment of September 10, 1973, renders the first paragraph of Grahame's original text, all about Mole's spring cleaning. But Chang's installment ends not with the closing sentence of the paragraph when Mole comes out into the sunlight and "found himself rolling in the warm grass of a great meadow," but instead with the beginning of the second paragraph, Mole's murmuring to himself, "This is fine! . . . This is better than whitewashing" (1). Such a division naturally leads on to the following installment, about what Mole is to experience on the meadows.

When necessary, Chang not only divided a paragraph and allowed an installment to begin in the middle of it, but also divided a sentence, so that some installments end in the middle of sentences while others begin halfway through. For example, to prepare for Mole's meeting with Water Rat, installment 3 describes how Mole spots a hole that is Rat's dwelling. However, the two animals do not meet until installment 4, during which they greet each other, and toward its end, Rat's boat is depicted. Then in the following installment, Rat and Mole begin to chat and step into Rat's boat. As the story unfolds, each installment shows something new, introducing the many events of the plot with a steady and gradually developing tempo. This way, the narrative seems to move smoothly and steadily onward, like a boat floating on the river.

Adding a reminder at the beginning of an installment to refresh the reader's memory of what has happened in the preceding one is a common technique many serial writers use. Interestingly, though, Chang did not adopt this convention, and it seems his method of beginning straightaway has not bothered his young readers. For example, in installment 74, Badger tells Mole of the ancient civilization that his home is built upon; the installment ends but the conversation doesn't. Then the following installment doesn't remind readers of what happened in the previous day's paper; instead, it begins with Mole asking, "But what has become of them all?" followed by Badger's explanation, which continues on into installment 76. Sea Rat's spell-like words to Water Rat are treated in the same way. Perhaps Chang felt that a devoted reader of a daily paper should not need a reminder; the short interval of time between installments would not cause any difficulties in following the plot. Or Chang may have believed that the internal structure of Grahame's narrative is so tight that even if he did not include reminders in the traditional style of serialization, the narrative would not feel fragmented.

Chang's translation is largely faithful to the content of Grahame's novel. Yet the serial is not without omissions and additions. For example, the serious talk Badger and others give to Toad in order to teach him to be sensible is much shortened in installment 107. Chang's readers never learn how Badger hears about Toad's having another "new and exceptionally powerful motor-car," or how the animals refuse delivery of the car, or how they hold Toad down on the floor to take off his motor-clothes. Nor do they hear how Badger blames Toad for squandering the money his father left him, or how Toad comes out in tears but soon recants his admission of wrongdoing and his apology. All Chang's readers hear is Toad's saying "O, yes, yes in there . . . . You're so eloquent, dear Badger, and so moving, and so convincing. . . ." (62).[5] Such omissions seem purposeful. The translator and editor would like to avoid the violent scene and skip Badger's grim reproach, the courtroom questioning, and corporal punishment. These omissions also tone down Toad's misbehavior, making him less of a negative role model and preventing children from imitating an antihero. Such a method conforms to the general editoral policy of *Mandarin Daily News* to keep the paper "morally correct"; social events such as scandals and crimes were typically left out to keep young readers' innocent minds untainted. The conservative social customs and high morals in Taiwan in the 1970s were reflected in the paper's editorial policies.

Other changes made by Chang relate less to morals and more to cultural contexts. Chang was aware that his audience might not understand all the English references in Grahame's text, so he added footnotes to explain the names of foreign countries or places (such as "the London River" [the Thames] and the Northern Seas) and historical figures (such as Sigurd). Chang was also conscious of the cultural differences between 1908 England and 1973 Taiwan, and included copious footnotes (sometimes as many as four in one installment) to explain English customs. For example, after installment 98, which depicts the Christmas carol scene, half of the next installment explains the background and meaning: the story about how Mary gave birth to Jesus Christ in a stable "where there were a lamb, a donkey and a cow around." Chang also provides his own interpretation of what a Christmas carol means: "if one cares for those who suffers or in misery, one will have happiness." Such an explanation is particularly helpful to Taiwanese children with no Christian background. The moral lesson the translator draws about helping people also makes the carol not exclusively for Christians, but allows it to appeal to any reader.

Another explanatory footnote is about the warder of the dungeon "anxious to be off to his tea" (86). To most readers today, the English custom of taking tea is familiar, but Chang felt that his 1973 audience might need an explanation of this national custom of the English because it differs from the way the Chinese take tea. He wrote that "[t]he author of this book is English, and what English people mean by 'having tea' is to have tea (black tea with milk and sugar), to have dessert, to talk and have a break" (installment 147). Chinese people have a longer history of cultivating tea and consuming it, but they take tea in quite a different way, without adding anything to it. Chang felt such an explanation should help his young readers understand how the guard's desire for tea provides a good chance for Toad to pass him easily. What Chang aimed for here was not just a literal translation, but a cultural translation.

Chang, however, did not intend to transform the foreign into the domestic for better understanding. Instead, he preserved the exotic taste of this very English novel. For example, in installment 150, rather than simply dropping the reference to a "pencil-case," or changing it into a more familiar item of stationery such as a pencil box, Chang meticulously added a footnote explaining, "[b]efore the invention of ball-point-pen, foreigners often took with them a case with a pen and a bottle of ink" (installment 150). Here he clearly indicates that it is the habit of "foreigners," and readers should know they are reading a story about "the others." Chang did not try to make the characters conform to the norms of a Chinese-language country nor to "domesticate" them.

The serial is, of course, not perfect, just like many journalistic writings in the daily papers brought out under the pressure of time. The most obvious flaw that occurred is a technical problem with installment numerical indexing. In one instance, the serial number disappears; in three other installments, wrong sequent numbers are given. It is hard to tell if it was Chang or the printer who made the mistakes.

Fortunately, the error was soon corrected four days after, but no explanation was given.

It is important to remember the time during which Chang's translation of *Wind* was published to understand its historical meaning to young Taiwanese readers. This translation was a part of a trend of systematic translation of Western children's books, and it appeared long before children in Taiwan started to be taught to speak and read English at a very young age. During this period Taiwanese people had no chance to buy foreign children's books at local book stores, at regular international book fairs, or through the Internet as we do today.

My own experience is typical. As a part of the generation of Grahame's first readership in Taiwan, I read the translated serial while living in a provincial town in the south of Taiwan, a town in which cultural literacy was limited. To me and to many of my generation, the serial provided not only the best material for learning Mandarin, which is different from my mother tongue, the Southern Min dialect, but also a source to get to know what an "English" lifestyle was like. Reading *Wind* cultivated my imagination and curiosity about a wider world. I then continued to read more translations of foreign children's literature in the paper and many more books in translation that the *Mandarin Daily News* published. No doubt, the success of *Wind* and other translations of English children's books also played a significant role in stimulating the growing market for children's literature in Taiwan in the 1970s, as *Mandarin Daily News* has also become one of the most important publishers of children's literature by Taiwanese as well as international authors up to the present day.

Translating English Culture

For many years, Chang's 1973 translation (published in book form in 1974) was the only version of Grahame's story available to Chinese-language readers. But since the 1990s, several new Chinese translations have been published in Taiwan and many more in Mainland China. In Taiwan, Hsiang-Tung Chiao's [喬向東] 1995 translation was quickly followed by Yu-Niang Yang's [楊玉娘] in 1996, while the twenty-first century brought Ho-Li Hsia's [夏荷立] 2002 translation, and Shih-Chien Hsieh's [謝世堅] in 2004. Unlike Chang's version, their translations are without phonetic symbols. In contrast to translations published in China and written in simplified Chinese, the above-mentioned Taiwanese authors' translations are written in traditional complex Chinese. By comparing their works, I aim to show how Grahame's text has gone through cultural transformation during the past three decades in Taiwan. Then I also examine how each translator, in his or her own way, interweaves personal interpretations into a text. Finally, I examine what may be the most challenging task for a translator: that is, how to evoke the style of a foreign writer. This investigation not only highlights Grahame's cultural contexts and his poetic style, but also the cultural differences between the English and the Chinese.

As translation theorist Lawrence Venuti has pointed out, there are two common strategies to adopt in translating a text: the "domestication" approach, or the "foreignization" approach. Domestication means "putting the foreign to domestic uses" (341); in other words, the translator "assimilate[s] a text to target cultural and linguistic values," changing terms unfamiliar to the supposed general readers into those which they can easily recognize (Oittinen 905). In contrast, foreignization means the translator will instead attempt to retain a "significant trace of the original 'foreign text'" in the target-language text as the result of translation (Oittinen 905). As is demonstrated later, translators of *Wind* in Taiwan, to different degrees and under different situations, have used both methods to suit their purposes.

Chang's newspaper serialization adopted the "foreignization" approach, so his translation includes many allusions and references rich with English cultural contexts (for example, the cultural meaning of having tea or of singing a Christmas carol as discussed above). His translation retains many of the original English references, and Chang simply provides footnotes to make them intelligible to his young readers. This way, there is no need for them to shift their ground from one culture to another, because they know they are reading a foreign story. Since the 1990s, however, people in Taiwan have had a lot more exposure to Western culture through media such as television and films. Therefore Chang's successors no longer feel the need to explain many cultural references that have become common knowledge today.

Comparing Chang's translation to other, later translators' works demonstrates that the latter exhibit a tendency toward domestication rather than foreignization. Each later translator, however, attempts to acquaint his or her readers with the foreign country of England via different strategies. Chang simply annotated, striving to assimilate, to imitate, and to connect to the foreign text; later translators, in contrast, represented, re-created, and enriched the source text to different degrees. But the level of domestication does not correlate precisely with an ever-increasing level of general reader knowledge of the West in Taiwanese culture, with the newest translation the most "domesticated." Each individual translator's grasp of Grahame's text also influences his or her translation choices, as does his or her skill as a prose stylist of Chinese. Overall, though, as can be detected in the following examples, the later translators tend to show more flexibility and variety in order to differentiate themselves from their famous predecessor Chang and establish their own identities.

One of the key issues in translating children's texts is related to what Göte Klingberg calls "cultural context adaptation"; that can be "names, appearances, habits which transcend the idiosyncratic, locations . . . flora and fauna, the food eaten, references to historical or cultural contexts, currency, weights and measures, etc. They are the aspects which make a text . . . recognizably foreign. . . ." (qtd. in O'Sullivan 154). When treating such material, translators' different backgrounds, as well as the readership they anticipate, will lead them to different degrees of fidelity, methods, and eventually effectiveness of translation. All such issues that translation theorists Venuti and Emer O'Sullivan have commented on, as well as the degree of the translator's invisibility in the target-language text, provide a practical theoretical framework for our assessing the many Chinese translations of Grahame's work.

The episode of Toad's escape in disguise provides a good example to demonstrate different translators' strategies in undertaking cultural context adaptation. The following table displays Grahame's text together with the different Chinese translations and their literal meanings in English to help an English native speaker's understanding:

Grahame's text

"even when he hesitated, uncertain as to the right turning to take, he found himself helped out of his difficulty by the warder at the next gate, anxious to be off to his tea, summoning him to come along sharp and not keep him waiting there all night." (2008 version, 86)

Chang (1974)

"甚至於他拿不定主意，到底該向轉哪一邊兒拐彎兒的時候，守在下一道門口的士兵也會自動地幫忙—就像是急著要去喝茶（註）似的，大聲吆喝著叫他走過去，生怕他會在那兒待一夜"

"As for his being unable to make his mind about which turn to take next, the soldier at the next door always volunteered to help—as if being anxious to have tea, they just shouted to let him pass, being afraid that he might want to stay for the night."

Chiao (1995)

"甚至當他猶疑不決，不知該朝哪個方向拐彎的時候，下一道門的守衛，正急於下班回家去喝茶的守衛，於是主動招呼她快走，以免自己整夜守在這裡"

"Even when he [sic, she] was hesitating and not sure of where to turn, the guard at the next door—who was anxious to be off and go home to tea—volunteered to beckon her to go quickly and to spare himself a whole night's watch here."

Yang (1996)

"即使當他舉棋不定時，也因為下個門口的警衛急著要去用茶點，招呼他快快通過別讓他乾等一整天，而讓他輕易擺脫困境"

"Even just as he was "holding a chess piece but being not sure of whether to make a move,' the warder at the next door was anxious to have tea and desserts. He beckoned him to hurry up and pass by quickly so that the guard won't have to wait for all day long. Consequently that enables him to escape the difficult situation easily."

Hsia (2002)	"有時遇到他在猶豫，不知道該轉哪一邊的時候，下一道門的守衛就會幫他解決問題。急著去喝茶的那些守衛會叫他手腳快點，不要讓他等到天黑"

"Sometimes when he was hesitating and not knowing which side to turn, the warder at the next door would help him to solve the question. Other warders anxious to have tea would hurry him off, so that he [sic, them] won't have to wait till it's dark."

Hsieh (2004)	"甚至當他猶疑不決，不知該朝哪個方向走的時候，下道關卡的看守也會給他指路。有個看守還大聲叫他快點走，免得他整夜守在門口，因為他急著下班回家喝茶"

"Even when he was hesitating and not knowing which way to go, the warder at the next gate would direct him to the way out. Being anxious to go home to have tea, one warder even hurried him off loudly so that he won't be waiting at the door for the whole night."

Interestingly, here in this passage, the word "warder" and the phrase "anxious to be off to his tea" are translated in different ways, and such differences to a degree reflect the larger differences of five translators' own backgrounds, cultural identity, and context adaptation. A closer look at the different translations can help us see how the translators grasp the source-language text and domesticate or foreignize it. Chang's translation of "warder," "士兵" ("soldier" in Chinese), may have something to do with his own military background, as he is known to have served in the Air Force before taking up editorial work. Then Chiao and Hsia translate the word into "守衛," while Yang uses "警衛"; both are in common currency. However, Hsieh's "看守" is out of general usage; it is typically used as a verb in Chinese. The first component word, "看," is a verb meaning "to watch," and the second component word "守," is also a verb meaning "to keep." This compound term may be chosen to visualize a warder's duty. Moreover, it is also worth noting that the last two translators consider the term plural. In Hsia's translation, one warder helps Toad solve the problem, and "other warders anxious to have tea" hurry him off so that "he [sic, should be "they" following the above "others"] won't have to wait till it's dark." In Hsieh's version, a warder directs Toad to the way out, while the other warder, "anxious to go home to have tea," just "hurrie[s] him off loudly" so that he won't be "waiting at the door for the whole night." One possibility for such discrepancies is that it is a common technique for the translators to divide a long sentence into two statements. Doing so, the two translators just change the single into the plural to reproduce a fluent and transparent sentence. Another reason may be that they create more warders to emphasize that what Toad is trying to escape from is a heavily guarded prison. Thus the translators' reproduction or supplement is to help the reader envision Toad's situation.

Like the last example, these translators also convey the meaning of "anxious to be off to his tea" differently. Chang again adds a footnote to introduce the cultural context of "having [English] tea." Both Chiao and Hsieh translate the phrase to mean "being off and going home," while Yang says, "having tea and desserts." Hsia simply provides a literal translation of the phrase, assuming that his readers would see it means being anxious to be off duty. Meanwhile, a vigilant translator might also pause and ask, who is the "he" who is "anxious to be off to his tea"? Usually pronouns are not a problem in English-to-Chinese translation, because there are equivalent Chinese pronouns for different forms such as the singular, the plural, the masculine, and the feminine. In this instance, however, because Toad is disguised as a washerwoman, should Toad be addressed as a "he" (as Grahame puts it) or "she"? Different translators have different judgments. Among the five translators, only Chiao uses the feminine pronoun "她" ("she") in describing Toad in disguise in the warder's eyes, and the masculine pronoun "他" ("he") in describing Toad's self and his action. Meanwhile, Hsia is verbose, using the pronoun as frequently as four times in a single sentence. Yang's translation is most different because she adds a concluding remark (meaning "that enables him to escape the difficult situation easily"). It seems, by spelling out Toad's situation, she is trying to emphasize Toad's easy rather than narrow escape. Distinctively, her use of a figurative idiom "舉棋不定" (meaning "holding a chess piece but being not sure of whether to make a move") to translate the word "hesitated" is a trace of the "domestication" approach and an effective as well as creative translation.

Even in translations of the above short passage, we observe many significant issues regarding translation. First, translation is also a kind of creation; when necessary, a translator still has much freedom to change the source-language text to make the meaning clear. Second, what one translator takes for granted may not be the same as what the others assume; often it depends on the translator's social and cultural background. For example, an early translator such as Chang may be more meticulous than contemporary ones and include footnotes to ensure the general readers' understanding. On the other hand, contemporary translations tend to be terse because many cultural references no longer need explanations following the growth of the reader's cultural literacy. Finally, a good translator should be able to take care of not only the denotation but also the connotation. While getting the meaning of the text right is no longer the most demanding task for the later translators, they may wish to focus more on the connotations; some might opt for a "domestication" approach such as using idioms to get closer to the original text's connotation.

To a great extent, Grahame's novel can be taken as a good guide to an authentic Edwardian life, since Grahame has incorporated so many household details and domestic scenes in his plots: food, kitchen gadgets, housework, and everyday life activities. Contemporary Chinese-speaking readers, despite their growing familiarity with some British customs, are still not familiar with them all. It is a demanding task for translators to translate such material into Chinese intelligible to children living in an oriental society with limited knowledge of what traditional English life is like, especially for those translators who themselves have little foreign experience. The lack of experience or the cultural gap presents a problem not only for readers, but also for translators, who sometimes make mistakes when translating cultural references.

One of the challenging references arises in translating food. We can see this in translations of the opening passage, when Mole jeers "Onion-sauce! Onion-sauce!" while passing by the rabbits asking for a toll: Chang's "臭小子" (3) means "smelly bloke"; Chiao's and Yang's

"洋葱醬" is a literal translation, but the latter includes a footnote to explain that onion-sauce is best for rabbit meat. Here Yang shows that Mole is mocking the rabbits. Hsia interprets such words as Mole's contemptuous comments "笨蛋，一堆笨蛋" ("fools, a great many fools") (7); Hsieh's "笨蛋，笨蛋" is similar (7). Although each translation makes sense, Yang's preserves the feel of Grahame while giving her readers the information they need to understand the implications of his words. But on another occasion, in translating the menu of the full picnic luncheon—"coldtonguecoldhamcoldbeefpickledgherkinssalad-frenchrollscressandwichespottedmeatgingerbeerlemonadesodawater," Yang obviously does not recognize the "potted meat" and "ginger beer" and instead writes "罐裝肉薑汁、啤酒" (meaning "potted meat in ginger juice and beer"). Chiao, too, has difficulty with this very English meal; he simply translates ginger and beer separately as two things (8). These translations were done before ginger beer was common in Taiwan, and in traditional Chinese cooking, ginger always goes with meat. Nevertheless, the most recent translator, Hsieh, gets the two things right: "罐裝肉、薑汁汽水" ("potted meat, ginger ale") (11).

Here we observe that the later translators tend to get closer to the original meaning of the source-language text. More such examples can be found. To translate "cabbage" literally into "甘藍菜" (Yang 152) or the common name "包心菜" (Hsia 135) is better than to transform it into a domesticated dish such as "捲心菜炒肉絲" (Chang) ("fried meat and cabbage"), "油煎馬鈴薯捲心菜" (Chiao 133) ("fried potato and cabbage"), or "捲心菜煎馬鈴薯" (Hsieh 121) ("cabbage and fried potato"). Because the story is self-evidently about English life and culture, a Chinese reader should find the food foreign; to "domesticate" the references of English food here takes away from the readers' experience of another country's culture. While not all translations must hew closely to an author's original words to be effective, in this instance, a lack of fidelity to the cultural difference in the source-language text clearly detracts from the readers' experience of encountering a different culture.

Another challenging task lies in translating relationships, also an important theme of the book. The animals' relationships are shown through their human-like conversations, conversations that make this story convincing and appealing. Therefore, to present their relationships, it is essential for the translators to be able to translate the terms of familiarity the characters use, especially under different circumstances, such as greeting each other or expressing appreciation, reproach, and even scorn. Because the translators are of different ages and from different backgrounds, they choose different terms for the animals to use. For example, upon being introduced to Mole, Otter says "Proud, I'm sure" (7). His words are translated into different degrees of formality: from the erroneous literal translation "我看是因為你太驕傲了" ("I think it is because you are too proud") (Chang 20), the archaic "堂堂儀表" ("Impressive look") (Hsia 16), the casual "很高興認識你" ("Glad to know you") (Chiao 13) and "認識你是我的榮幸" ("It is my pleasure to know you") (Yang 23), and finally to the terse "幸會，幸會" ("Nice meeting you, nice meeting you") (Hsieh 16). In Chang's translation, Rat often calls Mole "小老弟" ("Little Old Younger-brother"), or "夥計" ("Employee"), which can also mean "fellow" or "pal" in colloquial Mandarin. Mole and Toad address Rat in the same way. Chang also creates very terse and intimate terms of endearment by prefixing "老" ("old") to the species names (for example, "老獾," "老鼠" or "老水," "老鼴," and "老蛤") to express endearment—similar to the way Grahame adds a suffix to create the familiar "Ratty." In Chiao's translation, Rat often calls Mole "老夥計" ("Old Employee") (9, 12, 17, 81, 82, 83), which indicates that while Mole may be a "fellow" and "pal," Rat is the leader as the two explore the river. Similarly, when Badger is the leader, he uses the term to refer to Rat and Mole (101). Yang takes a different approach; most of the time Rat and Mole call each other by species names. But after the two are more familiar with each other, she has Rat call Mole "老兄" (literally "Old Elder-brother") in some situations, such as when complimenting Mole's "black velvet smoking-suit" (18) or inviting Mole to dig into their picnic lunch (21). However, when Mole is feeling homesick, Rat calls him "老弟" ("Old Younger-brother"). The former is slightly more respectful than the latter, but in a more colloquial sense, both terms mean "pal." By having the characters shift from calling each other by species names to using more intimate endearments, Yang shows she is conscious of the development of their relationship.

Hsia's translation is even less formal in its terms of address. When Rat proudly shows Mole his boat, and when he rejects Mole's request to

row, he calls Mole "小友" and "小朋友" (both meaning "Little Friend")
(Hsia 10, 19), a bit patronizingly; but when he is envious of Mole's
clothing, he calls him "老哥" ("Old Elder-brother") (Hsia 12). Having
something to ask Rat, Mole calls him respectfully "河鼠兄" ("Rat Older-
brother") (Hsia 21, 24). Toad is the most grandiloquent of all: trying to
persuade Rat to go on the road, he calls Rat "河鼠老好人" ("Rat the
Good Old Fellow"). Pretending to be ill asking for a doctor, he calls Rat
the slightly formal "親愛的朋友" ("Dear Friend") (Hsia 105).

The same approach of getting progressively more informal in showing familiarity is also adopted in Hsieh's later translation. He elaborates
more on Mole's calling Rat "河鼠兄，我寬宏大量的朋友" ("Brother
Rat, my open-minded friend") after his unsuccessful attempt to row
the boat, and the latter's addressing him "朋友" ("Friend") to express
forgiveness. When Badger is answering the door, he calls Rat "小老弟"
("Little Old Younger-Brother") (53). He has the habit of adding "older-
brother" or "younger-brother" as a suffix to the species names. Again it
is impossible to see any age differences in the ways they address each
other: "河鼠老弟" ("Rat Old Younger-brother") or "河鼠老兄" ("Rat
Old Elder-brother"), "獾老兄" (Badger Old Elder-brother), "蟾蜍兄"
(Toad Elder-brother) (Hsieh 16, 28, 191). "Old" and "young" here refer
to endearment rather than age.

Traditionally in Chinese writing and in colloquialism, differences
in age are indicated clearly. The young should speak to elders with
respect, and age difference between brothers should be indicated in
titles for decorum. In Chinese, there is no single word such as "brother"
to cover both the younger and the elder, unless the two words are put
together as a generic term. This is true not only of the word "brother,"
but also of other relationship words such as "sister," "uncle," and "aunt"
that are addressed with distinctions. So in Chinese there are two individual words to mean uncles younger and elder than one's father, and
two words to mean younger and older aunts. In contemporary Taiwan,
however, the age identity in colloquialism is becoming less and less important, especially when referring to relationships outside the family.

In addition to cultural issues inside the texts, it is also worthwhile to
look at those outside the texts, such as what translators think is suitable
material for children. For example, there are some episodes in Grahame's text in which sexuality seeps into the story through language.

When Toad is telling the barge-woman about his imaginary employees, he refers to them spitefully as "nasty little hussies"; the barge-woman, in turn, calls them "idle trollops" (Grahame 2008 version, 110). Chiao translates these appellations into "討厭的輕挑小女子" ("flirtatious little girl") and "懶惰的蕩婦" ("lazy lusty coquette") (Chiao 178), perhaps the most literal translations of "hussies" and "trollops." Chang, more decorously, translates them as "賤骨頭" ("wretched bones," a common curse in colloquial Mandarin) and "不正經" ("not decent") (installment 129). Yang keeps the gendered references, but deletes their sexual connotations: "輕浮挑桃達的小姑娘們" ("flippant and lazy little girls") and "懶惰兮兮的女孩" ("lazy girls"), as does Hsieh, "脾氣不好又輕挑的小女生" ("bad-tempered and flippant girls") and "不肯好好做事的女孩" ("unwilling to do things properly") (Hsieh 180). Even the contemporary translators (except Chiao) are concerned with the sexual implications of the original content and shift the focus to the girls' laziness rather than their promiscuity. Such a practice stems from how the translators (particularly those who hold a didactic concept of children's literature) view children and childhood. According to Roger Collinson, most translators believe that books for children "can and do influence outlook, belief and conduct" (qtd. in Shavit 39), so Taiwanese translators would rather find euphemistic ways of speaking or have the story completely free from sex, in order to conform with cultural constructions of childhood.

In addition to sex, another major concern is with the many scoldings and swear words that appear in Grahame's text. Most Taiwanese translators tend to edit out the more troubling swearing. For instance, sending Toad to prison, the police sergeant says to the gaoler, "Oddsbodikins!" The greatly different translations range from the highly insulting swearword "媽的" ("mother") (Yang 131), "奧茲博迪金斯" (Chiao 115) (a transliteration that only maps the letters of the source language to Chinese letters pronounced similarly that seems to mean the name of the gaoler), a simple word "喂" ("Hi") (Hsieh 105), to "老糊塗" (Chang 187) ("old bungler") which is perhaps most close to the meaning of the source language and also most effective. In order to reach their audience, translators must treat such material with discretion.

The above close reading shows how skilled these translators are in dealing with terms of familiarity, pronouns, sexuality, and swear words.

These are all what Anthea Bell calls "delicate matters" that demonstrate how "quite tiny things can affect meaning a good deal after all" (232). Handling such matters, the translators often step in to make changes to the original text in order to meet the requirements of social or moral codes. Almost all feel that it is legitimate to sacrifice fidelity to source-language text for a moral purpose.

Translating Style

Compared to translating the content, creating a translation that evokes the original author's style as closely as possible is far more challenging for a translator of literature. Grahame, in particular, is such a genuine stylist that most translators might feel they could not possibly translate his style effectively and precisely. In his introduction, Chang acknowledges this problem, writing that in order to ensure young readers' better understanding, he tries to "avoid using vague elegant classic Chinese," and has to "sacrifice the beautiful rhetoric of Chinese prose" (5). He considers it impossible either to present the elegant and poetic style that is so much a part of the appeal of Grahame's text, or to find stylistic equivalents in classic Chinese. Chang's disclaimer shows the style question any translator of Grahame is bound to face.

Grahame is very particular in his choice of words and often employs onomatopoeia to capture the sounds of nature. Mandarin is also rich with onomatopoeic words, but even a diligent and creative translator may not easily find an equivalent translation that conveys both the sense and sound effects of Grahame's poetic writing. Grahame's poetic prose is also full of rhythm and imagery, which appeals to a reader's senses of smell, sound, and sight. Take Mole's first impression of the river, for example: "[a]ll was a-shake and a shiver—glints and gleams and sparkles, rustle and swirl, chatter and bubble" (2). Grahame's sentence contains not only onomatopoeia, but also alliterated words and eye rhymes. The meanings cover the light, the shape, and the sounds of the river. To evoke the *feel* of Grahame's prose, as well as its sense, a translator must go beyond a simple literal translation. Looking at the different translations below, we can see that each translator has created in Chinese a distinctive grammatical structure with parallel syntax to present the moving and the shining water:

Grahame's text	"All was a-shake and a-shiver—glints and gleams and sparkles, rustle and swirl, chatter and bubble." (2008 version, 2)
Chang (1974)	"眼前盡是搖晃和閃動—閃閃的、亮晃晃的粼粼光影，匆促地、盤旋迴轉的水波，和咕咕噥噥，「波波」的水聲" (6)

noun and noun—adj. adj. noun, adv. adj. noun, and adj. adj. noun

"In front of the eyes see shakes and shivers—gleamy, sparkling light, swiftly, swirling water weave, and chattering, bubbling water sound."

Chiao (1995)	"整條河就像一條蛇，一堆碎片—閃閃發光、「嘩嘩」低唱；不斷地打著漩，冒著水泡" (5)

noun, noun—adv. verb, adv. verb; adv. verb, verb

"The whole River is like a snake, a pile of bits and pieces—gleamily sparkle, humming 'hwa-hwa'; incessantly swirling and bubbling."

Yang (1996)	"一切都是搖搖盪盪、抖抖顫顫—微光閃耀、浪光粼粼，打著漩渦、潺潺作響，嘰哩咕嚕、冒出水泡" (14)

noun and noun—noun verb, noun verb, verb object. adv. verb. verb. verb

"All are swings and shakes—the light shimmers, the weaves sparkle, making whirls, murmuring, rustling and bubbling."

Hsia (2002)	"一片搖盪和抖動，閃閃亮亮、微微爍爍和粼粼，沙沙作響，渦狀旋轉" (8)

noun and noun, adj. adj., adj. and adj. verb. verb. verb.

"All are swings and shivers, sparkling, shining, glinting, gleaming and sparkling; all are rustling, murmuring, and swirling."

Hsieh (2004)　　"所有這一切都抖動著河水發出嘩嘩的響聲" (8)

Subject, verb subject. verb. adj. noun.

"All shaking the river to make rustling 'hwa-hwa' sounds."

Here most of the translators use repetitions to create parallel patterns. Chiao's translation most differs from Grahame's original language in meaning and in style by using a simile: "整條河就像一條蛇" ("the whole river is like a snake"). While capturing the sense of Grahame's prose, Chiao's translation loses Grahame's poetic feel, because it completely leaves out the eye rhymes. Yang elaborates on the senses of light, sound, and fluidity, using four-letter phrases to build her sentence. Her parallel grammatical structure is well done, but it lacks rhymes to create rhythms and sound effects. Hsia's sentence also consists of a string of four-letter phrases and many rhyming words, including "盪," "亮," "響," and "狀" (pronounced as "dang," "liang," "shang," and "guang"). He also employs alliteration and assonance, using words with the soft pronunciation of "s" (閃閃 [san-san], 響響 [shang-shang], 爍爍 [suo-suo], 沙沙 [sa-sa]). But the meaning of Hsia's sentence is so vague that readers might not be sure what the narrator is describing. Hsieh's translation is in unadorned prose, with little feel for the poetic. Among all, in my opinion, Chang's translation, with its parallel structure, sensual images, rhymes and rhythms, is most effective in both conveying meaning and evoking a sense of Grahame's poetic style.

Another good passage to use when examining style is Grahame's memorable sketch of Mole's spring cleaning. Grahame creates much alliteration and repetition to show Mole's actions lively and vividly: "he scraped and scratched and scrabbled and scrooged, and then he scrooged again and scrabbled and scratched and scraped, working busily with his little paws and muttering to himself, 'Up we go! Up we go!'" (1). The target-language texts appear different in style. Chang's translation keeps Grahame's original sentence structure by using the two rhyming verbs "刨" and "挖" (pronounced as [pau] and [wa]). He repeats the same string of words twice, and in between, he inserts a phrase meaning "and then he takes a little break." Chiao adds another

"抓" (pronounced as [jwa]) to rhyme with the two verbs. These verbs have the same linguistic component, "扌," meaning "hand" in itself. This way, the image of Mole's "little paws" is embedded in the same pictograph of the Chinese characters. Yang not only retains the literal meaning of "little paws," but also creates an adverbial phrase, "七手八腳地" (literally "seven hands and eight feet"), to mean "busily" in Chinese idiom. She adds two more verbs, "摸索" ("touch") and "擠" ("push"), with the pictograph "扌" and an idiomatic adverbial phrase, "喋喋不休地," that means "chattering." Unfortunately her supplement ruins the original poetic structure even though her translation may emphasize Mole's labor more effectively than others do. Hsia also follows his predecessors, using the same verbs, but he adds one more verb, "揮" ("swing"), to the list, which may not fit in with other verbs for its meaning; his sentence structure ("．．．啊．．．的、．．．啊．．．的") is by no means superior to Chang's ("．．．了又．．．、．．．了又．．．"). Hsieh's translation, in his usual style, simply repeats one verb, "扒" ("dig"), in a simple structure, "．．．呀．．．," and skips all the repetitions and images. Because of his relish for complicated vocabulary and complicated idioms such as "入木三分" ("written in a forceful hand") and "引經據典" ("being pedantic") (Hsieh 201, 203), his translation seems to target adolescent readers more than young children.

To sum up, the above translators attempt to capture Grahame's poetic style, with varying degrees of success. Chang's faithful translation retains the author's tone and style better, while other translators experiment with diverse linguistic features and have their own voices heard. Some of them emphasize the rhythm more; others, the meaning. In Hsieh's case, the narrator and the implied readers he constructs turn out to be quite different from those of the other translations. Overall, the comparative study here does not necessarily provide a definite answer to which translator has achieved the best quality in terms of style, as our evaluation should be subject to not only textual fidelity, but also the translator's targeted readership and the degree of the translator's invisibility in the target-language text. It is well accepted today that translation *is* re-creation. A translator should be more active than a machine that can only translate word for word with precision but with little sense of an author's tone, style, or symbolic intent.

Conclusion

The introduction and serialization of The Wind in the Willows in Taiwan has become part of the collective memory of a generation of readers now already middle-aged. The book must have influenced its readers in Taiwan to be more open and liberal to the outside world. As Ronald Jobe remarks, "[c]hildren need to read the best literature other countries have to offer" (925). Encountering foreign literature at a young age will nurture universal understanding and a global view because such reading experience can enable them to accept the other cultures more easily. Grahame's The Wind in the Willows belongs to the global heritage that children of any generation of any country can inherit. In addition to arousing curiosity and wonder about the wider world, translations of children's classics can help children improve their reading ability and cultural literacy. A translation such as Wind relieves its readers of the boredom of the here and now, cultivates a better understanding of the foreign, and finally, advocates harmonious coexistence with other people and beings, an ideology that corresponds with many oriental philosophies such as those found in Taoism and Buddhism.

Notes

Sincere thanks to Mrs. Jenny Chung [鍾雪珍], librarian of the reference service division at the National Central Library of Taiwan, who kindly helped me to have the privilege of looking at the special collections of Mandarin Daily News, and to Dr. John Cruikshanks, who took me to Grahame's birthplace on Castle Road in Edinburgh, and showed me his own treasure of the old plaque of Grahame's house.

1. For English translation of Chinese names, the present article uses the Wade-Giles system that is most common in Taiwan.

2. For a brief introduction to the history of children's literature in Taiwan before and after the Second World War, see Desmet and Duh.

3. "Novel in teaspoons," a phrase coined by Thomas Carlyle to describe serial stories such as Dickens's A Tale of Two Cities; see Dickens 113, 145.

4. Chapter I: installment 1–17; Chapter II: 18–37; Chapter III: 38–56; Chapter IV: 57–78; Chapter V: 79–104; Chapter VI: 105–20; Chapter VII: 121–38; Chapter VIII: 139–59; Chapter IX: 160–88; Chapter X: 188–202, 402

[sic., should be 203, hereafter]–414; Chapter XI. 415–50, 251 [corrected]–61; Chapter XII: 262–81.

5. Here the quotations of Chang's translation are from his 1974 two-volume version and the page numbers are given. Otherwise, installment numbers are given if the quotations are from the newspaper version.

Works Cited

Bell, Anthea. "Translator's Notebook: Delicate Matters." *The Translation of Children's Literature: A Reader*. Ed. Gillian Lathey. Clevedon: Multilingual Matters, 2006. 232–40.

Chang, Chien-Ming, trans. [柳林中的風聲]. Trans. of *The Wind in the Willows*. By Kenneth Grahame. 1908. Taipei: *Mandarin Daily News* 10 Sept. 1973–3 June 1974.

———. [柳林中的風聲]. 2 vols. Taipei: *Mandarin Daily News*, 1974.

Chiao, Hsing-Tung, trans. [柳林中的風聲]. Trans. of *The Wind in the Willows*. By Kenneth Grahame. 1908. Taipei: Yeh Chung, 1995.

Chu, Chi-Ying, trans. [楊柳風]. Trans. of *The Wind in the Willows*. By Kenneth Grahame. 1908. Hsanghai: Pei-Hsin, 1936.

Desmet, Mieke, and Ming Cherng Duh. "Taiwan." *International Companion Encyclopedia of Children's Literature*. Vol. 2. Ed. Peter Hunt. London: Routledge, 2004. 1241–45.

Dickens, Charles. *The Letters of Charles Dickens*. Vol. 9. Ed. Madeline House et al. Oxford: Clarendon, 1997.

Grahame, Kenneth. *The Wind in the Willows*. Illus. Ernest H. Shepard. New York: Scribners, 1960.

———. *The Wind in the Willows*. 1908. London: Oxford UP, 2008.

Hsia, Ho-Li, trans. [柳林中的風聲]. Trans. of *The Wind in the Willows*. By Kenneth Grahame. 1908. Taipei: Fang Chih, 2002.

Hsieh, Shih-Chien, trans. [柳林中的風聲]. Trans. of *The Wind in the Willows*. By Kenneth Grahame. 1908. Taichung: Hsing Chen, 2004.

Jobe, Ronald. "Translating for Children—Practice." *International Companion Encyclopedia of Children's Literature*. Vol. 2. Ed. Peter Hunt. London: Routledge, 2004. 912–26.

Oittinen, Riitta. "Translating for Children—Theory." *International Companion Encyclopedia of Children's Literature*. Vol. 2. Ed. Peter Hunt. London: Routledge, 2004. 905.

O'Sullivan, Emer. "Does Pinocchio have an Italian Passport? What is Specifically National and What is International about Classics of Children's Literature." *The Translation of Children's Literature: A Reader.* Ed. Gillian Lathey. Clevedon: Multilingual Matters, 2006. 146–62.

Ransome, Arthur. Rev. of *The Wind in the Willows,* by Kenneth Grahame. *The Bookman,* January 1909: 190–91.

Shavit, Zohar. "Translation of Children's Literature." *The Translation of Children's Literature: A Reader.* Ed. Gillian Lathey. Clevedon: Multilingual Matters, 2006. 15–24.

Venuti, Lawrence. *The Translator's Invisibility: A History of Translation.* London: Routledge, 1995.

Yang, Yu-Niang, trans. [柳林中的風聲]. Trans. of *The Wind in the Willows.* By Kenneth Grahame. 1908. Taipei: Kuo Chi Shao Nien Tsun, 1996.

~

CHAPTER TEN

The Pursuit of Pleasure in *The Wind in the Willows* and Disney's *The Adventures of Ichabod and Mr. Toad*

Jennifer Geer

Although still watched and readily available, Disney's animated film *The Adventures of Ichabod and Mr. Toad* has never generated a large popular or critical response. Released in 1949, near the end of an eight-year decline in the studio's creative and commercial fortunes, the film is generally considered a pleasant but relatively minor work from one of Disney's less distinguished eras. In his study of the studio, Steven Watts dismisses *The Adventures* in a few lines as one of several "negligible" mid- to late-1940s productions (244), while Neal Gabler's recent biography of Walt Disney merely mentions it as the product of a "disengaged" period on the part of the studio and its founder (458). Although *The Adventures of Ichabod and Mr. Toad* does not break any new ground in terms of Disney's animation techniques, its cultural and historical characteristics certainly are worth examining in a collection devoted to the centenary of *The Wind in the Willows*.[1] This study will accordingly focus on these characteristics rather than making an in-depth analysis of filmic qualities. As children's literature becomes increasingly intertwined with other media products, film adaptations form a valuable part of the reception history of literary classics such as Grahame's novel—particularly when the film in question is produced by a studio whose influence on children's culture has been as far-reaching as Disney's.

Disney films are well-known for Americanizing their British and European source texts, but most existing studies of this process focus on fairy tale adaptations. These studies tend to discuss Disney's Americanization as part of a process of folkloric transmission, assuming that there are no fixed textual or historical points of origin with which to compare fairy tale films such as *Snow White* or *Cinderella*, for the literary fairy tales on which they are based derive from fluid international oral traditions. These studies thus tend to subsume the historically specific aspects of Americanization in the films while emphasizing other elements such as Disney's treatment of gender or the ways in which these films adapt the tales' narrative patterns.[2] Because *Mr. Toad*—as I will term the segment that *The Adventures of Ichabod and Mr. Toad* devotes to *The Wind in the Willows*—is based on a literary text, however, it facilitates a closer study of the ways in which Disney Americanizes a source text created by a known author in a single historical moment. Disney's film retains Grahame's thematic tension between upholding conservative communal values and pursuing individual adventure, but it places these elements in a context that is much more reminiscent of postwar America than Grahame's pastoral England. The film also makes significant changes to the very English character, Toad. While the adventures of Grahame's Toad speak to Edwardian anxieties about rural development, spendthrift squires, and working-class mobs, Disney's Toad is a creature of the postwar American middle class, with its irreverent energy, faith in technological progress, and concern about socialization and finance.

Critics have long noticed that Grahame's novel revolves around tensions between a desire for stable home life and a longing for peripatetic adventures, the pursuit of individual pleasures and the maintenance of social conventions, a love of tradition and a fearful fascination with modern technology. *The Wind in the Willows* develops these themes largely by intertwining two main narrative strands: Toad's comic adventures and the more introspective River Bank scenes focusing on Mole and Rat. The Toad chapters, which grew out of stories Grahame composed to entertain his son Alastair, are cheerful picaresques, extolling the hedonistic joys of travel and (often stolen) motorcars, while the River Bank storyline acknowledges the lure of adventure but focuses on pastoral pleasures and the security of traditional social ties.

Michael Mendelson has argued convincingly that much of the text's "special richness" derives from the ways in which it alternates between these two plotlines, setting up a perpetual "dialectic between" the values that they represent (128).

In order to manage these ongoing tensions, *The Wind in the Willows* "establishes a dominant mood of temperate indulgence" by beginning with Mole's strongly felt but "controllable" desire for adventure, which then leads to his friendship with Rat and incorporation into the larger River Bank social circle (Mendelson 130). Toad's solitary and far more hedonistic adventures, "while charming, see[m] nonetheless . . . aberrant" by contrast (Mendelson 130). His impulsive longing for anything that promises "[t]ravel, change, interest, [and] excitement" (Grahame 24) dismays Toad's friends and almost causes him to lose his home to the weasels, who invade Toad Hall while he is in prison for stealing a motorcar. *The Wind in the Willows* retains an underlying sympathy toward adventure, however, even while insisting that it should be contained within established communal norms. The final chapters about the battle for Toad Hall do not utterly disavow Toad's desires. Instead, the novel "enlists [his] adventurous impulse in the recapture of" his ancestral home, staging a rousing mock-epic battle that reestablishes community and tradition while granting plenty of excitement to Toad and his friends (Mendelson 141).

By concluding with the reclamation of Toad Hall, the restoration of Toad's good name, and his establishment as the "modest" and "earnest" host of a "strictly conventional" dinner party, *The Wind in the Willows* ultimately tells a tale of socialization (Grahame 242–3). At least for the moment, Toad has learned how to channel his desire for adventure and personal glory into socially acceptable forms. (His friends Mole and Rat, having gone through their own versions of this process in the earlier River Bank chapters "Dulce Domum" and "Wayfarers All," become two of his teachers, implicitly signaling their own successful integration into an adult social world.) Critics—and Grahame—remain ambivalent about precisely how thorough Toad's reformation is, however.[3] Sarah Gilead suggests that Toad ultimately is reformed and socialized, although she notes that the novel elsewhere depicts a darker side of socialization when a reluctant Rat is forced to give up his own dreams of adventure in "Wayfarers All" (155–6). Bonnie Gaarden, however, notes that

Grahame merely describes Toad as "altered," not permanently reformed (53). And Grahame himself, "when asked what became of Toad's good resolutions for the future, replied: 'Of course Toad never really reformed; he was by nature incapable of it'" (qtd. in Green 248).

Although the novel ends by celebrating Toad's return to Toad Hall and neighborhood respectability, it does imply that his socialization is tenuous at best. He may behave with conventional polite modesty at his dinner party—but largely because his friends intervened earlier in the day, marching him into a room, standing over him, and rewriting his original grandiose invitations in a more subdued style. Toad's struggle to comply with their wishes is evident; he succeeds only by giving himself the emotional outlet of singing an unrepentantly boastful "Last Little Song" in the privacy of his bedroom before the party starts. Significantly, Grahame reproduces the song and Toad's manner of singing it in loving detail, suggesting that his desires merit amused tolerance rather than censure. Even the novel's final paragraphs, which ostensibly reinforce ideals of socialization by showing how the weasel residents of the "successfully tamed" Wild Wood are teaching their "young ones" to admire "the great Mr. Toad, . . . the gallant Water Rat, . . . [a]nd . . . the famous Mr. Mole," remain slightly ambiguous (Grahame 244). Toad's greatness, after all, exists primarily in his own head, and the weasel mother's characterization of Badger is so exaggerated that the narrator terms it "base libel" (Grahame 244). In the world of *The Wind in the Willows*, successful socialization apparently depends on the vigilance of one's friends and the telling of tall tales, suggesting that it is not necessarily inevitable or natural.[4]

Overall, *The Wind in the Willows* seeks to contain rather than repress unruly desires, positioning them within a fictional world of regulated holiday where indulgence may take place within socially acceptable bounds. The River Bank is less a re-creation of traditional rural society than a vision of an upper-middle-class Edwardian gentleman's holiday: camaraderie with male friends, lavish picnics, and boating parties, with a few adventures to add spice (Green 248). As a banker from an upper-middle-class Scottish background who lived in London for much of his life and eventually became secretary of the Bank of England, Grahame himself was hardly a rural squire. Toad's reincorporation into respectable River Bank society thus represents not so much a return to traditional rural life as a reimagining of that life as a fin-de-siècle banker's holiday. The novel's final pages portray not a landowner earnestly collecting his rents, but a lighthearted group of friends who give dinner parties and go on excursions to the now-safe Wild Wood.

As critics such as Peter Green and Peter Hunt have pointed out, this fantasy world is suffused with Edwardian anxieties about rural development and social class. Green argues that Grahame's celebration of pastoral nature in the River Bank sequences may be traced to contemporary upper-middle-class anxieties about "the decay of rural England," whose (relatively) unspoiled nature and traditional squirearchy were seen as threatened by the rise of conspicuously consuming nouveau riche on the one hand and working-class radicals on the other (2, 242–47). Within this context, Toad's follies represent those of "the landed *rentier* squandering his capital on riotous pleasures" and his near loss of Toad Hall "constitute[s] a social object-lesson" in which such irresponsibility emboldens radical arguments against "inherited wealth and traditional class-values" (Green 245). Toad's reckless behavior and fascination with modern technology such as motorcars lead to his arrest, which then gives the weasels, ferrets, and stoats from the Wild Wood a pretext for taking over Toad Hall. The eventual recapture of Toad Hall and defeat of the ominously named Wild-Wooders may thus be read as "a fantasy in which country gentlemen finally triumphed over the unprincipled radical *canaille*" (Green 243). At the same time, however, the uncertain nature of Toad's reform reveals a nagging awareness that this dream of a return to a rural Arcadia safe from class conflict and motorcars is merely a dream, less grandiose than Toad's former imaginings but possibly no less fictional. *The Wind in the Willows* concludes by bringing the narrative lines of Toad and the River Bank back together (Mendelson 139), but it never quite resolves the tensions between the values that these two plotlines embody. Grahame suggests that an imagined truce in which traditional rural values temporarily contain the newer spirit of individualistic adventure is all that can be hoped for; at any event, he never told what he drolly termed the "painful" story of Toad's later adventures (qtd. in Green 248).

Disney's film adaptation shares the novel's tendency to sympathize with unruly pleasures even as it tries to contain them, but it adapts these themes to better fit the studio's house style and situates them within a distinctly postwar American context. Following a precedent set by the first nonliterary adaptation of *The Wind in the Willows*, A. A. Milne's stage play *Toad of Toad Hall*, Disney's Mr. *Toad* focuses on Toad and stresses the action and comedy of his adventures. In the introduction to his play, Milne argues that these changes arose out of dramatic necessity. He admits that "I have left out all the best parts of the book," but adds, "if he has any knowledge of the theatre, Mr. Grahame will thank me. . . . it seemed to me that Rat and Toad, Mole and Badger could only face the footlights with hope of success if they were content to amuse their audiences" (viii–ix). In keeping with his belief that "[t]here are both beauty and comedy in [*The Wind in the Willows*], but the beauty must be left . . . there" due to the exigencies of the stage, Milne omits Grahame's most strongly pastoral and introspective chapters, "The Piper at the Gates of Dawn" and "Wayfarers All," which detail Rat and Mole's mystical encounter with Pan and Rat's thwarted desire to travel to the South Mediterranean. Instead, Milne introduces a comic subplot involving the horse who pulls Toad's gypsy cart. *Toad of Toad Hall* also gives Toad the opportunity to sing his boastful "Last Little Song" in public after the recapture of Toad Hall. Milne's conclusion thus sanctions Toad's mischief much more openly than Grahame's: Rat, Mole, Badger, and the other animals eventually join in Toad's song, and the play ends with a merry dance.

Although animated film is a very different medium from the stage and Disney's strongly pastoral *Bambi* had been a great artistic and financial success in 1942, Mr. *Toad* tends to follow Milne's editorial practices rather than Grahame's original plotline. The film greatly condenses the novel's River Bank narrative, expands the roles of comic characters such as the horse, and provides a conclusion that indulges Toad's manic energy. Walt Disney had never shared Milne's reverence for Grahame's novel; as early as 1937, he "had . . . written to a fan who had suggested a film of *Willows*: '[W]e have never considered it particularly well suited for cartoon material" (Gabler 458). Disney's reference to "cartoon material" presumably indicates what Steven Watts has called the "unique blend of music, mischief, dance, comedy, and heroic melodrama" that had marked Disney films since the advent of Mickey Mouse in the 1920s (33). Toad's adventures are better suited to this overall aesthetic than are the novel's River Bank sequences.

The studio's house style of the late 1940s and early 1950s also supported a decision to follow Milne's precedent and focus on Toad's picaresque adventures. During this period, the muted pastels that helped create the pastoral mood of *Bambi* and parts of *Snow White and the Seven Dwarves* gave way to a "sharper, flatter" aesthetic in which "all the figures are tinted with clear, bright colors, and delineated by simple black lines," which help create a distinctly unpastoral sense of "demarcation between characters and their environment" (Wood, "Domesticating" 28–9). This visual style lends itself more to the bright, busy comedy of Toad's adventures than to the bucolic reveries of the River Bank. Disney animated films from the postwar period also tend to be more episodic than earlier works such as *Snow White* and *Bambi*, and more dependent on sentimental melodrama, cute animal characters, and increasingly fast-paced comic gags (Watts 248–51). With these character types, narrative preferences, and visual styles in mind, Disney's Mr. *Toad* condenses Grahame's leisurely novel into a thirty-five-minute romp.

Disney's film intensifies the focus on Toad by omitting all of Rat's and Mole's adventures unless they are directly connected with Toad's. In contrast to Milne's play, which includes the novel's opening chapter in which Mole abandons his spring cleaning and the episode in which he and Rat stumble upon Badger's house in the Wild Wood, Mr. *Toad* omits these episodes entirely. Instead, it elevates Toad's passion for gypsy carts and motorcars, his escape from prison, and the final battle for Toad Hall into extended action sequences, replete with rousing music, melodramatic near-disasters, and slapstick visual gags. These scenes replace the predominantly verbal humor of Grahame's descriptions with audiovisual spectacle and greatly increase the pace of the film as compared not only to the novel, but also to Milne's play, which keeps many of the action scenes offstage until its third act. The film's conclusion, too, is more reliant on action and comic reversals than the play's. Just as Rat, Mole, and Badger are declaring Toad "completely reformed, through with gypsy carts and motorcars," he appears at—and very nearly shatters—the window in an airplane. To a greater extent than the play and certainly than the novel, the film is a comedy with one central protagonist: Toad.

More fundamentally, Disney replaces many of the British cultural references of the novel and play with American ones. As critics such as Richard Schickel, Eric Smoodin, Steven Watts, and Nicholas Sammond have pointed out, the studio has always tried to situate itself and its products as models of American middle-class values. Toad, his friends, and the narrator of the Mr. *Toad* segment, Basil Rathbone, may speak in British accents, take tea, and admire the quasi-feudal architecture of Toad Hall, but the film addresses an American implied audience. This process is most noticeable in the framing devices. Although Grahame does not provide any frame narrative for *The Wind in the Willows*, both Disney's film and Milne's play frame the animals' adventures with scenes featuring human characters. Milne's and Disney's frames address very different implied audiences, however. Milne presents the adventures of Toad and his friends as the dream of a little girl named Marigold. The dream frame recalls Lewis Carroll's *Alice* books, which had been adapted to the stage quite successfully, as well as the fairy plays that had been a Christmas tradition for British families since the early nineteenth century. Marigold's flower-derived name also links her to the heroines of popular children's plays such as *Bluebell in Fairyland* (*Toad of Toad Hall* opened in mid-December, the height of the season for this type of play). Milne thus situates *Toad of Toad Hall* within a specifically British tradition of children's entertainment: Christmas fairy plays.

Disney, on the other hand, presents Toad as a charming literary-historical artifact, forming part—but only a part—of a broader Anglo-American cultural heritage. *The Adventures of Ichabod and Mr. Toad* was the last of several animated "package films" released during the 1940s that mixed disparate segments "to lure an audience by . . . offering something for everyone" (Watts 249). The first half of the film features Mr. *Toad*, while the second half focuses on Washington Irving's "The Legend of Sleepy Hollow." The opening frame is set in a library and uses ideas of literary heritage to link the two segments. After the opening credits, Basil Rathbone intones, "If you were asked to choose the most fabulous character in English literature, who would it be? Robin Hood? King Arthur? Becky Sharp? Sherlock Holmes? Oliver Twist, perhaps? . . . I would nominate a toad." The segment devoted to Irving's story is narrated by the American Bing Crosby, who pointedly notes that "we here in the colonies" also have "fabulous characters" and picks Irving's Ichabod Crane from a list including Paul Bunyan, Davy Crockett, and Daniel Boone. The use of "we" and "here" to refer to the United States indicates an American implied audience, as does the fact that the American Ichabod gets top billing in the film's title and theme song. Indeed, Toad and his friends do not even appear on the front cover of the U.S. DVD release of *The Adventures of Ichabod and Mr. Toad*; that position is Ichabod's alone, with Toad relegated to a small portion of the back cover.

Within the Mr. *Toad* segment, middle-class American values pervade Disney's portrayal of Toad and his friends. Naomi Wood's studies of the studio's fairy tale adaptations reveal its consistent tendency to Americanize European and British source texts. Films such as *Cinderella, Snow White,* and *Sleeping Beauty* emphasize the tales' comic and romantic aspects, deflate the pretensions of royalty and rank, and celebrate "hard work, clean living, self-control" and belief in one's dreams ("Domesticating" 34, 29–33 and "Walt" 132). These general patterns are also evident in Mr. *Toad,* though the romantic and domestic themes Wood notices in the fairy tale films are virtually absent. This absence is probably due to the gender of the protagonists; while the fairy tales revolve around heroines, *The Wind in the Willows* has only a handful of female characters, who play small supporting roles and are of a lower social class than Toad, Rat, Mole, and Badger. Disney retains Grahame's focus on genteel male characters—the four friends are never shown working for wages and the novel's few women are omitted altogether in the film, making it an exclusively male affair. Mr. *Toad* alters the social context in which Toad and his friends move, however; instead of presenting them as London gentlemen on holiday, the film evokes a middle-class American male ideal, the boyish adventurer whose energy may lead him to excess but who is ultimately forgivable and even charming.

In keeping with Disney's tendency to poke fun at Old World pretensions and affirm its male protagonists' comic energy, Mr. *Toad* alters the novel's attitude toward traditional social structures. *The Wind in the Willows* sympathizes with Toad's longing for grandiose adventures but ultimately offers the hope that this adventurousness might help restore a dream of traditional British rural life. The film, on the other hand, portrays British traditions and the animals who try to uphold them as charming but somewhat too rigid. The narrator introduces Rat as a "bit stuffy of course, but really a fine fellow"; the casual "of course," Rat's subsequent displeasure at Mole's being late for tea, and Badger's nervous irritation work to position the film's version of traditional British society as a foil for Toad's comic actions rather than an ideal in its own right. Even though Disney critiques Toad's worst follies, the film's comic sensibilities favor his effervescent individualism.

The film's final comic twist about Toad's new passion for airplanes thus settles the question of Toad's reform firmly in the negative. This scene also undercuts Toad Hall's ancestral opulence by using it as material for a punch line. After reclaiming Toad Hall from the weasels, Rat, Mole, and Badger are celebrating the New Year by admiring its portraits and heraldic banners. "Auld Lang Syne" plays on the audio track as the narrator intones, "Toad's friends were dreadfully proud of him. . . . He was a new Toad now, completely reformed." In the next frame, however, all hope of Toad's becoming respectable is literally shattered when his plane clips Toad Hall, scattering bricks and knocking the head off a statue. As Toad flies off into the sunset, the narrator merely chuckles indulgently and says, "But let's weigh our judgment carefully, we moles and rats and badgers. Really now, don't we envy him a bit? I know I do." This concluding comment, which is the narrator's final word on the subject, nicely demonstrates the film's attitude toward British traditions and cultural authorities. They are not discounted; Rathbone's status as a famous British actor and his position as the narrator who chooses and presents this classic tale establish him as their spokesman. Yet instead of using tradition to provide a necessary counterweight to Toad's excesses as in the novel, the film invokes tradition to sanction viewers' sympathy for his freewheeling impulses. By having Rathbone's kindly, paternalistic narrator approve Toad, Disney suggests that he has entered the canon of classic literary characters precisely because he is incorrigible.

Mr. Toad does not discount all social and cultural authority, however. It merely shifts the locus of that authority from the British squirearchy to the American middle class. Rural chase scenes, manor houses, and gloomy Dickensian prisons may dominate the film's visual elements, but the screenplay presumes a setting much more reminiscent of twentieth-century America.[5] Nicholas Sammond has traced the ways in which other Disney films of this period reflect and help assuage postwar American anxieties about rapidly growing suburbs, the pleasures and perils of readily available consumer goods, and an increasingly bureaucratic mass culture (195–206); the changes that Disney makes to Grahame's setting and plot elements align Mr. *Toad* with this larger pattern. The world of Mr. *Toad* is implicitly suburban. There is no Wild Wood in Disney's film, and although the River remains, it functions as a visual backdrop rather than as a central element in the animals' lives, as it does in the novel. Disney's Toad and his friends retain the genteel social status of Grahame's animals, but do not lead rural lives; instead, Toad's adventures play out against a backdrop of tabloid newspapers, Byzantine legal systems, and worries over personal finance.

This backdrop certainly existed in Grahame's day, but *The Wind in the Willows* specifically excludes it. In the novel, such things form part of the Wide World, a misty horizon that may be "the smoke of towns" or "only cloud-drift" and that Rat dismisses as "something that doesn't matter" (10). His later attempt to see the Wide World in the "Wayfarers All" chapter suggests it does indeed matter, but even this episode presents the Wide World and its towns as an illicit temptation, a distant presence beyond the bounds of the animals' daily lives. In Disney's film, however, the separation between the Wide World and the River Bank becomes a moot point. A postman visits Rat's home on a regular basis, and creditors clamor at the front doors of Toad Hall. The film uses newspaper stories about Toad's trial as a convenient narrative shorthand; the fact that the animals would appear in a newspaper is assumed as given. These newspaper stories about the legal appeals Toad's friends mount on his behalf, as well as their later attempts to regain the legal deed to Toad Hall, implicitly position Disney's animals as members of postwar mass society, not as rural squires who may take the law into their own hands on their own property. To reclaim Toad's good name and property, he and his friends rely on the court system, their actions duly reported in the mass media.

Viewers are free to enjoy Toad's exploits because he is presented as a basically law-abiding member of the suburban middle class. Disney's film, which was produced during a period that saw "cohesive social activity and infrastructural development [on] a scale and pace never before imagined" in America (Sammond 206), grants far more importance to legal and financial institutions than Grahame's novel does. In the novel, Toad steals a motorcar, is sent to prison, escapes with the help of the gaoler's daughter, then encounters the motorcar and its owners a second time—at which point he promptly steals it again.

The police never catch him after his escape, and neither he nor his friends seem worried about the possibility. Humphrey Carpenter points out that *The Wind in the Willows* is not especially interested in the police or the human world they represent; the other animals' main concern is that Toad has betrayed the traditions of River Bank society by "letting down his class and exposing it to danger" from the weasels, who use his disgrace as a pretext for taking over Toad Hall (164). Rat, Mole, and Badger persuade Toad to thank or compensate the individuals he has encountered during his adventures, but they never address the legal charges against him, nor do they invoke the rule of law to evict the weasels who have taken over Toad Hall. Instead, they act as traditional landowners might. They are paternalistic and generous toward friendly members of the working class, giving the gaoler's daughter who helped Toad escape from prison "a handsome gold necklace and locket set with pearls" (Grahame 243), but have no qualms about using brute force to rout unfriendly working-class characters such as the weasels. In the novel, Toad's status as a gentleman implicitly places him above the law.

Disney's Toad is far more law-abiding than Grahame's; he and his friends exist squarely within, rather than above, middle-class systems of law and finance. Although Toad is imprisoned for stealing a motorcar, the film later reveals that he was merely caught in the stolen car. The true thieves are the weasels and a crooked barman named Mr. Winky. Disney's Toad is not guilty of theft, but of impulse buying: he sees the car, falls in love (levitating off the ground in bliss when he smells its exhaust), and upon finding he has no ready cash, offers the deed to Toad Hall in trade for it. Toad has no idea that the car he "purchases" from Mr. Winky has in fact been stolen, or that he is acting in any way against the law.

Disney shares Grahame's broadly comic attitude toward the court system. In keeping with what Watts has called Disney's characteristic "suspicion of big bureaucratic institutions" (288), the prosecutor resembles a stereotypical villain, with his billowing black robes, cruel-looking face, and supercilious voice. He and the judge are easily swayed by Mr. Winky's oily compliments. Still, Disney's Toad and his friends remain generally mindful of the law, rather than above it, as are Grahame's characters. It is the horse Cyril, whose status as a comic sidekick and self-proclaimed "bit of a rotter" places him outside polite society, who engineers Toad's escape from prison. Rat, Mole, and Badger, the respectable characters with whom the narrator aligns himself and the implied viewers in his closing comments, act quite differently. Their initial efforts to free Toad are strictly legal, conducted through the appeals process and duly reported in the judicial columns of the newspapers. When Toad does escape, Rat sternly disapproves, threatening to call the police and telling Toad that "You owe a debt to society, and you've got to pay." He only relents after Badger confirms Toad's version of events by giving an eyewitness account of Mr. Winky's presence at Toad Hall and possession of the deed. With Toad established as a foolish and impulsive consumer but a basically law-abiding citizen, his friends—and the film's viewers—are free to sympathize with him and his efforts to reclaim his home and good name. Mr. *Toad* conveniently ignores the problem of Toad's receiving stolen goods; once he and his friends prove that he did not steal the car himself, the scene immediately cuts to a newspaper headline proclaiming, "Toad Exonerated!"

The film's final battle for Toad Hall thus plays out rather differently from the novel's. In *The Wind in the Willows*, the four friends reclaim Toad Hall by forcefully teaching the weasels, ferrets, and stoats their place in the social order. Rat, Mole, Badger, and Toad sneak up on the boisterous but cowardly Wild-Wooders, and "whack 'em" until they flee or become more than happy to act as humble servants (Grahame 218). Grahame's mock-epic motifs—the title of this final chapter is "The Return of Ulysses"—position Toad and his friends as righteous heroes, reclaiming their own property from a disorganized, dishonest rabble.

Mr. *Toad* also presents its four protagonists as heroic, but in a much more unassuming American way. They have no intention of defeating the weasels and Mr. Winky in battle; they mount their expedition to Toad Hall in order to reclaim the deed that is Toad's legal proof of innocence. Unlike the novel's Wild-Wooders, the film's weasels are much more heavily armed than Toad, Rat, Mole, and Badger. Most of Grahame's weasels, ferrets, and stoats have no weapons, and their rude bravado quickly turns "panic-stricken" beneath the protagonists' "terrible sticks" (Grahame 230). Disney's weasels, on the other hand, are in a drunken stupor at first but soon wake up and acquire a seemingly unlimited supply of weapons with which to attack Toad and his friends, who carry no arms during the main battle. By portraying the weasels as formidable opponents, Disney situates its protagonists as the classic American underdogs, who overcome an enemy's superior force by using wits and teamwork. When their original plan to lower Mole over the balcony so that he can slip the deed from Mr. Winky's pocket fails, the four animals must outrun and outwit their opponents in order to retrieve it. They finally succeed not by instilling righteous terror into the usurpers, but through a clever stratagem of Toad's: after seeing Mole fold the deed into a paper airplane to send it out of the weasels' reach, Toad launches a dozen more paper airplanes at them, confusing them until he and his friends can escape with the real deed.

Toad's clever use of technological toys—paper airplanes—to defeat the weasels and his final appearance in an airplane also speak to a postwar American audience by displacing anxieties about technological progress. In *The Wind in the Willows*, Grahame's language displays an uneasy fascination with the car. It is "dark" and "brazen" but also "magnificent . . . immense, breath-snatching, [and] passionate" (31). The novel is in no doubt about the car's effect on older forms of transport such as the gypsy caravan, however; after the car passes, the caravan is "an irredeemable wreck," a symbol of the past made obsolete and literally thrown into a ditch by newer technologies (Grahame 32). Yet in the final chapters, the motorcar is curiously absent. Toad's impulsiveness remains, but once he and his friends begin their efforts to recapture Toad Hall, Grahame's cultural allusions become almost entirely preindustrial, focusing on epic conventions and the duties of landed gentry. Even Toad's final flashes of grandiosity ignore twentieth-century technology. The bombastic dinner invitations that his friends confiscate include "An Address. By Toad" lauding his adventures as those of "A Typical English Squire," an expert on "Our Prison System—The Waterways of Old England—Horse-dealing, and how to deal—Property, its rights and its duties." Toad's reformation may be doubtful, but he does seem to have forgotten motorcars and resolved to go "Back to the Land" (Grahame 236). *The Wind in the Willows* acknowledges the simultaneously fascinating and disruptive emergence of modern technology, yet ultimately attempts to efface technological progress and return to a vision of a preindustrial England powered by waterways and horses.

Disney's film, in contrast, presents Toad's fascination with new technologies as an ongoing progression: he moves from gypsy caravan to motorcar to airplane. Furthermore, the horse Cyril—harness collar still firmly in place—remains at his side throughout. In *The Wind in the Willows*, the horse who pulls the gypsy caravan is horrified by the motorcar and remains so, a reaction that Grahame describes as "natural" if inconvenient (32). Cyril, however, while momentarily startled by the first motorcar he sees, soon learns to enjoy the new adventures open to him; he casually lounges in the stolen motorcar, front hooves behind his head, while Toad begins his ill-fated negotiations with Mr. Winky and the weasels. As many Disney films do, *Mr. Toad* uses such comic scenes to "transform intimidating, even frightening" machines "into fascinating and laughable images" (Watts 75). Placing a comical horse (and toad) in a motorcar and airplane suggests that tradition and new technologies can coexist happily. *Mr. Toad* thus speaks to the postwar American faith that technological progress and affordable consumer goods could improve users' quality of life and perhaps minimize social divisions; instead of working to pull a caravan, the horse is relaxing as a passenger, right along with Toad. Cyril and Toad's enjoyment naturalizes technological progress, reassuring postwar audiences that these innovations are compatible with traditional figures and supposedly natural desires.

Disney's faith in technological innovation, its tendency to poke gentle fun at Old World traditions, and its delight in comedy combine to paint a picture of Toad that is even more sympathetic than the novel's. *Mr. Toad* does not entirely abandon Grahame's thematic tensions or his emphasis on socialization, however. The film's portrayal of Toad aligns him with other typical Disney heroes of the period, "innocents in search of happiness" with "boyish high spirits and a propensity for mischief, a dislike of hard work, and a sweet attractiveness that draws other characters to them" (Wood, "Walt" 133). In *Mr. Toad*, this general pattern—which Wood traces in films from *Pinocchio* (1940) to *Aladdin* (1992)—is linked to particular ideals of socialization that were emerging in postwar America.

Nicholas Sammond's study of the ways Disney has positioned itself as a defender of American childhood argues that the studio's products of the late 1940s and early 1950s "resonated . . . with a postwar shift in ideas about child-rearing . . . [and] also with larger concerns about American culture and character" (197). During and after World War II, popular models of American child-rearing often stressed "the central dilemma" of "balanc[ing] the needs of an orderly and rational society against those of individual freedom in the production of future" citizens (Sammond 193). Such a balance, it was felt, would give children enough individual self-reliance to thrive in a free-market system and to reject Communism and totalitarianism, while also fostering the self-discipline necessary to function in an increasingly bureaucratic "and standardize[ed] . . . infrastructure, educational syste[m], and economy" (Sammond 252, cf. 210–11). Because the majority of these commentators believed that American children were natural individualists and thus "resistant to authoritarianism and totalitarianism," postwar theories of child-rearing often were marked by "a search for a means of behaving naturally" (Sammond 211, 201). In this view, "the proper boundary between the natural and the cultural occurred midway between the authoritarian and the anarchic. . . . The child whose natural impulses were respected but who experienced sensible restraint would be best prepared for democratic capitalism: able to compete, but mindful of the needs of the larger community" (Sammond 271–72). Mr. *Toad* filters Grahame's thematic tensions through this American model of socialization; Toad's impulses are portrayed as natural and worthy of respect, even though they remain in need of "sensible restraint."

Because the film omits most of the novel's River Bank narrative, it does not develop this dialectic by intertwining plotlines as Grahame does. Instead, it relies on its framing devices and character relationships to suggest the contrasting claims of home and adventure, the individual and the community, and tradition and modernity. These contrasts are evident from the first scenes. The film's opening shots are saturated with references to literary traditions and cultural heritage. After the opening credits, the film cuts to a shot of a stained-glass window portraying a book and a candle, then moves inside to the library where Rathbone presents "J. Thaddeus Toad, Esquire," an imposing figure embossed in gold upon the spine of a leather-bound book. Yet when Toad steps out of the book and becomes active, literary elegance immediately gives way to slapstick comedy. Toad's first major scene sees him careening madly around the countryside on a gypsy caravan, a short, squat figure brilliantly dressed in a red jacket, yellow waistcoat, and gray trousers—which soon go missing to reveal bright red underclothes. The library's polished shelves and orchestral music disappear in favor of frightened ducks, smashed hedges, splashing water, and the sound of Toad and Cyril singing a rousing comic song. Mr. *Toad* oscillates between a reverence for cultural traditions and a delight in anarchic comedy while encouraging viewers to enjoy both; the lushly painted interiors of the library and Toad Hall are as carefully animated and scored as the bright, busy chase scenes.

The film also uses its supporting characters as foils that validate Toad's comic energy while tempering his excesses. Toad's relationships with the other characters tend to place him roughly in the middle of a continuum between anarchy and stuffy conformity. As in Grahame's novel, the weasels occupy the anarchic end of this spectrum: skulking, slouching figures who are introduced as an undifferentiated mass of eyes peering out from the interior of the stolen motorcar. Mr. *Toad* partners the mob of weasels with Mr. Winky, a Disney-created character who embodies the figure of a crooked businessman. Like Toad, he is given to grandiose statements and schemes, but he makes that animal's exploits look positively harmless by comparison. Mr. Winky is even more vain and loudly dressed than Toad, and his greedy calculation seems far more dangerous to middle-class legal and financial stability than Toad's impulsive naivety. He apparently helps the weasels steal the car, then gains the deed to Toad Hall by taking advantage of Toad's foolishness, and finally perjures himself in court by claiming that Toad had tried to sell *him* the stolen motorcar. Toad looks the picture of honesty and taste by comparison.

On the other hand, the film criticizes Toad for leaving himself open to Mr. Winky's schemes: if he had been a responsible consumer and property owner, he never would have been tempted to trade his home for a car in the first place. His foolish trade of Toad Hall ("an estate worth thousands") for a red motorcar is only the latest in a long line of poor financial decisions. The film portrays Toad as a spendthrift from the start; the first scenes of Toad Hall show not Toad but Badger, despairingly going over his friend's accounts and fending off creditors before exclaiming, "Something's *got* to be done about Toad!" Thus, although Mr. *Toad* excuses most of its hero's emotional excesses, it does criticize his financial ones.

Toad's friends in the film are much more concerned about his financial and legal woes than his loss of respectability. In *The Wind in the Willows*, Rat and Mole do worry about the fines and repair costs that attend Toad's reckless driving, not to mention his personal safety, but they appear to regard these as only "part of the trouble" (61). The fact that Grahame frames these concerns with discussions of "animal-etiquette" (62) and loving descriptions of Badger's modest but impregnable ancestral home suggest that the primary objection to Toad's behavior is its implicit threat to the rural squirearchy and its social traditions. In keeping with its attempts to appeal to the postwar American middle class, Disney's Mr. *Toad* indulges its hero's disregard for social mores that are identified as traditionally British but criticizes his financial mismanagement and emphasizes the legal troubles that result from it. Toad's main fault is that his desire for adventure has led him to "costly follies [that] had brought him to the brink of bankruptcy"—a financial crisis more severe than the one that Grahame's Toad faces. If the novel's Toad betrays the ideals of the traditional English squirearchy by leaving his property open to the claims of lower-class mobs, his filmic counterpart betrays the ideals of the American businessman by his reckless spending and destruction of property.

Still, the film maintains that Toad's impulsive energy merely needs to be harnessed, not eradicated. Rat and Badger, while far more sympathetic characters than Mr. Winky or the weasels, are subtly criticized for being too anxious about property and propriety. Although they sometimes mentor Toad as in the novel, they more often function as comic straight men. The film introduces Rat as he is fretting over Mole's being chronically late for tea, a scene that does not appear in the novel but corresponds to American stereotypes about British gentlemen. The narrator's description of Rat as a "bit stuffy of course, but really a fine fellow" reinforces this suspicion of traditional British society as overly proper and lacking in innovation. Badger, too, is a lovable but stereotypically irascible and thrifty Scot, who often faints in horror at Toad's more spectacular exploits. Unlike Milne, who concludes his stage adaptation of *The Wind in the Willows* by allowing all of the animals to shrug off their inhibitions and sing along with Toad, Disney never suggests that Rat or Badger will enjoy life as freely as their friend does, however kind and sensible they may be.

Mole and Cyril—a character whose expanded role derives from Milne's play but whom the Disney film adapts to its own ends—occupy positions closer to acceptable norms and serve to balance some of Toad's more problematic traits. Both are likeable characters whose strengths and weaknesses complement Toad's. Mole is introduced as a "gentle creature, kind and sympathetic," and his consistent sympathy for Toad during his trial and imprisonment functions as an emotional touchstone for the film's viewers, who are encouraged to feel similarly. Yet although Mole has the emotional sensitivity to others that Toad lacks, the screenplay and visual elements suggest that he is too meek and too easily swayed by others' opinions. He generally looks somewhat overwhelmed by his surroundings and tends to change his opinions based on which of his friends speaks first. If Mole is sensitive but rather too refined, Cyril is his opposite, just as adventurous as Toad but even more outspoken. As the working-class comic sidekick, Cyril functions as Toad's partner in crime, able to instigate many of the "chaotic 'gags' and sexual 'cuteness'" that Wood has identified as so crucial to Disney's comic sensibility, even as his social inferiority reassures viewers that the "true" middle class characters—including Toad—remain essentially respectable ("Domesticating" 43).[6]

Overall, the Mr. *Toad* segment indulges Toad's actions; he is foolish and exasperating but always kind-hearted, and his delight in comic adventure and new technology is infectious. The film as a whole, however, suggests that its audience can afford to be amused by Toad precisely because they are not like him. The Mr. *Toad* segment may poke fun at Rat and Badger's obsessive regard for tradition and propriety, yet the framing devices presuppose an audience with enough respect for cultural traditions to be interested in fantastic characters from classic literature. The narrator's concluding comment that "we moles and rats and badgers" should temper our judgment of Toad clearly positions the viewers as proper, rational members of polite middle-class society. Toad may remain imperfectly socialized and prone to fits of comic anarchy, but viewers are free to "envy him a bit" because they already have internalized a respect for community and middle-class American traditions.

Indeed, the film as a whole subtly indicts irrational behavior such as Toad's. To a certain extent, both Toad and Ichabod function as "comic anti-types showing us the results of improper behavior," because they conspicuously lack the rational self-control that is lauded in other Disney films from this period (Wood, "Domesticating" 26). The root of their troubles is an absence of reason and self-control. Toad nearly loses his home, his freedom, and his good name to what his friends and the narrator describe as his "mania" for new hobbies and adventures. When he sees a motorcar, his eyes spin in fuchsia swirls and he goes, as the narrator puts it, "completely mad." Ichabod's irrational impulses also lead him to misfortune. First, his blind and overambitious love for Katrina sparks the jealous rivalry of Brom Bones. Ichabod reacts to Katrina just as Toad does to motorcars; both rise off the ground in senseless bliss at the scent of an exhaust pipe or a handkerchief. As a thoughtless coquette, Katrina is a time-honored (if misogynistic) symbol and enabler of irrationality. She flirts with both Ichabod and Brom, until Brom resolves to drive the newcomer Ichabod out of town. He finally does so by exploiting Ichabod's second irrational trait: superstition. Ichabod is terrified of ghosts, so Brom primes him with horrifying tales of the Headless Horseman, a spirit who is searching for a mortal to kill so that he can replace his missing head with theirs. Ichabod may be a schoolmaster, but he symbolically loses his head; he believes the tales and is so frightened by Brom's impersonation of the Horseman that he flees town and is never seen again.

At the same time, however, Ichabod's story makes Toad's seem all the more appealing by contrast. Toad's impulsiveness may cause chaos, but his friends' loyalty and his genuine delight in adventure and technology remain attractive. The *Ichabod* segment paints a much more cynical picture of small-town rivalries and superstitions. None of the characters is particularly sympathetic. Although the narration initially introduces Brom as having "no malice" and Ichabod as peculiar but meriting "no complaint" from the townspeople, their later actions suggest otherwise. Brom takes ruthless advantage of Ichabod's superstitions, and Ichabod's pursuit of Katrina seems crassly ambitious; his fantasies about kissing her transform comically (but unsettlingly) into dreams of owning her father's rich farm. Katrina herself is a flirt who seems to enjoy creating rivalries among her admirers, while the other townspeople are as superstitious as Ichabod and even more comically uncultured than Brom.

Tellingly, the narrator makes no mention of envying Ichabod at the end of the segment. He simply says, "I'm getting out of here," as the "Headless Horseman" theme strikes up its refrain, "You can't reason with a headless man." The world of Disney's Ichabod, which the narrator describes as "a remote period in American history," makes a fine ghost story—the dramatic scene in which Ichabod is pursued by what he believes is the Headless Horseman is beautifully animated and exciting to watch—but it is best left in the past and only visited in the pages of fantastic literature. Paradoxically, *The Adventures of Ichabod and Mr. Toad* aligns the ostensibly British Toad, not Ichabod, with twentieth-century American values. Toad's irrepressible delight in "travel, change, excitement," and new technologies is presented as worth envying, even if it needs to be tempered with reason and good financial sense.

Of course, Rathbone's comment about envying Toad also suggests that the film's well-socialized, rational audience might benefit from a bit of Toad's comic energy. Disney's implied viewers may be too sensible to act like Toad, but their less prudent impulses need not be completely repressed; as they watch the film, they can live vicariously through his exploits, which seem as alluring as they are unrealistic. In its own very American way, *The Adventures of Ichabod and Mr. Toad* is as invested as Grahame's novel in creating ongoing dialectics between tradition and modern technology, individual pleasures and communal responsibilities. Ultimately, the film concurs with postwar American models of socialization that urged parents to praise both "natural impulses" and "sensible restraint" (Sammond 272). Disney's film, like Grahame's novel, hints that its careful balance of contraries can only exist in the imagination: an animated vision of Toad triumphant, giddily (if unsteadily) flying off to new adventures before being returned to his place in the pages of a literary classic. It insists, however, that the pleasures of that fantastic image remain well worth pursuing.

Notes

1. Throughout, I will be using the term "Disney" to refer to the studio's creative team and/or corporate persona as a whole, including but not limited to its founder.

2. See Stone; Wood, "Domesticating" 26–33, and Wood, "Walt."

3. For more extended discussion of Toad's (possible) socialization and its relation to the other animals' character development, see Gilead, Mendelson, Gaarden, and Kuznets 97–112.

4. Rat, too, only abandons his dream of traveling South with the Sea Rat after Mole physically restrains him and then encourages him to sublimate his adventurousness through writing poetry.

5. In his discussion of the True-Life Adventure series of nature documentaries that Disney released from 1948 to 1953, Sammond argues that this tendency to situate animal characters in an implicitly suburban American milieu was typical of the studio's products during this period (202–5, 225–27).

6. It is Cyril, for instance, who characterizes Toad's desire for the red motorcar as implicitly sexual, telling the court that the car "was big, it was red, it was beautiful. A motorcar? Bit of all right! Toad was transfixed with, uh, rapture."

Works Cited

The Adventures of Ichabod and Mr. Toad. Dir. James Algar and Clyde Geronimi. 1949. DVD. Disney, 2000.

Carpenter, Humphrey. *Secret Gardens: A Study of the Golden Age of Children's Literature.* Boston: Houghton Mifflin, 1985.

Gaarden, Bonnie. "The Inner Family of *The Wind in the Willows.*" *Children's Literature* 22 (1994): 43–56.

Gabler, Neal. *Walt Disney: The Triumph of the American Imagination.* New York: Knopf, 2006.

Gilead, Sarah. "The Undoing of Idyll in *The Wind in the Willows.*" *Children's Literature* 16 (1988): 145–58.

Grahame, Kenneth. *The Wind in the Willows.* 1908. New York: Dell, 1969.

Green, Peter. *Kenneth Grahame, 1859–1932: A Study of His Life and Times.* London: John Murray, 1959.

Hunt, Peter. "Language and Class in *The Wind in the Willows.*" *Children's Literature* 16 (1988): 159–68.

Kuznets, Lois R. *Kenneth Grahame.* Boston: Twayne, 1987.

Mendelson, Michael. "*The Wind in the Willows* and the Plotting of Contrast." *Children's Literature* 16 (1988): 127–44.

Milne, A. A. *Toad of Toad Hall: A Play from Kenneth Grahame's Book.* 1929. New York: Scribner, 1957. *Universal Library.* 30 Dec. 2003. Internet Archive. 23 June 2009 <www.archive.org/details/toadoftoadhall002025mbp>.

Sammond, Nicholas. *Babes in Tomorrowland: Walt Disney and the Making of the American Child, 1930–1960.* Durham, NC: Duke UP, 2005.

Schickel, Richard. *The Disney Version: The Life, Times, Art, and Commerce of Walt Disney*. 1968. 3rd ed. Chicago: Ivan Dee, 1997.

Smoodin, Eric. "Introduction: How To Read Walt Disney." *Disney Discourse: Producing the Magic Kingdom*. Ed. Eric Smoodin. New York: Routledge, 1994. 1–20.

Stone, Kay. "Three Transformations of Snow White." *The Brothers Grimm and Folktale*. Ed. James McGlathery. Urbana, IL: U of Chicago P, 1988. 52–65.

Watts, Steven. *The Magic Kingdom: Walt Disney and the American Way of Life*. Columbia, MO: U of Missouri P, 1997.

Wood, Naomi. "Domesticating Dreams in Walt Disney's *Cinderella*." *The Lion and the Unicorn* 20 (1996): 25–49.

———. "Walt Disney." *The Oxford Companion to Fairy Tales*. Ed. Jack Zipes. London: Oxford UP, 2000. 129–33.

Index

~

About the Contributors

Deborah Dysart-Gale is a rhetorician of science and technology in the faculty of engineering and computer science, Concordia University, Montreal. Her PhD is from the University of Pittsburgh. Her research focuses on the ways in which children's books predispose audiences for the persuasive messages of medicine, science, and technology.

Catherine L. Elick is professor and chair of the English department of Bridgewater College in Virginia, where she teaches courses in children's, British, and modern literature. She has published on the work of twentieth-century writers of children's fantasy, including articles on C. S. Lewis, P. L. Travers, and Hugh Lofting.

Jennifer Geer is an assistant professor of English at the University of Louisiana at Lafayette, where she teaches children's literature and Victorian British literature. She has published on Lewis Carroll, Jean Ingelow, and the film *Finding Neverland*, and is working on a book about nostalgia in Victorian children's fantasy fiction.

Jackie C. Horne worked as a children's book editor before returning to academia to earn her PhD at Brandeis University. She has taught graduate and undergraduate courses as an assistant professor at the Center for the Study of Children's Literature at Simmons College. Her published work has appeared in *Children's Literature Association Quarterly*, *Children's Literature*, *Children's Literature in Education*, and *Women's Writing*; she is currently working on a book about shifting models of exemplarity in British children's fiction of the early nineteenth century.

Karen A. Keely earned her PhD from the University of California, Los Angeles, and now teaches English at Dana Hall School in Wellesley, Massachusetts. She usually publishes on American literature and culture but could not resist the lure of writing about one of her favorite novels for this collection.

Shu-Fang Lai is an associate professor at National Sun Yat-Sen University, Taiwan. A Dickensian, she lectures on Victorian literature, the nineteenth-century English novel, and literary translation. Winner of the Liang Shih-Chiu Literary Translation Prize, she was also commissioned to be on the jury for Best Children's Picture Books and Juvenile Literature of the Year in Taiwan in 2002 and in 2005.

Ymitri Mathison is an associate professor of English at Prairie View A&M University. Her current areas of research are in British children's literature and postcolonial literature. She has published articles on Hanif Kureishi and nineteenth-century British children's fiction. She has a book chapter forthcoming on the British missionary project in children's literature.

Jonathan Mattanah is an associate professor of psychology at Towson University. He received his PhD in clinical psychology from the University of California, Berkeley. His research focuses on parent-adolescent relationships and college adjustment. More recently, as a fellow in the Honors College, he has developed a scholarly interest in applying psychological theories to understanding classic works of children's literature.

David Rudd is professor of children's literature at the University of Bolton, UK, where he runs the master's program in children's literature and culture. He has published some 100 articles on children's literature and related areas. Most recently he has edited the *Routledge Companion to Children's Literature*.

Donna R. White teaches young adult literature, linguistics, science fiction and fantasy, and writing at Arkansas Tech University. She is the author of *A Century of Welsh Myth in Children's Literature* (1998) and *Dancing with Dragons: Ursula K. LeGuin and the Critics* (1999), and has also coedited two books: *Diana Wynne Jones: An Exciting and Exacting Wisdom* (2002) and *J. M. Barrie's Peter Pan In and Out of Time* (2006).

Meg Worley is an assistant professor of English at Pomona College, where she teaches courses on Chaucer, graphic novels, and the Bible as literature. Her research focuses on the translation of medieval literature and on translations of the Bible.

Wynn Yarbrough teaches children's literature, advanced composition, and British literature and culture courses at the University of the District of Columbia. He is the book review editor for *Interdisciplinary Humanities* and serves as an associate editor for *California Arts and Letters Magazine*. He has published articles on Rudyard Kipling, Langston Hughes, Kenneth Grahame, and teaching nonfiction composition. He is currently researching jazz poetics in young adult poetry.